Fifties Ethnicities

SUNY series in Multiethnic Literature
Mary Jo Bona, editor

Fifties Ethnicities

The Ethnic Novel and Mass Culture at Midcentury

Tracy Floreani

SUNY PRESS

Cover photo: Annie and Sarah Jane from *Imitation of Life*. Courtesy of Photofest.

Published by State University of New York Press, Albany

Printed in the United States of America

For information, contact State University of New York Press, Albany, NY
www.sunypress.edu

Production by Dana Foote
Marketing by Kate McDonnell

Library of Congress Cataloging-in-Publication Data

Floreani, Tracy.

Fifties Ethnicities : The Ethnic Novel and Mass Culture at Midcentury /
Tracy Floreani.

pages cm.—(SUNY series in Multiethnic Literature)

Includes bibliographical references and index.

ISBN 978-1-4384-4769-8 (hc : alk. paper) 978-1-4384-4768-1 (pbk : alk. paper)

1. American literature—Minority authors—History and criticism. 2.
American fiction—20th century—History and criticism. 3. Ethnicity in
literature. 4. Immigrants in literature. I. Title.

PS153.M56F57 2013
810.9'920693—dc23

2012040583

10 9 8 7 6 5 4 3 2 1

Contents

Illustrations

Acknowledgments

I offer sincere thanks to friends, colleagues, and mentors whose diverse, yet complementary, personalities and intellectual perspectives have been a great resource over the course of this project. The earliest versions of this manuscript owe much to the people willing to exchange ideas, read pieces of drafts, and challenge my thinking and writing in productive ways: Cheryl Lester, Philip Barnard, Giselle Anatol, Barry Shank, Catherine Preston, Andrew Hoberek, Fred Gardaphé, Anna Neill, Janice Radway, Maria Elena Buszek, Jesse Alemàn, Cotten Seiler, Douglas Steward, Roberto Marsengo, Michael K. Johnson, David Goldstein-Shirley and Audrey Thacker. Many thanks, too, to reference librarian Cindy Pierard for enthusiastic, often unsolicited, library sleuthing on my behalf in the early days of research, to the librarians at Baker University and Oklahoma City University for unfailing help in tracking down and obtaining many sources, and to Danielle Kutner for proofreading. For more recent input I thank Beth Bouloukos, for her sharp and timely editorial work, as well as Joe Kraus and SUNY Press's anonymous reviewers, who provided really useful feedback for revision. I especially thank Mary Jo Bona for her encouragement and steady advocacy for this manuscript.

I am also indebted to other academic acquaintances with whom I have regular, energetic exchanges, the results of which may not appear directly in these pages but do always influence my work and my thinking on the complicated nature of race and ethnicity in the culture of the United States. These fine people include Michele Fazio, JoAnne Ruvoli, Derek Parker Royal, Sterling Bland, Matthew Calihman, Tim Buzzell, and Jim Buss. This list would not be complete without a shout-out to all the good people who make up MELUS, the Society for the Study of the Multi-Ethnic Literature of the United States, an organization without whose community I cannot imagine my work evolving.

Versions of chapters 3 and 4 first appeared in other publications, and are reprinted here by permission. "What's for Sale: Consumer Fantasy, American Women, and Social Mobility in Gwendolyn Brooks's *Maud Martha* and the *I Love Lucy* Show" was originally published as "*Maud Martha* vs. *I Love Lucy*: Taking on the Postwar Consumer Fantasy" in *Complicating Constructions: Race, Ethnicity, and Hybridity in American Texts*, ed. David Goldstein-Shirley and Audrey B. Thacker, University of Washington Press, 2007. "The Celluloid Fantasy: Negotiating the Ethnic Male Star Image in William Saroyan's *Rock Wagram*" first appeared as an article in the special issue *Fifties Culture* of *the minnesota review*, ed. Andrew Hoberek, ns. 55–57 (October 2002), copyright Virginia Polytechnic Institute and State University / Duke University Press.

Finally, I want to express the deepest gratitude to family. My parents, Annette and Walter Floreani, provided unflagging support, and my brother Michael came up with the idea for me to study English and become a professor before I even knew I wanted to. Credit for my sanity goes primarily to Mike Hoffman, for needed distractions and support that helped me get through various incarnations of this manuscript over many years. I dedicate this book to the memory of my father, whose personal experiences with the ever-changing notions of race and ethnicity inspired this research.

1

Introduction

Cultural Narratives and American Identities

In *Notes of a Native Son*, James Baldwin writes, "I think that the past is all that makes the present coherent, and further, that the past will remain horrible for exactly as long as we refuse to assess it honestly."[1] Part of what makes the period after World War II so fascinating is that the oppressive and the rosy seem to have existed simultaneously and consistently in balance for so many years. When I began this project years ago and would mention that I was examining narratives about ethnicity in the 1950s, the response from colleagues and friends was often the same, a joking bewilderment: "There was *ethnicity* in the fifties?" While only anecdotal evidence, the frequency of this response hints at the ways in which the forces of mass culture have elided ethnicity from much of popular memory, and the irony of the remark also belies a cynical awareness of the forces that have resulted in such an elision.

We scholars of the period need to do more than simply point out how and why whiteness has been privileged and where ethnic citizens were denigrated or ignored within the popular imagination, of course. By reinserting the perspectives that seemingly have been denied spaces in the creation of this popular imagination, I demonstrate some of their implicit roles within its very construction. In other words, we cannot simply write off invisibilities as symptomatic of cultural chauvinism; we must investigate further the media through which such invisibility was brought into very real existence.

Moreover, we must find the spaces where ethnic subjects knowingly engage that invisibility in meaningful—sometimes challenging—ways, while also engaging the meanings at work within national discourses.

This study builds on previous studies of literary and mass culture narratives of the period through a detailed study of ethnicity. I examine how novels specifically frame the consumer and gender imperatives within popular configurations of American identity, calling into question the ways in which the privileging of these enactments of citizenship also inherently privilege whiteness. In doing so, these "ethnic novels" participate dialogically with mass culture to offer additional voices in the construction of ethnicity and American identities. I focus on five novels written by American ethnic minorities, immigrants, and the children of immigrants that engage the image-laden commercial culture surrounding them. Chin Yang Lee's *Flower Drum Song*, Vladimir Nabokov's *Lolita*, Gwendolyn Brooks's *Maud Martha*, William Saroyan's *Rock Wagram*, and Ralph Ellison's *Invisible Man* constitute a critical engagement with and critique of ethnic invisibility, and they converse with various forms of visual mass culture narrative. The novels discussed here are limited to those by ethnic minority and immigrant writers that offer some sort of negotiation of racial or ethnic subjectivity and that also specifically and directly engage mass culture within the narratives. In this, they work well together not because of thematic cohesion but in the variety of ways they perform the same kind of cultural gesture and offer a set of "case studies" in the potential cultural work of the ethnic novel at midcentury. The mass culture narratives I have chosen for this study also hold no claim on representing all of midcentury mass culture. Some of the texts discussed here were best sellers or box office smashes—canonical texts revisited—but others were quietly shelved in libraries and have only received new critical attention within the past two decades. All are worth revisiting and reexamining in light of the potential re-readings of mass culture narratives the novels themselves invite. Cultural texts constantly work together in a variety of ways; "any one text is necessarily read in relationship to others and . . . a range of textual knowledges is brought to bear upon it." John Fiske argues that the "space *between* texts" is as important as the texts themselves.[2] That in-between space should be imagined here as the kind of understanding of history that comes into being not from traditional empirical evidence but from the meanings found when cultural texts are read in reference to one another.

Reading ethnic representations in such narratives must also go beyond an assessment of how progressive or stereotypical a portrayal of a racialized or ethnic subject seems. Michele Wallace rightly asserts that the positive/

negative binary is one that has tended to dominate cultural criticism, but it is an ultimately limiting mode of analysis because it oversimplifies our considerations of the complex nuances that go into the production and reception of these representations and the generic differences within them.[3] In placing mass media and literary texts into comparative readings, I attempt to move beyond such binaries to show how they work both against and with each other toward a more complicated, sometimes inconsistent, set of identity discourses and constructions in the national public arena.

All sorts of narratives permeating midcentury American culture converged in an overarching interpretation of what it meant to be American, and participating in national culture became an important enactment of citizenship. The concept of citizenship held power not only as a legal identifier or patriotic title, but also in more abstract forms that implicated certain types of expected behavior for participation in a mainstream national culture. The visual mass media served as major avenues through which the forms of cultural participation were imagined and projected, from overtly anti-Communist detective films to Betty Crocker lay-outs on the importance of convenient but nutritious meals. The everyday political that occurred tangentially with foreign policy and legislative debates visibly manifested itself in the promotion of personal behaviors that would contribute to national ideals of unity, namely, through active participation in the consumer economy and strengthening the American family.

Commercialized mass culture presented an undeniably engaging vision of American success and national belonging, but, at the same time, minority writers and artists, too, were in the process of engaging that vision and implicitly participating in its construction. While the Cold War was a significant influence in how cultural production and consumption worked, as Evan Brier rightly notes, it was not *the* influence in regard to the midcentury narrative.[4] The expansion of consumer culture and the entrenchment of gender roles (into what might now be understood as a romanticized throwback to Victorian ideals of the public and domestic spheres) are the two major elements that continually appear in all of the narratives under examination in this book. Like the Cold War atmosphere, these elements not only function as tropes through which to understand the period's cultural narratives but also serve as bridges between various narratives and the public and private understandings and articulations of identity. In visual mass culture, where the white, middle-class nuclear family became symbolic of American identity on the whole, the privileging and construction of a "dominant culture" is obvious—but not uncomplicated.

Because of the social and political pressures typical of depictions of the Cold War United States, we have tended to think of cultural resistance and real cultural diversity as near impossibilities. The 1997 collection of essays *The Other Fifties* was one of the earliest midcentury studies to challenge the wholly nostalgic, conformist image of the era, and editor Joel Foreman argued that progressive cultural texts of the period were actually a launching site for the progressive movements of the 1960s. He argues that many artists of the period managed a subtle, "pragmatic balance of subversion and accommodation." More recently, studies like those collected in *American Literature and Culture in an Age of Cold War* and *Invisible Suburbs* challenge the tendency to frame midcentury analysis in ways that perpetuate binary thinking about the era, that texts represent either cultural "containment" or "emergence." Editor Joshua Lukin writes, "Emergence risks a parallel excess to that of Containment: it can fall in the everything-is-subversive school of cultural studies and ignore oppressive ideological forces, or at least overestimate the freedom fifties Americans had to move outside them." Ultimately, there are "risks inherent in any historical generalizations: the farther its claims stray from analysis of specific experiences and movements, the more likely they are to make errors of rhetoric, emphasis, or characterization."[5] The period following World War II possesses the ambivalences of any historical period in a nation so varied and large.

Leerom Medovoi cautions, too, that we should not read resistance narratives as separate from, or simply in opposition to, the conformist elements of the culture:

> Tacitly, this approach presupposes that postwar radicalism was extrinsic to Cold War culture because it expressed a psychopolitical refusal to be "contained." If we approach the Cold War as producing something other than just a "containment culture," however, we can begin to understand the emergence of identity discourse, not as an extrinsic response to Cold War culture based on the ontological truth of identity, but rather the production of identity itself as the dialectical antithesis of containment within a cultural matrix of the Cold War world. If "containment" offered a rhetoric of repression, identity countered with a rhetoric of "liberation."

Thus, Medovoi argues that through the new explorations of the concept of "identity" during this period, we can understand the paradoxical coexistence of both a conformist culture and a culture that resists conformity in various forms of narrative, since both cultures are engaged in examining articulations of national and individual identities, respectively.[6]

All of the aforementioned studies have ventured into examinations of race and ethnicity (primarily African American and Jewish); likewise, various studies in ethnic literature contain explorations of the 1950s. There is certainly more work to be done with these questions of identity in relation to race and ethnicity at midcentury, however, and this book attempts to offer a sustained joining of ethnic studies and midcentury studies in order to deeply explore the constructions of ethnicity within a period that has informed American cultural identities in significant ways. Ethnicity itself was being thought about in new ways during this period. With the arrival of newly displaced Jews from the European war and the beginnings of the civil rights movement, this was a period when "ethnic" or "immigrant" writers were being "elevated to a position of prominence as definitively *American* writers."[7]

What the following chapters explore is a grouping of voices from the period's definitively American ethnic margins. While the novels negotiate their cultural context in diverse ways, from apparent accommodationism to metaphorical critique, they add to the conversation on identity that Medovoi invokes. Jinqi Ling, drawing on the work of Gayatri Spivak, argues for an understanding of hegemonic processes in a way that provides the "'crucial middle term'" of an "oppositional cultural politics," "an account of the production of ideology as an emancipatory process of identifying and unpacking historically produced conditions of *fundamental power imbalance*" (original emphasis).[8] This is the stance that "ethnicity" offers here, part of the important cultural work that these "ethnic novels" do. Simply writing as—and creating—an ethnic identity inflects the configurations of national identity circulating within the larger culture.

These chapters examine the ways in which novels engage aspects of mass culture and then analyze the ways in which novels and nonnovelistic texts are simultaneously and dialectically in the process of articulating notions of American identity or "cultural citizenship." Though my use of this term does not derive directly from Toby Miller's work on citizenship, my focus falls within the larger scope of his definition: "[A] public is formed and governed via a technology of the cultural subject known as the cultural citizen, the virtuous political participant who is taught how to scrutinize and improve her or his conduct through the work of cultural policy."[9] The chapters consider the specific "technology" of cultural narratives, from mass culture and book culture, that serve as vehicles through which to examine identities within the postwar United States. These narratives may not always read as overtly "protest" or political in tone, but in my readings of them I try to highlight ways in which they specifically respond to cultural "policies" from ethnic perspectives.

The five novels at the core of this work function as an important space for, in Stuart Hall's words, "playing with the identifications" presented within mass culture. Much like the texts comprising Jinqi Ling's study of Asian American writers, the novels I focus on reveal how "these texts' ideological tendencies and formal characteristics, as well as the specific forms of their social imagination, were shaped not by any single determinant but rather by the complex interplay between authorial design, available social space, and accessible cultural resources—on a social-material terrain that was only partially open, conditionally heterogeneous, and dynamically fluid yet frequently inhospitable to the voices of the emergent." Ling's comments are intended to highlight the specificity of the cultural history influencing one set of immigrant groups, but this convergence of the social and imaginative spaces applies across ethnic canons more generally, as well. While continuing to investigate the specificities of ethnic experience in the United States, it is also important to continue exploring the ways in which ethnically marked narratives cross cultural boundaries to partake in articulating different versions of national identities at significant points in American history. As noted earlier, the novels and visual narratives discussed here are not all-inclusive and cannot claim to represent all novels of the 1950s nor the experiences or representations of all ethnic groups during this period. While we should not "homogenize" ethnic experiences, we do need to recognize, in Manning Marable's words, "the profound divergences *and* the parallels in the social construction of ethnicity."[10] The cultural work these texts perform together and the questions they inherently ask about ethnicity, identity, and cultural citizenship do highlight the connectedness of many ethnic American experiences and, consequently, contribute to a further understanding of some of the ways in which identities have been configured within American culture writ large.

Because of this project's evocation of a particular cultural context for reevaluating ethnic novels, my textual choices necessarily exclude some important narratives from the literary canon. For example, I do not discuss in detail midcentury Anglo-American authors who dealt with institutional racism (William Faulkner, Harper Lee, Lillian Smith) or works by ethnic minority authors that do not deal explicitly with ethnic identity (for example, James Baldwin's *Giovanni's Room* or William Saroyan's *The Human Comedy*). For the purposes of this project, I focus on the insights provided by novels that *name* ethnicity as a significant factor within the narrative and do so while engaging commercial, visual narratives. As Fredric Jameson famously contends, we can meaningfully access history through its "textualization, its narrativization in the political unconscious."[11] Novels and other major narrative forms are constantly positioning themselves vis-à-vis one another within American cultural life, and reading them in conversation with one another opens new interpretive avenues for contemplating the ethnic "textualizations" of social history. By incorporating various mass-culture narratives in comparative readings with these novels, I further promote the notion that the period is not just a "context" (read backdrop) for the novels, but that these texts are all engaged collaboratively in constructing or revising ethnic American identities at a crucial point in history.

Written and Visual Narratives at Midcentury

Two well-known films of the post–World War II era, *A Face in the Crowd* (1957) and *The Manchurian Candidate* (1962), contain scenes that frame television as a potentially troublesome site for the misuses of power and manipulation of the public.[12] Framing screens within screens, they offer sophisticated metacommentaries on the medium in its early years. Within the first film's narrative, Andy Griffith's seemingly down-home TV host character, Lonesome Rhodes, is framed and climactically exposed as a demagogue when his vengeful manager pulls up the sound in the studio to block out the show's exit music, revealing his flippant off-air comments about how easily he can dupe the audience. In a similar vein, *The Manchurian Candidate* contains a behind-the-scenes vision of demagoguery waiting to be exposed: Angela Lansbury's double-agent character, Mrs. Iselin, skulks conspiratorially in profile next to the television monitor on which her McCarthyesque husband announces the number of suspected Communists in the federal government. Both films rely on these critiques of television to forward messages about the power and malleability of image and rhetoric that threaten the very principles guiding American life. These commentaries seem especially clever in feature films appearing in the aftermath of the television boom, which noticeably challenged the popularity and productivity of the Hollywood movie industry in ways that caused major revisions in movie making and marketing practices.[13] While the above metaframes question the politics behind representation on television, "film" seems to ignore the fact that it, too, is engaged in these same kinds of politicized activities.

Novels began paralleling the gestures in these two films in prior decades, framing and calling into question the representational practices at work within movies, which were in the process of shifting the cultural position of the novel as the dominant form of entertainment narrative. One of the most famous examples appears in Richard Wright's *Native Son* (1940), as the narrative frames the movie screen flickering before Bigger Thomas's eyes, offering him images of white femininity and desire that he can only temporarily consume but never really possess.[14] These kinds of novelistic framings are not usually inflected with the same tones of conspiracy and paranoia as the above filmic counterparts; however, they do raise the same kinds of questions about the rhetorical power of images within the public and private spheres of American culture. Still, novels are not always consistently acknowledged as "products" themselves. Evan Brier notes the ways in which the growth of mass culture in the postwar era influenced the American novel, both in that it became a subject for novelists and in that it altered the ways in which books functioned as commodities: "As there is no categorical separation between mass culture and other forms of culture, there is no such divide between the marketing of postwar American novels and the novels themselves; marketing went, as it were, all the way down, and novelists were, in effect rather than by design, essential collaborators in the project of producing belief in the novel's cultural value." He aptly demonstrates that novels are "still often treated solely as commentators on the commodification of culture" as opposed to participants within a commodity culture.[15]

While this book works to create dialogue between visual and written narratives, the novels are a starting point. The novels provide an impetus for reexamining familiar visual narratives, whose readings are then afforded a disruptive potential that may not have been there without the novel in question. My work on these novels is based on several premises about the functions of literature and other narratives within American culture. Foremost is the assumption that almost all cultural products reveal some kind of narrative, and all narratives produced within the national boundaries of the United States are in some way *about* American identity, as, in the words of Lisa Lowe, "it is through culture that the subject becomes, acts, and speaks itself as 'American.'" Furthermore, Edward Said argues that the connections between imperial expansion and culture are found within narratives, as "nations themselves *are* narrations" (original emphasis).[16] As noted earlier, the psychological and cultural concept of "identity" became a crucial force of inquiry within narratives in the period following World War II. Ralph Ellison once stated that the search for identity is "*the* American theme. The nature of our society is such that we are prevented from knowing who we are. It is still a young society, and this is an integral part of its development." Moving beyond the alienation that became the focus of much modernist writing, many postwar works explore the multiple and complex identities operating within what was once seen as "the unified subject." Joseph Urgo describes the postmodern stance as one that implicitly acknowledges that there is no "original" (or "authentic") identity from which to be alienated, and narratives work through a process of "self revision and cultural interrogation."[17] The period immediately following World War II remains integral to further interrogations of these trends within literary history because of the boom in production of, and sheer cultural saturation by, visual narratives that vied for a contributive space within the larger national "search for identity" at the dawn of a new technological age—even as the new media were representing the old and vice versa.

While other literary forms also provided spaces for marginalized writers, I focus on novels because of their significance as the predominant form of print entertainment narrative in the modern age. Until the advent of films, and then television, the novel was the most-consumed narrative across class and gender lines for almost a century. While there is not space to examine the complete institutional history of the novel in this project, it is important to acknowledge its unique cultural position within literary production as other major entertainment narratives entered the scene, all of them in discursive circulation within the postwar American public, and sometimes in collaboration with one another as novelists became increasingly involved in theatrical and film work through adaptation and script writing. Of the novel's social role, Jonathan Arac notes, "In that age of the novel in the United States, say from about the time of *Moby-Dick* and *Uncle Tom's Cabin* to that of *Invisible Man* and *Lolita*, the novel had a special relationship to what we now call the national imaginary, and that special relationship has now passed from print, in particular the novel, to other media forms." It is at midcentury we see the growth of technologies and distribution that move visual media ever more firmly into the private space of the home, right alongside the novels on one's bookshelf or nightstand, and a shift in the headquarters of the "national imaginary." This period is fruitful for further exploration of the cultural functions of the novel in a culture in which visual narratives are increasing in number and vying for space within the larger public arena, and also of how these different types of narratives work together toward more multifaceted understandings of that culture.[18]

In a sense, the writers of this period perform the same cultural gesture as the previous century's writers examined by Priscilla Wald in *Constituting Americans*. She describes creative prose as a common medium to which people have continually returned for working out questions of Americanness. Though the specific rhetorics in question after World War II differ from the early legal documents forming the backdrop of Wald's study, the questions she asks still apply: "What are the limits and boundaries of We the People? What is the role of the writer in the constituting of Americans?"[19] The increasingly significant position of mass media within American culture shifted these issues of democratic theory into different arenas and discourses, but the same impulses found themselves still paradoxically entrenched in postwar culture, in a nation striving toward an idealized all-inclusive, egalitarian society while also promoting individual success at the expense of the whole.

Race, Ethnicity, and Context

The postwar period saw a convergence of related forces that changed American lifestyles for the latter half of the century, including demographic and geographic shifts, changes in thinking about the family and education, shifts in work and class structures, and the rise of leisure culture and mass consumption. So what did it mean to be "ethnic" at midcentury? There were various events and social changes taking place during this period that expanded the possibilities for ethnic minorities to participate fully in cultural citizenship and some others that maintained limits upon them. The social progress that is popularly understood as the labor of the 1960s is now well documented as having been in place before and during the 1950s, with, for example, the legal fights for educational desegregation and early civil rights actions.[20]

Mainstream mass culture began to change with the insurgence of African American and Chicano music stars and the inclusive casts of characters in youth gang novels and films (though often in stereotypical criminal roles). Even scholastic juvenile literature celebrated the contributions of immigrants to the United States with such titles as *We Came to America* (1954) and *Nine Who Chose America* (1959). At the same time, though, such cultural inclusions were counterbalanced by circumstances like continuing discrimination and violence against African Americans; "Operation Wetback," which deported thousands of *bracero* residents of the Southwest for fear of Communist infiltration; the federal government's undertaking of major expulsions of American Indians from treatied lands; and the execution of the Rosenbergs accompanied by a persistent paranoia that associated Communism with intellectuals and Jews. "Ethnic pride" movements were not yet on the national scene.

Ethnicity certainly does not hold a particular, coherent political expression between the calendar dates of 1948 and 1963 (or whatever parameters one uses to define "midcentury"). This book does not attempt to define all "ethnic writing" of the period nor to argue for all ethnic minority writers as embodying progressive political views.[21] Yet the period after World War II was a pivotal era in new conversations and thinking about ethnicity, in both political and popular arenas. Simultaneously, institutional segregation was still practiced—legally and not. Questions arose then and remain today about how to define race, how to define ethnicity, and to what extent either category matters to American cultural identity.

One certainty is that the definitions of these terms have always been in flux. Scholars such as Michael Roediger and Clara Rodriguez are two of the more recent to explore how definitions have shifted due to changing sociohistorical contexts for how Americans think about race and ethnicity. For example, Rodriguez studies in detail the history of the U.S. Census to examine how these definitions have evolved over time. She documents that the 1950 Census was the first that tried to explain the concept of "race" within the Census form, in language that revealed how little the United States understood its own conceptualizations of race and how definitions still varied from state to state because of historical precedents. Roediger carefully examines how, in the first half of the twentieth century,

> [a]lthough World War II was a watershed, . . . [there was a] gradual series of changes in urban race relations, housing, and state policies causing new immigrant communities to want and win a firmly white identity. Ironically, the nadir of new immigrant existence—the racial attacks culminating in restricted immigration in the 1920s—ushered in a period in which the "immigrant problem" seemed relatively settled and assimilation to whiteness could occur; at the same time, the great liberal mobilizations of the New Deal and industrial unionism in the 1930s made space in which new immigrants could mobilize as whites and exclude others. As they lived with race and called on the state for aid, the immigrant house, increasingly defined as the "white" house, became a key site for the making of race. As houses were constructed, so too was the idea—validated by popular campaigns for segregation of neighborhoods in the 1920s and then by the New Deal housing policy—that African Americans were "antineighbors"; and that all Europeans could unify around that realization.

His work shows the various processes by which the idea of "ethnicity" as an aspect of whiteness came into being and was already in place by the war.[22]

A study that nicely demonstrates the strength of fluctuating definitions at midcentury in particular is Karen Brodkin Sacks' "How Did Jews Become White Folks?" Sacks traces the coincidental circumstances resulting in a situation in which "[s]uddenly the same folks who promoted nativism and xenophobia were eager to believe that Euro-origin people whom they had deported, reviled as members of inferior races, and prevented from immigrating only a few years earlier were now model middle-class white suburban citizens." These disparate factors were the post–World War II easing of anti-Semitism in the United States, new economic opportunities, federal educational initiatives, and suburbanization. What Brodkin Sacks documents here, parallel to Roediger's work, is the process in American culture by which "race" metamorphoses into "ethnicity" for certain groups by means of particular sociohistorical circumstances. Similar scholarly work has been done to trace these processes for other specific groups, as well, such as the Irish and the Italians. Arlene Dávila shows, too, how the shift from racialized to "ethnic" over time is not unidirectional: "Already, even if only categorically, Mexicans were regarded as white prior to the 1930s, as were many Latin Americans in the United States prior to the official 1970s institutionalization of 'Hispanic' to include all peoples of Spanish heritage and origin." Now, the twenty-first century sees the political atmosphere around immigration reracializing Mexicans. Such studies reiterate precisely Ronald Takaki's point that "race" has been an inherently more powerful category for exclusion than ethnicity has been for inclusion because of the power differential at work. Categories based on physiognomy or phenotype, like "black" or "Asian," have remained in inferior hierarchical relation to "white" and have historically lent those categories less malleability for cultural redefinition.[23]

As such, "race" serves as a public and political category more than as an individual descriptor of identity. "Ethnicity" has come to represent the identity variables at work within a set of geopolitical boundaries, based on cultural practices, language, nations of origin or ancestry, and religion. Using ethnicity in this sense, one might argue that everyone is ethnic, because everyone draws on culture and ancestry for identity. "Yet," warns Rey Chow, "if everyone is ethnic, no one is," so we have to think carefully about how we use this term.[24]

What case studies on the topics of race and ethnicity seem to collectively assert is that *context* has everything to do with how these categories are defined and play out within the real social arena. Where Irish may have been a distinct "race" in the early American Republic, the abstract processes of acculturation had taken place so thoroughly by the mid twentieth century that "Irish" became a nominal ethnicity. Meanwhile, the federal watchfulness over potential domestic enemies during World War II highlighted as "racial" Americans of Japanese and Italian heritage because the context provided for them to be seen as "alien." Despite a continuing general suspicion toward foreigners during the Cold War, many refugees from Communist-led countries were welcomed to the United States, and the McCarran-Walter Act of 1952 eased the heavy immigration restrictions of previous decades and lifted racial qualifications for citizenship eligibility.[25] Even with these legal maneuvers, the categorical influences of "race" did not quickly disappear for new immigrants. These metamorphoses of official identities speak to Ralph Ellison's apt definition of the American nation as "more of a process than an isolable set of characteristics." As Rey Chow puts it, "ethnicity is not simply a static space occupied by ethnics who are, somehow, already there but, more important, also a relation of cultural politics that is regularly being enacted by a Westernized, Americanized audience with regard to those who are perceived and labeled as being ethnic." And from a historical perspective, Roediger argues, "the ambiguities [of definition] spoke to how ethnicity tortuously emerged as a term registering uneven and unpredictable changes in how new immigrant communities and communities of color existed in a changing social structure."[26] While both race and ethnicity serve as important identity-influencing factors within this project, my more frequent use of the term "ethnicity" imparts an interest in the cultural identities that are always in progress within the parameters of—and apart from—the legal racial categories.

Worth considering, however, is the attention some theorists pay to the ways in which the concept of race has been glossed over because of a privileging of "ethnicity" as an all-encompassing term. Michael Omi and Howard Winant, for example, caution that people too easily view race as a "variety of ethnicity," which draws attention away from the very real power differentials at work within a culture that functions with a "ubiquitous racial logic." It is a concept that has become increasingly difficult to define, they continue, but "how one is categorized is far from a merely academic or even personal matter" because of the real-world ramifications race has within public and private sectors. Similarly, anthropologist Roger Sanjek contends that in scholarship seeking to further our understanding of global racial formations "it clarifies nothing to euphemize race with 'color caste,' 'ethnicity,' 'plural society,' 'duality,' or similar evasions." While this is true, it is also important to examine the ways in which all the social concepts and formations Sanjek lists do interact variously on personal and social levels. We must not overlook the significance of race within world history, and we must also not allow it to become an overly deterministic or reductive consideration. Chow reaffirms this in her contention that the "frequent conflation of [these terms] is not the result of mental sloppiness on the part of scholars but rather a symptom of the theoretical fuzziness of the terms themselves, and fuzziness that, moreover, must be accommodated precisely because of the overdetermined nature of the issues involved."[27]

Turning to economic concepts as a means of understanding how race and ethnicity have been artificially constructed within the modern era, like Chow and Roediger, theorists Etienne Balibar and Immanuel Wallerstein explore these definitions in relation to labor and class. Wallerstein positions "race" and "ethnicity" primarily in relation to the division of labor within the "economic machinery" of the modern nation-state. Balibar adds that ethnicity is a "fictive" set of categories devised for the purposes of producing a sense of "natural" and "transcendent" belonging to a community. Similarly, Werner Sollors asserts, "The forces of modern life embodied in such terms as 'ethnicity,' 'nationalism,' or 'race' can indeed be meaningfully discussed as 'inventions.'" Seeing less manipulative hegemony at work than Balibar and Wallerstein, he still implies the constructedness of such concepts, describing them as "widely shared though intensely debated, collective fictions that are continually reinvented."[28] The work of these three theorists is useful in demonstrating the arbitrary nature of categories devised as a means of assessing "identity," but these definitions are also somewhat narrow and overly deterministic for encompassing the social implications of such structures.

To claim that ethnic identities are, at base, artificial constructs is to imply that ethnicity does not *really* exist. As slippery, arbitrary, and temporal as its definition might be, the idea of ethnicity has long held—and continues to hold—power in the material world. Of course, to argue the polar opposite, that these identifiers are not "fictive" or "invented," is to inherently fall into the trap of defining ethnicity and race according to nonsocial structures, to look for the problematically "natural" origins of identity. Essentialist definitions of identity leave little influence to historical and cultural environment and can, at worst, perpetuate stereotypes and assumptions about identity-related predilections. Sollors admits that, while understanding the constructedness of these identity categories, "it must be possible to acknowledge and describe concrete ethnic differences without necessarily reifying the concept of ethnicity." And while it may be useful to parse out and challenge these loaded terms in various ways, a terminology is still necessary for tagging a set of lived experiences. "Ethnicity" is indeed an apt term here, for in Chow's words, it "voids replicating the residual biologism that is inerasably embedded in the term 'race,' situates the problems at hand within culture and representation, [and] marks the discrimination entrenched in dominant ways of thinking and talking about so-called minorities."[29] In contrast, I occasionally use the term "racial*ized*" in my discussion to indicate the very purposeful, institutional categorization of an ethnic subject based on physiognomy.

Snapshots of an Era: Mass Culture and National Cultural Shifts

"[S]eeing is absolutely central to the meaning of the 1950s."
—Karal Ann Marling

The emphasis on mass culture within this book is not meant to serve simply as a social context. Instead, we should see it as a kind of commercial narrative force circulating within the culture, one that projected, reflected, and evolved with popular thinking on a variety of subjects. Joel Foreman describes mass culture of the era as "a living information system" that, "through the medium of exchange relations, pricing mechanisms, resource allocation, and productive activities organized and maintained itself as a distinct entity."[30] The images of Donna Reed in an apron, hula-hoopers, screaming Elvis fans, Lassie, and teenagers necking in huge convertibles have endured within our culture because they were so engaging and novel, and they conveyed the exuberance with which people wanted to live everyday life after two decades of economic depression and war. They are also largely responsible for a rather homogenous nostalgia about the era because of the facility with which they were mass produced, preserved, and made mainstream; the newer technology that enabled them to stay in circulation has kept them in our collective line of vision, and the fact that the majority of the faces in these images appeared Anglo has kept that collective image as majority white.

Because it is for sale, mass culture is presumably "for" everyone. This is an aspect of midcentury mass culture that is so fascinating: while it became ever more widely available, not everyone was directly and visibly included in the invitation to consume, and not everyone had the financial means to do so.[31] Several studies have noted that much of the economic prosperity we associate with the period was artificial. The period immediately following the war witnessed an understandable slump in production without the war machine. The government instigated production initiatives and new lending policies that created a general sense of optimistic financial upswing. The reality is that, while the middle class was rapidly expanding, prosperity did not set in fully until midway through the 1950s and experienced some hiccups later in the decade.[32] Before the war, there were various avenues that really did cater to all kinds of people. The "race record" industry promoted early jazz and blues performers to mass audiences; immigrant neighborhoods and the movie industry enjoyed a symbiotic link; and, as Richard Polenberg notes, hundreds of foreign-language radio programs existed for immigrants nationwide. Some of these ethnic-targeted marketing strategies were altered by the war or simply slipped away, as was the case of much radio programming, when replaced by emergent technologies. But these avenues for representation were not necessarily replaced with equivalents after the war. In the late 1940s, marketers started to consider ethnic-specific advertising, but it was limited. Lizabeth Cohen notes, "In 1948, when Pepsi-Cola became one of the first mainstream advertisers to 'discover' the Negro market and mount an advertising campaign in over fifty black newspapers, it set a precedent that would continue through the 1950s of major companies increasingly pursuing African Americans' rising spending power, but without substantively reorienting their 'one-size-fits-all' mass marketing campaigns." It was not until the ethnic pride movements of the 1960s that such advertisers stopped running in ethnic media the same ads with white models they ran in mainstream magazines. As the postwar years wore on, the mass media narratives became ever more "white," middle-class, nuclear family oriented, traditionally gendered, and consumer oriented. This resulted in a series of what Alan Nadel calls patriotic "tropes" that "performed the ideological task of constructing narratives that allowed a significant portion of the population to link its sense of self—the story of its life—to national history"—that is, national history as renarrativized by Anglo-Americans.[33]

The term "white middle class" has become a problematically homogenizing descriptor in itself. My use of it is intended not to oversimplify a set of real identities, but in the sense best articulated by Lynn Spigel, as a "set of social identifications encouraged by the media rather than to real individuals whose identities were more fractured and complex. Still, the term has real meaning because it was the particular aim of the mass media—especially television—to level class and other ethnic differences in order to produce a homogenous public for national advertisers."[34]

Part of this leveling was due to the major shifts in the cultural geography of the United States, with vast numbers of families moving away from urban centers to the suburbs. An increased need for housing after the war resulted in the mass production of new neighborhoods in previously rural areas, most of them using the assembly line method devised by William J. Levitt (of Levittown fame) to crank out hundreds of homes each week. The increased availability of housing, along with new lending initiatives developed by the government, resulted in a mass migration of young families and couples away from the urban centers, away from distinctly ethnic neighborhoods and extended family structures. Historians have noted that this is one of the major ways in which a younger generation from Eastern European and Mediterranean immigrant families became absorbed within "whiteness." Roediger, for example, argues that this shift was set in motion well before the war: "The FHA, [Home Owners Loan Corporation], and VA actually ensured that new immigrants and their descendants would have less and less ability to choose to develop their own urban neighborhoods. New Deal housing policies empowered and advantaged new immigrants, but as whites, not as new immigrants." Ironically, notes Polenberg, "just when the government and the civil rights movement appeared to be moving the nation toward integration, the flight to the suburbs was pulling it even more strongly in the opposite direction."[35] While these demographic shifts provided some ethnic groups with a sudden social mobility, the zoning regulations and by-laws in many new subdivisions prohibited home sales to some groups, particularly African Americans and Jews. The Veterans Administration and Federal Housing Administration did not inherently combat the exclusionary codes of specific housing developments, as their rules and lending practices discriminated against investment in private ownership of homes in many ethnic minority neighborhoods. Cohen notes, "In theory, veterans who were first-time home buyers of all races were able to get low-interest mortgages guaranteed by the Veterans Administration or the Federal Housing Authority. . . . But to get such a loan, a veteran needed a willing lender and a willing seller—both difficult to find, especially in the South. Loans were limited to single-family homes, not urban apartments or town houses." In fact, only a tiny percentage of VA loans went to African American veterans. Even for nonveterans, federal and private lending guidelines favored mortgages in white, middle-class, suburban neighborhoods. In the end, "The landscape of mass consumption created a metropolitan society in which people were no longer brought together in central marketplaces and the parks, streets, and public buildings that surrounded them but, rather, were separated by class, gender, and race in differentiated commercial sub-centers."[36]

For those who could buy new homes there came a consequent imperative to outfit the home with furniture and modern appliances, to provide vehicles for transport to the centers of work and commerce. Martyn Lee locates the birth of a "fully fledged regime of accumulation" in the 1950s and 1960s within the earlier twentieth-century phenomenon of "Fordism" (named after the innovator capitalist responsible for the development of modern mass production methods). This force not only changed production and labor practices; it also instigated "the emergence of modern consumer society and a whole raft of corresponding social and cultural changes." Further, Medovoi argues,

> the postwar suburb must be understood, not simply as a geographical phenomenon, nor even as a new mode of mass consumption, but as a primary Cold War ideological apparatus. A "machine for living," the suburban home . . . hailed its subjects not as a multiracial working class with common laboring interests to defend, nor even as citizen members of a heterogeneous public, but instead as white Americans participating in a national ideal (the much ballyhooed "American Dream") that itself needed defending against its communist enemies. Moving to the suburbs was tantamount to doing one's national duty by building the affluence and strength of America's Fordist order.

The groundwork of these postwar marketing successes, whether rhetorical or commercial, was established in the 1920s and '30s. An existing consumerist rhetoric, then, along with perceptions of household need in the new suburbs, and new technologies to attract purchasers, came an increased accessorizing of the new majority white-collar lifestyle and its accompanying leisure culture. Thus, conspicuous consumption gradually became part of the fabric of American life for more families, who, practically speaking, could afford more purchases because of the lower cost of cheap goods via mass production.[37]

Participation in a vital consumer economy was envisioned not only as a personal fantasy, but also as a patriotic duty and national privilege. The rhetorics reveal both a sense of shared excitement about new technologies and the ways in which it might help society progress and an imperative to participate in growing the capitalist economy as a response to Communism. A perfect example of combined patriotic and consumerist rhetoric appears in one television program that ran a dramatization of the hypothetical takeover of an American town by Communists. In the middle of the militaristic dramatization, the host breaks in with a commercial intermission to promote two new shopping centers. He claims that this is a worthy pause because the malls are "concrete expressions of the practical idealism that built America. . . . with

Figure 1. Picturing immigrants: Ethnic Americans as "social problems" in documentary photojournalism. Here, a family of immigrants files paperwork with Alien Registration. New York City, 1951. "Alien Registration." Photographer Burt Glinn / Magnum Photos.

more than four-score beautiful stores . . . and plenty of parking for all the cars that we capitalists seem to acquire. Who can help but contrast the beautiful, the practical settings of Arcadia Shopping Hub and the Whittier Quad with what you'd find under communism?"[38]

On television programs, on product packaging, on cookbook covers, the bodies of Americans were primarily envisioned as white and middle-class. Ethnic subjects appeared now and then, of course, as caricatures, logos, entertainers. Issues facing ethnic Americans were broached, but often in the context of "social problems" in film dramas or photo-realist journalism. Some ethnic minority stars did have their own television shows (Molly Goldberg, Nat King Cole), but they were often short-lived programs, as I will discuss in further detail in chapter 4. The visual, institutional, and social messages were convoluted and sometimes self-contradictory. These narratives were circulating as rapidly as prefabricated houses were going up, and they were all vying for attention through a variety of semiotic appeals, on new television sets, at the drive-in movies, in Technicolor, in more and more teen magazines.

While this was the case, there were also some narrow avenues for diversity within the consumer logic. The large number of mass culture products in constant circulation provided many opportunities to go beyond the stereotypical or status quo. Foreman notes that because of a "spontaneous emergence of desires and demands that cannot be predicted with certainty," the market and its "millions of constituents preclude central control and provide the enabling conditions for cultural change." Not only is there space for the production of new, potentially progressive, cultural forms, there is room for interpretation. Stuart Hall maintains that mass culture is not all bad; it "is profoundly mythic. . . . It is where we discover and play with the indentifications of ourselves, where we are imagined, where we are represented, not only to the audiences . . . but to ourselves. . . ."[39] Through the novel, as well, midcentury ethnic writers were very much engaged in playing with the mythologies set out within mass culture, in engaging the real estate of representation occupied most visibly—but not solely—by mass media, and in offering additional narratives for reimagining the American self.

In this cultural milieu, the chapters that follow offer investigations into how various narratives question and prod these definitions and boundaries of performances of cultural citizenship in the 1950s. These textual case studies begin with the positioning of recent immigrants within postwar American culture in "The Land of Plenty: American Mass Culture and the Literary Immigrant in C. Y. Lee's *The Flower Drum Song* and Vladimir Nabokov's *Lolita*." A comparative reading of the novels, published in 1957 and 1955, respectively, this chapter differs from the ones after it in that it focuses on two novels' engagement of mass culture in general rather than focusing on a novel/nonnovel dialogue (though both novels were eventually adapted to film). In terms of narrative development, language, audience, and ideology of citizenship, these two novels delineate the extremes in representing immigrant subjects. They offer very different takes on cultural self-definition, influenced by the tensions between assimilation and cultural preservation in relation to gendered and ethnicizing identity practices within American culture. My readings of immigrant subjectivities here function as an analytical "hinge," extending the ideas of the first chapter and providing groundwork for the subsequent ones. First, the readings introduce how a novel can engage mass culture in ways that both affect narrative structure and serve as implicit social commentary; second, they highlight the ways in which ethnic subjects may participate in midcentury cultural citizenship; third, they theorize the role of mass culture forms in accomplishing this kind of cultural participation. In both novels the immigrant is portrayed as facing an obvious set of decisions regarding his relationship to American cultural practices. Because identity is so obviously based on decisions in these narratives, and the two novels attempt to work out these decisions in narrow (and contrasting) ways, this chapter functions as an important first step in theorizing the roles of popular and mass cultures in identity formation that come into question in the subsequent chapters. In each of those, I then focus on a novel in conjunction with a major visual narrative medium (respectively, television, magazine/star marketing, and film).

Chapter 2 also begins the work of examining the gendering of the consumer imperative, which is taken up further through the perspective of ethnic womanhood in chapter 3, "What's for Sale: Consumer Fantasy, American Women, and Social Mobility in Gwendolyn Brooks's *Maud Martha* and the *I Love Lucy* Show." This chapter examines the roles of gender and ethnicity within class and domestic ideals by reading Gwendolyn Brooks's short 1953 novel against one of its most culturally influential televisual counterparts. Here, the public and private spheres become spaces for thinking through identities and cultural capital. This chapter offers *Maud Martha* as a resolution of the contradictory tensions for the ethnic subject through writing the struggle with, and final rejection of, an identity enmeshed in consumer fantasy.

Transitioning from the private spaces of identity reinterpretation offered within *Maud Martha*, the next two chapters examine ethnic subjectivities under scrutiny within public spaces. They further take up the issue of performing cultural citizenship, the perspectives shifting as the subjects attempt to insert themselves within mass culture in the form of celebrity. In this light, I reconsider the possibilities for "passing" into national culture based on the sociohistorical forces of ethnicity and the ways in which ethnic subjects contribute to the construction of (ethnic) American identity.[40]

The first of these, "The Celluloid Fantasy: Negotiating the Ethnic Male Star Image in William Saroyan's *Rock Wagram*," examines the 1951 novel's fascinatingly complicated portrait of an Armenian American actor in Hollywood. This chapter considers the relationship between mass media institutions and the identities constructed and manipulated therein by positioning the novel within a contemporaneous constellation of popular narratives about ethnic masculine celebrity. Saroyan's novel somewhat reverses the perspective of the previous chapter, moving from a contemplation of the ideals for sale to the public to an examination of the politics of "being the product." At the same time that these theatrical institutions anglicized and incorporated ethnic male stars, such as Desi Arnaz, Frank Sinatra, and Danny Thomas, the same institutions utilized the "exotic" qualities of their ethnic masculinity to market popular desires, and the celebrities contributed ethnicity to the construction of popular desire itself. I use the novel's own theories of identity to engage and reassess the history and role of ethnic actors in Hollywood at midcentury, analyzing those processes of manipulation as they are problematized within the novel and as they occurred historically through the marketing of ethnic male star images in movie magazines and in Hollywood. In the end, this chapter takes on the notions of "artificial" versus "authentic" (or "assimilated" versus "preserved") ethnic culture by examining how Saroyan's protagonist works through multiple notions of identity that undermine the ability of these terms to encapsulate identities at all.

Finally, chapter 5, "Leaving the Dark Room in a Lighter Mood: Narrating Invisibility in Douglas Sirk's *Imitation of Life* and Ralph Ellison's *Invisible Man*," joins the various ideas at work within these chapters by further investigations into the notion of cultural performance through a reading of Ralph Ellison's well-known 1952 novel *Invisible Man* in conjunction with the 1959 film version of *Imitation of Life*, directed by Douglas Sirk. Sorting through notions of ethnicity, gender, and narrative medium to assess the avenues for public articulations of identity, this chapter engages two popular forms that directly take on ethnic and social conflict as a topic in widely consumed narratives. Through the metaphor of moviegoing, the analysis begins with an examination of the film's work on identity and the Ellisonian notion of invisibility in the character of Sarah Jane. Sarah Jane then engages in a kind of dialogue with Ellison's famous protagonist. Like the other novels in this study, *Invisible Man* portrays the tension between resistance and capitulation to participation in the larger culture and the cluttered alleys by which one may move within it. Furthermore, the Sirk film and Ellison novel appear last within this study because together they provide a sort of response to the questions raised within the other novels: if to become visible within American culture is to perform an imitation of cultural citizenship, how might the models provided for simulation be changed, too? Is it possible to go beyond rejection or critique to a real cultural revision in which ethnic Americans contribute to the discourse on what it means to be American?

While I want to evaluate the aspects of medium and genre that affect the cultural work a narrative does, I do not claim that one kind of narrative is inherently better than another. Novels are the starting point for me, but the narrative forms are not in competition. Simply put, by understanding the ways in which a narrative medium functions, and putting it into dialogue with another medium, we might gain a broader set of voices contributing to what Leerom Medovoi calls the "collective we" under scrutiny in this period.[41]

2

The Land of Plenty

American Mass Culture and the Literary Immigrant in C. Y. Lee's *The Flower Drum Song* and Vladimir Nabokov's *Lolita*

Vladimir Nabokov's *Lolita* (1955) and Chin Yang Lee's *The Flower Drum Song* (1957) both engage in contemplations of the ways in which mass culture forms hail individuals into a space of national participation. Though the two novels are very different from one another in terms of narrative development, language, audience, and the ideology of citizenship, they both rely on mass culture within the narrative structure and theorize the role of mass culture as instrumental to postwar American identity formation. Both were also adapted into contemporaneous visual narratives, Lee's as a popular Rodgers and Hammerstein Broadway musical (1958–59) and Hollywood film (1961), and Nabokov's as Stanley Kubrick's *Lolita* (1963). The novel *Lolita* (through the perspective of its recently immigrated, upper middle-class narrator) derisively portrays a nation in which identities are almost completely erased and reformulated through proliferating mass culture forms. This contrasts *The Flower Drum Song*, which presents the overt message that embracing the ideals and icons within American mass culture can serve as a vehicle through which immigrants may pursue assimilation, individual success, and consequently, identification with "nation."

These contrasting subjectivities provide an interesting study in the politics of self-representation, the cultural capital tied to perceptions of ethnicity, and the tensions between notions of assimilation and cultural preservation in relation to commercial consumption. The idea of immigrant subjectivity appears separately from other American ethnicities in this chapter because the negotiations between participation in American public culture and private identity become magnified for subjects newly immersed within the postwar American cultural context. Here, looking at the ways in which mass culture informs immigrant subjectivities provides a basis from which to work in examining the negotiations of ethnic identities in subsequent chapters. The postwar era offers no short supply of published immigrant stories, and the two novels chosen for this chapter might make an unlikely choice for "representative" immigrant narratives. However, they both explicitly utilize American commercial culture in enlightening ways within their explorations of cultural self-definition.

In *Immigrant Acts*, Lisa Lowe examines the often paradoxical rhetorics and political philosophies that have surrounded Asian American immigration to the United States, observing that "the legal and political forms of the nation have required a national culture in the integration of the differentiated people and social spaces that make up 'America,' a national culture, broadly cast yet singularly engaging, that can inspire diverse individuals to identify with the national project." While her study focuses on the ways in which immigrants have created alternative spaces to counteract the legislative determination of immigrant subjectivities through cultural production, her formulation of the national culture is also useful in understanding the formations of immigrant subjectivities more generally. A particular paradox she works with is how the economic and the political, which complement one another in theory, effectively contradict one another in a "racially differentiated nation": "[C]apital, with its supposed needs for 'abstract labor,' is said by Marx to be unconcerned by the 'origins' of its labor force, whereas the nation-state, with its need for 'abstract citizens' formed by a unified culture to participate in the political sphere, is precisely concerned to maintain a national citizenry bound by race, language, and culture." Lowe's formulation is complemented by Toby Miller's, which describes the capitalist nation-state as relying upon consumerism, among other means, "to produce a sense of oneness among the increasingly heterogeneous populations" and "forge a loyalty to market economics and parliamentary democracy, as well as a sustainable society through the formation of cultural citizens, docile but efficient participants in that economy-society mix." Lowe's project translates work like Miller's into a more specific application, not to examine the theoretical processes by which these abstract citizens are formed, but to examine the working definitions that help to inform such notions of citizenship when, inherently, ethnic and racialized subjects are treated differently. Lowe examines how the imperative to bind an "abstract citizenry" became heightened in the mid-twentieth century with the onset of the Cold War and found an important avenue for implementation within the commercial fields that permeated everyday life. In thinking through how Lee's and Nabokov's novels articulate this consumerism-as-citizenry narrative, I add more explicitly mass culture to Lowe's discussion of the legal and political, with Pierre Bourdieu's configurations of the interdependent fields of cultural production in mind. The various institutions, while serving different social functions, inherently and always position themselves in relation to one another, dependent on the others for some of their forms of expression.[1]

I should qualify here why it is that I am reading *Lolita* as an immigrant narrative. Nabokov and his narrator, Humbert Humbert, are most often referred to by critics as *émigré*, or occasionally as "expatriate," terms that immediately call attention to the class issues implied in the term "immigrant." Most people do not think to group a book like *Lolita* with "immigrant literature" precisely because of the European origins and academic class positions of Nabokov and his narrator—which brings to light the ways in which class has largely been overlooked in immigrant literary studies. The term "immigrant" carries with it political connotations because of the history of immigration law and ethnic and cultural politics within the United States. While *émigré* possesses the erudition of its French intonation, "immigrant" has most commonly implied marginalization, exclusion, poverty, and (sometimes romanticized) suffering.

Considering the cultural implications of ethnicity in the context of immigration, the term "immigrant" has become a powerful, often marginalizing, cultural category with very real conditions for certain individuals and groups, and the term has taken on connotations specific to American immigration history.[2] In the two novels discussed in this chapter, for example, Humbert Humbert would seldom be called "immigrant," while the characters of *The Flower Drum Song* are unquestionably incorporated within bibliographies of immigrant literature because of their ethnic, non-Western origins. Yet their non-Western origins seem to be the only aspect that truly differentiates them from Humbert in this classification, for, like him, the Wang patriarch is highly educated and relatively well off. Instead of editing a volume on French poetry (as Humbert does), a kind of scholarship that translates into a revered form of "high culture" within the United States, Wang Chi-yang is an expert in Chinese calligraphy and the studies of Confucius, which, in the world of the narrative, have an audience only within his home and are portrayed as the kinds of "work" that have no real value in the modern American, protestant-work-ethic setting. Wang Ta, the second generation immigrant, has multiple degrees and attends medical school, yet he still reads as "immigrant" because segregating practices do not allow him to use his education in significant, participatory ways.

These examples highlight the ways in which the perceptions of immigrants are influenced by context-specific notions of ethnicity and class. The loaded term "immigrant" has taken on political connotations, but I also use the term here equitably to describe a literary genre simply for its basic denotation: narratives by those who leave countries of origin to live in another country. In this, *Lolita* is an immigrant novel, and that being the case, almost any immigrant narrative is capable of offering a useful perspective on the culture of the United States—both despite, and because of, its ethnic/class positioning.

With diametrically opposed narratives and styles, the two novels in this chapter serve as a kind of meter by which to examine the encounter of the imagined immigrant and American mass culture. They illustrate the basic either/or that has structured much of the mainstream discussion of ethnicity in the twentieth century: either one assimilates, or one strives to maintain his or her cultural heritage. Of course, much of the work of cultural studies has been to highlight the ways in which this binary is an oversimplification. Locating the either/or extremes within these novels, however, works as a foundation from which to examine the ways in which various levels of negotiation play into ethnic identities. As demonstrated throughout this study, the "choices" are much more complex than those embodied within the assimilate/preserve scenario.

One of the problems with the notion of assimilation is that it presumes the individual or group's culture of origin to be static, as if the country of origin is not also in a state of political, cultural, linguistic flux or one of multiple ethnicities itself. It also assumes that assimilation is a one-way process, that the "host culture" of the United States remains unchanged with the introduction of various immigrant groups and each new group simply has to adapt to an already existent and stable monoculture. Obviously, if the culture of the United States has been under constant revision for its centuries as a nation, the understanding of "assimilation" needs to be used in relation to the cultural, political, and linguistic practices within particular sociohistorical contexts.

"Let Me Take You to an American Movie."

The Flower Drum Song is a novel that (when it does receive critical attention) is often lambasted as pandering to Anglo audiences with stereotypical, offensive portrayals of Asian Americans in an overtly assimilationist tale. The story receives most of its critical attention for the musical stage version rather than the novel, whose libretto cuts most of the original story's commentaries on discrimination and the inequalities found in American culture. Understandably, many critiques come from other Asian American writers, but even some mainstream reviewers of its day found the staged version objectionable because of the Asian stereotypes it perpetuated. While I agree with most of these assessments, I also think that the novel has been overlooked for some of the possibilities it provides for exploring the configurations of these kinds of stereotypes within American culture and in examining how the novel may have been attempting to speak about immigrant identity to an Anglo audience within a certain sociohistorical context. Pausing to investigate obviously stereotypical portrayals may be risky in that it requires that we link our analyses to the discriminatory ideology in which such portrayals originate. But failing to examine them in more depth—just dismissing Lee's novel as unworthy of discussion because it relies on stereotypes—also overlooks possibilities for further critiquing the power dynamics within American history that allow for these representations. For this reason, we do continue to study texts imbued with problematic ideologies, such as the unabashedly racist works of Thomas Dixon and D. W. Griffith. *Flower Drum* provides a useful case study within the postwar context because of the ways in which the narrative attempts to engage and validate isolated pieces of American culture in a rather apologist immigrant narrative—at a "distinct cultural moment," according to Christina Klein, when "Americans turned their attention eastward."[3]

Focusing on the Wang family in San Francisco's Chinatown, the novel offers a typical story of generational conflict, one that, Klein argues, serves to "ethnicize" and Americanize a previously racialized, Othered group in the interest of promoting positive relations between the United States and Asian nations who were allies during the war: "*Flower Drum Song* should be read as both a cultural narrative and a social practice—as a popular story and as an investment of capital, a body of hiring practices, and a series of marketing decisions. As it circulated around the country on stages and movie screens, *Flower Drum Song* created a focal point around which the integration of Asian Americans was enacted, performed, promoted, and publicized." The novel's opening phrase, "To the casual tourists," hails Anglo readers into the narrative space as just that, casual tourists in the lives of a Chinatown family. In a more recent interview, the Chinese immigrant author C. Y. Lee describes what was at the time a desire to write "to a mainstream audience," implying his goal as one of the first Chinese American authors published in English to introduce an accessible version of Chinese culture into the then-contemporary melting-pot approach to immigrant cultures. Klein refers to this trend in Asian American literature of the time as "a touristic quality": "Motivated by an educational and sociological impulse, they guide their readers like privileged tourists through the inner workings of Chinese families, businesses, social relations, and customs" in a literary fashion that dated back to the nineteenth century. The novel's opening phrase signals the intended audience of the novel, for whom an insider's view of Chinatown is promised. But that view does not go too far "inside," as the characters are kept at a relative distance through the third-person narrative perspective, a focus on plot rather than psychological conflict, and cursory accounts of relationships outweighed by detailed attention to the "exotic" accessories surrounding the relationships: physical settings (homes, bars, restaurants), Chinese cultural practices (the herb shop, the curio shop, the tea house), and especially lavish descriptions of food and eating. The tone maintains a "quaintness" and relies on simplified language and a limited amount of dialogue, which is written in basic vocabulary and somewhat broken form as if translated from Chinese. The most extreme of these is found in the character of a waiter, whose speech is transcribed thus: "You've come the wlong day. . . . come to this loom please, the best loom—like it is leserved for you."[4]

The novel's almost naïve tone is undercut with the occasional sensationalist plot development, such as when one of Wang Ta's past girlfriends becomes involved in a love-triangle intrigue and a shooting at a nightclub. In the end, *Flower Drum* reads something like an attempt at what Ta's friend Chang says he would like to create, "a book packed with romance and action and mystery, entitled, *Chinatown after Dark*."[5] (Lee's own novel reads as a pretty tame pot boiler, though.) These are the same aspects of the narrative that Rodgers and Hammerstein played up and boiled down into an even more stereotypical spectacle of Chinatown in their popular Broadway musical version of the book, further hinting at the ways in which Lee's novel made itself available for mainstream consumption. While this novel may have given some voice to Chinese American authors, for the above reasons it may be the least qualified to perform the kind of cultural work that Lisa Lowe seeks in her attempt to uncover Asian American narratives that create alternative spaces for identity formation within the historical and official contexts of American culture.

The novel's elderly widowed father, Wang Chi-yang, is the most traditional of the characters, making every attempt to live his life as he lived it in China, in a house "decorated with Chinese paintings and couplet scrolls, furnished with uncomfortable but expensive teakwood tables and chairs, and staffed with two servants and a cook whom he had brought from Hunan Province." He speaks almost no English, does not work outside the home, and spends his days counting his money, practicing Chinese calligraphy, and taking walks through a limited section of Chinatown. His sons are described as "the only 'impure elements' in his household." The eldest son, Wang Ta, becomes the center of the narrative and the center of familial conflict. A medical student, he is caught within a web of conflicting impulses: old-world definitions of respectability, desire for an American lifestyle (especially when it comes to romantic matters), and discontent about the ways in which young American-educated men like himself are excluded from professionalization in the institutions that have trained them. The younger son, Wang San, is the most Americanized and has "learned to act like a cowboy and talk like the characters in a Spillane movie. At thirteen he had practically forgotten his Chinese."[6] San's role is relatively small in the narrative, but he is significant as the greatest source of shame for his father and the greatest source of "culture clash" comedy for Anglo-American readers. The narrative joins the family's American acculturation midstride, as they are already well settled in San Francisco's Chinatown. We are given no reason for the family's emigration from China, but they do refer to themselves as "refugees," most likely of the pre–World War II Japanese invasions of China and, later, Chinese Communism.

More than through the linguistic makeup and structure of the novel, its accessibility for "mainstream audiences" is built upon the illustrative function of mass culture and commercial ideologies within the narrative. The story persistently refers to and compares "American" and "Chinese" cultural practices regarding food, clothing, transportation, finances, leisure hobbies, courtship, and marriage practices. This is not an uncommon motif in immigrant novels, but here the balance weighs in particularly ideological ways, as all American practices are seen as either beneficial or innocuous, while most Chinese practices are seen as limiting and lacking progressive potential. (The exceptions here are food and, an aspect to which I will return later, gender relations.) Throughout the novel, American mass culture is championed as the vehicle through which one successfully assimilates. Those characters who are unable or unwilling to assimilate by these means meet an unhappy end.

The character who plays the unhappiest of these roles is the father, Chi-yang. He begins the novel as described earlier, attempting to replicate his life of upper-class privilege as lived in China. His values and daily routines are portrayed as backward, often by means of a foil, his sister-in-law Madam Tang. On one hand, she sides with Chi-yang and tradition in certain matters, such as her support of arranged marriage and belief in the Chinese horoscope's importance in making life decisions. Conversely, she also represents (in the world of the novel) a first-generation immigrant who is succeeding in her adaptations to American culture because of her willingness to learn English, take citizenship classes, and wear "Western dress." She constantly tries to intervene in Wang family matters to help them achieve an ideal middle ground that honors their heritage but, more importantly, works to fit those remaining pieces of "Chinese-ness" comfortably into American mainstream culture. Kathryn Edney's study of African American audience reception demonstrates how this intermediary character (called Madam Liang in the stage and film versions) served an important role during the civil rights struggle: "[Juanita] Hall was an African-American woman cast in the role of a Chinese woman in the process of becoming an American citizen at precisely a point in history when African-Americans were regularly denied their civil rights." As such, her performance complicates what seems like a stereotypical portrayal of Asian Americans because she links two ethnic groups' struggles for greater cultural access—a fact not lost in the black press coverage of the original performances of the musical.[7]

In the novel, Madame Tang demonstrates Chi-yang's inability to fit in with American culture through two details: "'Aiyoo, my sister's husband,' she often said, 'please put your money in the bank. And buy yourself a suit of Western dress. In this country you truly look like a stage actor in that satin gown.'" Such a comment belies the (probably accidental) irony of the situation in the author's narrative construction, since the one place Chi-yang would seem to be able to wear traditional dress without getting strange reactions is Chinatown. With the Western-suit scenario, he is made the butt of a comic motif, as he is unable to comfortably wear the American suit and, after much hassling by Madam Tang, burns it in an elaborate ruse to avoid wearing it.[8]

While this scene reveals an "innocent" inability to adopt a custom, he is more soundly punished for not adapting to American attitudes about personal finance. Knowing that he hides a fortune in cash within his home, Madam Tang tries to talk Chi-yang into opening an account at an American bank. He refuses, distrusting the strangers who would handle his money. Shortly after this decision, he is robbed on the street and sees his error. He naively believes that the American government should know about the episode and should guard him, to which his sister-in-law responds in her best citizenship class rhetoric, "You just cannot order the government to send you two soldiers to guard your house day and night as though you were a feudal lord. This is not China. You had better get that idea out of your mind. Besides, the American government has three departments: the legislative, the executive, and the judicial. All you can do is to ask the police department of the Executive Department to catch the thief. As for your money, it should be kept in a bank, as I have repeatedly told you." He eventually does agree to put the money in the bank, after which he sleeps much better, implying the soul-deep security of the American financial system.[9]

Financial planning is Chi-yang's only successful foray into American culture in the story. More often than not his interactions with the culture outside of Chinatown are disastrous, as exemplified by his one venture away from Grant Avenue. Feeling more confident after having safely deposited his money, he breaks his routine walk and decides "to venture farther north to the foreign territory called North Beach." He immediately finds himself in an uncomfortable situation, affronted by the number of bars and the alcoholic smell of the neighborhood as well as the seemingly amoral atmosphere supporting beatnik bars and nude dance clubs. Through a series of misunderstandings, he follows a woman and ends up at a club "with pictures of nude foreign women hanging outside the doors like the poetic banners posted outside the Chinese stores during the New Year." After enduring a brief episode involving an unpalatable "foreign concoction" and a stripper, he rushes home "to bathe himself and fumigate his head with incense."[10] This scene encapsulates the book's dual view of Chinatown as both a sanctuary for the immigrant and, simultaneously, a physical limitation upon the immigrant's ability to adapt to American life. The version of American life in this scene is a subcultural one, but it signifies all of life outside of Chinatown for Wang the elder. In contrast to his experience, the characters who seem happiest in the novel are those who leave Chinatown frequently to seek external relationships and adventures, which fits with Klein's view that many Asian-related narratives of this era promoted integrationist rhetorics. Ta's interactions with friends almost always contain a reference to what kind of car they are driving, which represents their embracing of the new car culture and the physical and social mobility associated with it. In contrast, Ta's father travels everywhere on foot and covers little ground, symbolizing the slowness with which he adapts to becoming American. Because of this slowness, Chi-yang is only beginning to change by the novel's end because he has to: he no longer occupies the "master" position of his household, all of his plans for his sons are in ruins, and his declining health mandates that he seek help from Western medical practitioners.

The most carefree in the Wang family is San, the youngest son, who, in the mind of this father, "talked a foreign tongue, ate with his hands, read strange picture books, and tossed an ugly ball around every day." He imagines training these tendencies out of San with instruction in "the fundamental Chinese morals."[11] An embodiment of the generational culture clash within the Wang house, San best plays his role when reciting his lessons. His father requires him to recite in the style of traditional Confucian education what he has learned at the American school. However, because San spends more time going to the movies, reading comics, and playing baseball, he studies very little and, knowing his father does not understand the content of the English recitations, comedically slips through his recitations by repeating the Declaration of Independence over and over, no matter the subject his father has requested. (He is later physically punished because he cannot recite the maxims of Confucius in Chinese, and his father realizes the boy has been faking all along.) Though this scenario is intended as comedy, the rote memorization of the Declaration here also is ideologically linked with San's participation in American mass culture, for the lines of the Declaration and American leisure activities are portrayed as those aspects that come "naturally" to him—in contrast to the "unnatural," uncomfortable physical setting and the Chinese cultural practices that require extensive, repetitive, "unproductive" work, such as calligraphy and the rote memorization of Confucian maxims.

Of all the family members, however, Wang Ta is the most thoroughly developed character and serves as the most complex element of the story in terms of the levels of cultural ideologies at work within the book. As noted earlier, he is a character torn between the traditional values and proprieties represented in his upbringing and the American lifestyle and worldview he encounters on a daily basis. Unlike his father, who finds Chinatown to be a sanctuary, Ta constantly seeks to remove himself from the enclave, both physically and psychologically. This disruption is presented in terms less political than personal, for the moments of serious critique are few. For example, the first half of the novel contains one serious discussion between Ta and his confidant, Chang, in which they bemoan the paradox of being able to pursue advanced degrees in the United States while being blocked from entering American institutions as professional white-collar workers. The conversation is downplayed, however, by many more detailed discussions of romantic matters and the problem that Chang sees as the root of all difficulty for Chinese immigrants: the high proportion of men to the small number of available Chinese women.[12] Chang is a character who constantly spouts practical advice and wisdom about survival in the United States, and Ta eagerly absorbs the advice because Chang has been in the States longer, is older and more experienced, and has removed himself completely from Chinatown by moving to Los Angeles, revising his career goals toward the service industry, and remaking his life from the kind of food he eats to the non-Chinese woman he marries. (He does not marry an Anglo woman, it is worth noting, but one of the group that they call "foreign foreigners"—other immigrants. He marries a Mexican American woman at the end of the novel.)

Seeking him out frequently, Ta progressively adopts Chang's Americanized philosophies, best represented in his discourse on bowling. Claiming that Chinese refugees "take life too seriously," Chang offers his own life as a model: "You know what I've been talking about since I became a grocery clerk? Bowling. Now I'm a bowling expert. I'm the leader of the Black Dragon team, organized by my grocery colleagues. Don't despise bowling. Besides being good exercise, it's also good for the mind." Espousing the benefits of the growing postwar leisure culture, bowling becomes his metaphor for a larger philosophy of life, which celebrates the "simple working people" of America instead of intellectualism (though not enough to "sound like a communist," he is quick to point out) and "moments of happiness and relaxation." In all of this, he explains, he is trying to "sell" Ta "a new attitude."[13] Over the course of the narrative, then, Ta chooses to ignore the exclusionary practices of American institutions and work toward his own version of Chang's outlook.

What results is a narrative that offers American mass culture as the primary vehicle for acculturation—more so than any educational facility or citizenship class. Like San's recitation of the Declaration of Independence, what seems like an innocent cultural gesture on Ta's part often carries ideological import. Among his increasing forays to dance halls and clubs outside of Chinatown, most notable is his mantra throughout the novel, "Let's go to a movie." His movie-going begins as a form of entertainment, a favorite thing to do on a date. As the novel progresses, however, he comes to think of movies in the same way that Chang views bowling, which, in turn, leads to his espousing of non-Chinese practices within his family, as he increasingly stands up to his father about such conflicts as how the spaces within the house are used, how his younger brother is disciplined, and the superiority of Western medicine over Chinese herbal cures. This narrative agenda is the complete reverse of that which I will discuss in the book's last chapter. While *Flower Drum* provides a view of mass culture as an unproblematic distillation of American values, *Invisible Man* exposes the impermanence of the comfort a marginalized subject may find in such cultural forms.

When political issues do play into the narrative structure, they appear in the form of critiques of the Communist regime in China. These appear mostly in the second half of the novel, with the increase of Ta's indoctrination into the "democracy of bowling." Unlike his father, who dislikes Communism "for one reason only, that it destroyed Chinese tradition and turned the Chinese social order upside down," Ta comes to see the Communist system as a problematic undoing of that which Chang has been trying to "sell" him. In his monologues, Chang associates his own happiness with the relaxed forty-hour American work week and the individualistic, entrepreneurial spirit that allows him to save up and become a grocery store magnate with a PhD in political science. Ta sees this contrasted in a Russian movie: "In that picture, everybody is a hero. He works twenty hours a day, seven days a week. He salutes his comrades tirelessly. When orders come, he raises his arm and flag with a battle cry, dashes to the battlefield and dies."[14] What he describes is, essentially, propaganda—an element he does not seem to find in American movies.

The anti-Communist rhetoric in the novel is mostly oblique, but there is one scene in which political ideologies are analyzed overtly—again, by Chang. At a culminating moment of frustration with his romantic, familial, and professional prospects, Ta briefly considers emigrating back to China. Chang reacts quickly as the spokesperson for the American system, noting that while an immigrant may be "'only refused the opportunity to do what [he] want[s] to do,'" in China he "'will be forced to do'" what the government wants. After a lengthy comparison of Communism and American capitalism, he concludes in rhetoric similar to that of the "Whittier Quad" promotion cited in the introduction: "This sounds like propaganda, but it's a fact we have to face; and you have to constantly bear in mind that communism and capitalism are like fire and water, they will never mix. As long as there is capitalism, communism will fight it. And you can assure yourself that capitalism isn't some back-yard weed that can be uprooted easily."[15] Such elements within the narrative contribute to an overall tone of reassurance (toward its Anglo audiences) of the loyalty of Chinese immigrants. Despite the Communist take over of China, Anglo-Americans can be assured that the Chinese on postwar American soil are those same Chinese who were allied with the West against Japan during World War II.

Figure 2. Asian American culture as spectacle, as interpreted by Rodgers and Hammerstein in *Flower Drum Song*. Courtesy of Photofest.

The late introduction of the characters Old Man Li and his daughter May Li seems to reinforce the palliative purpose of the novel. They are newly arrived in the United States, having been brought over by their employer, a retired U.S. Army general who lived in China but was driven out by the Communist regime. He has died since their transfer, and the father and daughter go to Chinatown in search of one of the general's contacts to help them get established in America. Their appearance coincides with the Chinese New Year celebration, and they decide to get in on the festivities and make some extra money by working as street performers. They perform a traditional operatic skit, a flower drum song. This type of performance is repeated several times in the second half of the book and seems to serve no real purpose in the narrative other than to render the father/daughter pair charming to those around them. The flower drum song lent itself easily to the stage adaptation, as Rodgers and Hammerstein played up the spectacle as part of the "exotic" pageantry and a basis from which to develop their original songs in the score. That "Flower Drum Song" becomes the title of the book, then, links to the "reassurance" at work within the novel: not only are these immigrants willing allies of the United States, but those aspects of their culture that remain apparent are benign and commodifiably "exotic"—essentially, Chinese culture as mere spectacle.

Not surprisingly, the spunky May Li becomes the main love interest for Wang Ta. Her presence resolves the many conflicts at work within his romantic life: first, she is unlike the Chinese American women he has dated previously, because, in her newness to the scene, she is "uncorrupted" by the practices common to the other women, who "overestimated [their] value" because of the shortage of Chinese women and date many men at once.[16] Second, his proposal to her rescues Ta from an arranged marriage being plotted by his father and Madam Tang. Third, his interest in May Li allays the fears of Ta's father that his son wants to date "foreign she-demons."

Throughout the story, the treatment of gender falls along traditional and moralistic lines, with women who play the field and engage in premarital affairs finding their fates in jail or death, as do two previous women in Ta's life, Miss Tung and Madam Chao. Chang's marriage, too, reads as a politically gendered move, as he marries because "some immigration investigators or inspectors . . . seem to have a tendency to think that all bachelor aliens over forty are homosexuals. In order to have my immigration status adjusted, I decided to prove to them that I'm a normal human being." Not only is his rationale homophobic, but it is aimed at alleviating the doubly politically suspect identifiers of "Chinese" and "homosexual," associations that carry particular weight for a group that has been not only ethnically othered, but also coded as effeminate within Western culture.[17]

May Li, as a young and innocent woman, reverses Ta's unhappy romantic life and, for the presumably Anglo-American audience, offers assurance that immigrants can find a happy Technicolor ending within their own cultural group. Ideologically, May Li also serves an important purpose in the pro-American narrative ideology surrounding the Wang family. As the heroine, it is relevant that she is both a refugee from Communism and an outspoken challenger of the old-world caste system replicated in the Wang household. She proudly performs her Chineseness in the form of a "Flower Drum Song" spectacle, but she also balances this expression with overt gestures to embrace budding democratic ideals and the Protestant work ethic, an important set of values as the young bride-to-be and implied procreator for the next generation of American Wangs.

Of course, American movies become the primary device through which Ta enacts his courtship of May Li. After she begins living with his family as a domestic, he frequently talks her out of working in order to go to movies. In this, he initiates a relationship in which he is for May Li what Chang was to him, immersing her in mass culture as a way of immersing her in American cultural values. He first argues the superiority of American films over those from Communist countries: "In an American movie, everybody has a beautiful car; in every car there is a beautiful woman. And the heroes don't die so often, as the Chinese heroes do. Sometimes they do die; if they don't, they always end up the whole thing with a long kiss. You know what a long kiss is, don't you?" As the courtship continues, he takes May Li to movies so that she may study how to kiss American style and practice on him. Though "the foreign movies [are] colorful and exciting," she does not understand the language, but this proves a momentary delay in the process that is well underway by the novel's end, the development of an ideal immigrant wife "whose words and deeds conform."[18]

That Asian American playwright David Henry Hwang initiated a revival of the musical version of *Flower Drum Song* in 2001 says something about the power of the narrative, despite its controversies. Hwang and his collaborator Robert Longbottom worked to preserve the charms of the Rodgers and Hammerstein spectacle (often with "retro" irony) while also reclaiming the meat of the immigrant narrative from the original novel; they cast more Asian American actors in the play than had been cast in the past and worked to update the representations of ethnicity and gender. The controversies over past productions certainly did not disappear with the revival, of course, because of the origins of the production in an ethnically and gender-stereotypical stage show. However, Hwang's revision inflects the meaning of Lee's original novel by demonstrating how the various versions—compositely—contribute importantly to an articulation of ethnic immigrant subjectivity in the 1950s.[19]

"The Holy Spirit of Huncan Dines"

Through its parodic allusions to American name brands and its mostly denigrating view of popular culture, *Lolita* reads as a kind of self-aware theorization of what occurs in *The Flower Drum Song*. Protagonist Humbert Humbert's running commentary succinctly divides "high" and "low" cultures and implies that American popular culture forms work to instill "low" cultural values in the masses. He does not seem surprised, either, that the American masses willingly consume whatever is offered to them on billboards or through their radios. Even Charlotte Haze's attempts to participate in postwar middle-brow culture are seen as low-brow gestures in Humbert's opinion. "She was, obviously," he writes, "one of those women whose polished words may reflect a book club or bridge club, or any other deadly conventionality, but never her soul."[20] Unlike the kind of ideal, capitalism-defending immigrant consumer represented in *The Flower Drum Song*, *Lolita*'s narrator sees himself as above participation in consuming American culture, overtly criticizes such consumption, and, thus, implicitly attempts to critique the larger set of practices that facilitate cultural citizenship.

This stance is rather ironic, however, considering that Humbert has come to the United States by way of a "soft job" offered by an uncle, consisting of "thinking up and editing perfume ads." In essence, mass culture is the main conduit to his "fateful" meeting of Lolita. In addition to the class status afforded by his job, his racial status seems to be read as "white" because of his European origin, which lends him access to cultural power not available to the Chinese characters. This power also affords him the ability to maintain his ironic distance from the culture he now lives in. Despite that ironic distance and, often, disdain, Humbert's narrative is one that "lays bare a sophisticated European's ravishment by Truman-era Americana—by the vulgarity of American beauty and, equally, the beauty of American vulgarity."[21] There are many elements that complicate his unfavorable views of mass culture, not the least of which is his own desire and its requisite forms of consumption—an important aspect of the narrative to which I will return shortly.

His participation in the production of perfume ads and the fact that his critiques primarily derive from his observations of his desired Lolita and her mother, Charlotte Haze, with whom he has taken a room as a boarder, point to a crucial qualifier in his implied theory: the consumer imperative is configured within and aimed at the American female. He articulates this most clearly while on his first road trip with Lolita, when he observes that "she believed, with a kind of celestial trust, any advertisement or advice that appeared in *Movie Love* or *Screen Land*." After spending weeks humoring her constant urge to buy "'novelties and souvenirs,'" magazines and candy, and to put coin after coin into juke boxes, he concludes, "She it was to whom ads were dedicated: the ideal consumer, the subject and object of every foul poster."[22] His choice of the word "dedicated" seems especially appropriate, as it connotes a loyalty on the part of the advertising companies to the teenage and female consumers they target.

Before midcentury the concept of "teenager" did not exist as a distinct social and age group. The postwar era witnessed a boom in teen culture, and cultural historians have noted that mass culture producers explicitly sought to win over the now-distinct group that, for the first time, had its own spending money and few responsible imperatives for how to use it. Nabokov astutely picks up on this in his portrayal of Lolita, and this also makes for one of the stronger elements in Kubrick's adaptation of the book, as it is layered with visual and audio montages of teen culture, from bubble gum pop music to excessively chiffoned school dances. Many scholars have also examined the ways in which mass culture producers targeted women—especially through visual narratives that found their way into the domestic space. According to consumer theorist Martyn Lee, print advertising "became both the means by which women could be educated into the correct modes of consumption and shown the ameliorative benefits to be found in the functional and constantly improved use-values of new consumer goods, as well as a force by which those goods could be culturally legitimised within everyday life." To its influence I would add postwar television programming, which presented intertwined narratives of advertisement and entertainment within the domestic space and increasingly functioned, too, as a "critical intermediary agency bridging the industrial process and everyday life" in reinscribing the social roles of women.[23]

Drawing on a more psychoanalytic model, Lynne Joyrich theorizes the process by which these gendered configurations take place as one that "ruptures the boundary between subject and object." She argues that "the discursive link between consumerism and femininity, both related to an overidentification with the image or commodity object, affects the whole of Western culture. Not only are women presumed to be the best consumers, but all consumers are configured as feminized—a situation yielding tension in a culture desperately trying to shore up traditional distinctions even as its simulations continue to destabilize such attempts." Joyrich's analysis, while at times too deterministically oriented, allows for a more comprehensive understanding of the dynamic in which psychological, economic, and material histories intersect and influence gendered subjects. In contrast, Lynn Spigel insists on acknowledging the presence of a multifaceted discourse about mass culture (especially via the television set) that resulted in "ambivalence and hesitation" when it came to assessing one's private identity in relation to such public institutions. One of the main ways in which she pursues this discourse is to separate out the rhetoric of advertising from the other narratives within women's magazines: "[W]e need to give the sales effort a less deterministic role and to remember that while magazines and advertisers might work in mutual relations of support, they are relatively autonomous institutions whose strategies might sometimes be at odds." JoAnne Meyerowitz's research on women's magazines—particularly magazines targeted at African Americans—affirms Spigel's assertions, arguing that an inventory of articles reveals many stories focused not on the domestic and consumerist, but on public service, careers for women, and involvement in community and politics.[24]

Still, as scholars like Lizabeth Cohen and Marianne Conroy illustrate, the consumerist rhetoric at work in the period was pointedly aimed at women—and not just through domestic magazines and advertising. Cohen notes how the changing suburban landscape itself was gendered, and commercial developers, "in feminizing public space, . . . enhanced women's claim on the suburban landscape but also empowered them more as consumers than producers." Conroy identifies a "status panic" that was peculiar to postwar American culture. Describing the "instabilities" of class identity during this period of economic and social change, she notes how contemporary social critics David Reisman and Betty Friedan immediately picked up on the gendered element within class status concerns in their respective descriptions of the socio-psychological needs for women to feel "competent" as consumers and publicly affirm their class positions.[25]

Charlotte Haze's urgent work to identify her class position for Humbert by attempting to speak French, discussing books and social clubs, making pointed comments about the maid, and so on, fits easily within this notion of a gendered, class-status panic. Quickly disparaging the cultural practices in which Charlotte partakes, Humbert maintains an academic take on Lolita's penchant for mass culture goodies and the processes that have helped her arrive at such desires, without judging her for it. Enshrouded within his own desires to consume her, he only later realizes that Lolita is well on her way to becoming like her mother, whom he sees as the archetypal American housewife and purveyor of domestic kitsch. Moreover, Humbert comes to rely on mass cultural processes in order to "consume" Lolita, not recognizing his own complicated relationship to the consumer imperative.

John Haegert argues that "[f]rom Humbert's point of view, it might be said, all regions of America are necessarily middle class, in the sense that they seek to mimic in a makeshift and thoroughly middling way the ostentatious splendors of Europe." Humbert sees in Charlotte, I would add, a perfect representative of the middle-brow culture much maligned by contemporaneous culture critics. In her study of middle-brow culture, Joan Shelley Rubin details the ways in which such phenomena as Great Books series and programs to expose the arts to mass audiences were denounced as "vulgarizations" of "High Culture." The spread of middle-brow culture after World War I, in the minds of high-culture critics, was linked to growing consumerist practices, and "'the successful launching of the Book-of-the-Month Club' and the spread of 'other packaged cultural experiences,'' were embraced "merely as 'symbols of social refinement' that could be purchased in the same way as toasters and model T's."[26] Humbert Humbert's analyses of Charlotte seem excerpted straight from the pages of Clement Greenberg and Dwight MacDonald (the more famous of the post–World War II critics Rubin discusses), from his mocking of her attempts to speak French to his "solemn exasperation" at her attempts to "glorify the home" after their marriage. In fact, the marriage exposes to him the very façade that was her participation in "culture," and he notices, "the novels I had found her reading when I moved in were now replaced by illustrated catalogues and homemaking guides."[27] Linked as we readers are to what some of my students have called "Humbert-vision," the narrative asks that we see "poor, sad Charlotte" in this way, too—regardless of what we end up thinking of Humbert (genius or pervert, or both). He kills her off before we can assess her ourselves, though. From what we do see of her, she echoes Wang Ta's attempts to learn to "be" American through mass and middle-brow cultures and their material tools for learning to perform the ideals of refinement, femininity, and domesticity.

Humbert maintains his denigrating view of American culture throughout most of the narrative, from the moment he steps on American soil to his later reunion with Lolita and her new working-class husband at the novel's end, the three acting out what Humbert calls "a beer ad" in the living room of the young couple's Coalmont shack. The strength of his derogatory tone, however, falters at times, since "there can be no doubt that his denigration of America is designed, at least in part, to rationalize his relationship with Lolita and endow his criminal conduct with a sense of high heroic conduct."[28] There are brief moments when, in his reveries, he actually aestheticizes pieces of the American landscape, mostly in an attempt to recreate the idealized scenes of the Europe of his past. One such scene occurs in the midst of his extensive list of American roadside scenery during their first year on the road, self-consciously and allegorically marking the mournful difference between his European perspective of the landscape and that narrow focus of consumerist young America, embodied in the young Lolita. Seeing Claude Lorrain in the clouds and El Greco on the horizon, he writes, "A great user of roadside facilities, my unfastidious Lo would be charmed by toilet signs—Guys-Gals, John-Jane, Jack-Jill and even Buck's-Doe's; while lost in an artist's dream, I would stare at the honest brightness of the gasoline paraphernalia against the splendid green of oaks, or at a distant hill scrambling out—scarred but still untamed—from the wilderness of agriculture that was trying to swallow it."[29] This is only one of many other moments in which we see the overt acknowledgment of this entire narrative as "an artist's dream." As is obvious from the outset, the narrative is a construct, assembled by Humbert from memory. In this reconstruction, he neatly distinguishes himself, the discerning *émigré* aesthete from the undiscerning American consumers.

Yet his choice to participate in consumer travel inserts him within the leveling public space of the American highway system and travel/tourist culture. This public positioning becomes the source of his growing paranoia and the backdrop against which his psyche plays out the Doppelgänger scenario with Clare Quilty, who eventually lures Lolita away from her stepfather. Within the public space, Humbert must train himself to perform the domestic male, father to Lolita, rather than the openly "perverse," manipulative, and statutory rapist "lover" that Quilty comes to embody. In order to maintain this performance, Humbert begins an avid participation in American commodity consumption.

His adoption of that which he critiques occurs as an almost inadvertent impulse, spawned by the complications of his desire for Lolita. He maintains that Lolita is the reincarnation of his childhood sweetheart Annabel and, initially, indicates his own projection of this image upon the American girl when he overtly states that "he broke [Annabel's] spell by incarnating her in another." Regardless of his constant attempts to maintain control of the relationship and Lolita's very identity for his purposes, what becomes increasingly obvious throughout the narrative is that Lolita exerts her Americanness within his fantasy construct to the extent that Humbert ends up needing the very consumerist accessories of her being that he purports to hate. This need manifests itself most obviously in his own consumerism, which is linked with his lust for nymphets, as illustrated in the scene where he devotes an entire day "to buying beautiful things for Lo" just before their trip to the Enchanted Hunters Lodge. "What crazy purchases were prompted," he admits, "by the poignant predilection Humbert had in those days for check weaves, bright cottons, frills, and generously full skirts!" On the surface, these clothes purchased for the girl are intended as tools of seduction, but his adoption of the language of a teen magazine fashion spread reveals his real thrill in the act of shopping, just as does his adoringly detailed list of the other material comforts he purchases for Lolita: "four books of comics, a box of candy, a box of sanitary pads, two cokes, a manicure set, a travel clock with luminous dial, a ring with a real topaz, a tennis racket, roller skates with white high shoes, field glasses, a portable radio set, chewing gum, a transparent raincoat, sunglasses, some more garments."[30] As the narrative progresses, though, we see these commercial transactions take on a seedier tone (primarily once they have settled in the prep-school town of Beardsley), as Lolita's recognition of the commercial nature of their relationship results in her demanding money for sexual favors. In this scenario, he is as much the commercial consumer as Lolita is because he cannot stop paying for "the product."

While Humbert might rationalize his shopping as a vehicle through which to pursue his "artistic" endeavor to fill "the gap between the little given and the great promised" of "nympholepsy," his own adoption of other mass culture ideals infects the entire retelling of his story in a series of "cinematographic still[s]." Even before meeting Lolita, he recounts his break-up with his first wife and "the backhand slap with which I ought to have hit her across the cheekbone according to the rules of the movies." That he is disappointed in himself for not following through on this melodramatic violence with her reveals that the "rules of the movies" are, despite his pretentions, something to be taken relatively to heart in matters domestic. After arriving in the United States, he seems truly thankful that his own looks fit within Hollywood's definitions of handsome, cultured men so that his pursuits among American girl-children will be the more successful: "I have all the characteristics which, according to writers on the sex interests of children, start the responses stirring in a girl: clean-cut jaw, muscular hand, deep sonorous voice, broad shoulder. Moreover, I am said to resemble some crooner or actor on whom Lo has a crush."[31] He adapts easily into this system of desires because class signifiers and his physiognomy facilitate a nonethnic immigrant status and access to those performances (romantic lead, legitimate stepfather, professor) that will implement the fulfillment of desire.

Humbert's own fantasies also derive from the cinematic, as he imagines Lolita "clos[ing] her eyes as Hollywood teaches" for a kiss, or "as if she were a photographic image rippling upon a screen" even as he physically incorporates her into his masturbatory fantasies. Finally, he ends with a fantasy of heroism as he prepares to kill Quilty while readers are cued to "recall at this point the obligatory scene in the Westerns of their childhood."[32] Humbert's allusions to the cinematic are too numerous to list in full here, but they persist throughout the book at a level almost equal to the number of literary and artistic allusions, rendering the role of mass culture as crucial as that of high culture in articulating Humbert's memorializing metanarrative of a love gone astray. Indeed, he is as indebted to mass culture for his sense of identity as Wang Ta is. Of course, Clare Quilty's presence as Humbert's Doppelgänger also contributes to the undermining of Humbert's pure elitism, as he boorishly displays for Humbert (and his readers) all of those characteristics he does not want to see in an Americanized version of himself: a not-so-movie-star-handsome corporate spokesman (for Drome cigarettes) with a love of popular theater, pornography, and conspicuous consumption (emblematized by Quilty's Aztec Red convertible).

Another way in which the narrative undermines its own snobbery is to slip in minor, almost imperceptible comments on interethnic relationships within America. This is an important aspect of the novel that, even with all the adoringly detailed analyses of its language, has been mostly ignored by Nabokov scholars. Humbert's relatively unkind representations of ethnic Americans exist with those flagged moments when readers are reminded that we are not really supposed to be rooting for him (as, for example, when he admits that Lolita cries every night after he has sex with her). The first of these occurs within a comment revealing a misogyny that he reserves not only for the adult women his life (Valeria and Charlotte) but also for nymphet-aged girls of non-European origin. Shortly after arriving in North America and spending some time in a "sanatorium," he mentions his accompanying an arctic expedition as part of a psychological remedy, one that temporarily relieves him of his desires because "Nymphets do not occur in the polar regions": "The plump, glossy little Eskimo girls with their fish smell, hideous raven hair and guinea pig faces, evoked even less desire in me."[33] Unlike this overtly xenophobic comment, other commentaries occur within the space of the suburban Ramsdale neighborhood, where the inhabitants are white middle-class Anglos and the domestic workers are African American.

He first meets Leslie, "Miss Opposite's" chauffeur who "cheerfully" conveys Humbert to the Haze home. Leslie reappears later as the subject of gossip among Charlotte and her friends after having been spotted "taking a dip 'in the ebony'" at the local lake. Charlotte assesses this behavior as evidence of Leslie's being "subnormal" and expresses concern that her own maid, Louise, "is in love with that moron." Almost all of the derogatory comments on ethnicity occur within the suburban setting, and one must wonder what they are really doing within Humbert's narrative at all, since he has had the liberty of revising and recreating the story of his love affair with Lolita to include what he sees as the necessary evidence to persuade his "dear readers" to sympathize with him. Why, for example, should he include the neighbor's comment that "too many of the tradespeople here are Italians" or make note of the "hunchbacked and hoary Negro in a uniform of sorts" who takes his bags at a hotel? Douglas Anderson has also noted the hinted allusions to anti-Semitism in the novel, as in the gleeful description of his Eastern European ex-wife Valeria's death during a ridiculous scientific experiment to test "racial reactions" to an all-banana diet and living on all-fours, echoing the extreme and absurd experimentations of Nazi scientists upon Jews. More than simply demonstrating the small-mindedness of the Ramsdale social set, these comments together serve a couple of purposes: first, they seem to point to—and implicitly critique—the employment of ethnic domestic workers as a middle-brow pretention; second, they point to the failed project of democracy within the middle-class culture, whose idea of cultural inclusion is represented in superficial terms, like "those American ads where schoolchildren are pictured in a subtle ratio of races, with one—only one, but as cute as they make them—chocolate-colored round-eyed little lad, almost in the very middle of the front row."[34]

Such comments should not be read as Nabokov's, though many people still insist on reading Humbert's perspectives into Nabokov's own. In fact, Nabokov's position as an immigrant highlighted for him one of the more nonsensical taboos within American society: "a Negro-White marriage which is a complete and glorious success resulting in lots of children and grandchildren."[35] This brief comment supplies an awareness of the unnecessary legal and social segregations in place when Nabokov arrived in the United States to the extent that we must read brief commentaries on ethnicity as drawing attention to the illogic of suburbanite chauvinism and a critique of the limited access to cultural citizenship within the increasingly suburbanizing American landscape.

Through Humbert's unreliable narration, *Lolita* simultaneously attempts to theorize the problematic relationship among suburban American consumers, ethnic Americans, and mass culture forms, and it also encourages us to laugh at Humbert and his opinions. However, while we may laugh at his slapstick and half-drunken mimic of a suburban man's lawn maintenance, "lurching" along with the mower and getting caught up in lawn chairs, the language with which he relates his "eructations" may have removed the comedy from a wide audience in its day. That is to say, despite the comedic and ironic tone of the novel, it replicates the very elitism it mocks through a persistent "high-brow," allusive, and academic diction. Erik Martiny notes how Nabokov's language did not translate to the visual all that well (though he adapted one script himself), resulting in a much different narrative rendering of the characters and purpose than the novel's original. The novel's dense language and Humbert's elitist tone do exclude the "middle-brow," which probably contributed to its attracting a very different kind of audience (in its own era) than that of *The Flower Drum Song*. Humbert's desire reveals self-contradictions that allow us to read him as not entirely above that which he mocks, but perhaps these are over-ridden by what seems like an anti-assimilationist narrative. This is highlighted further when compared with *The Flower Drum Song*'s mainstream appeal. Intending to ingratiate the immigrant to American audiences, C. Y. Lee admits, "I exaggerated it a little, perhaps, made it a little more quaint."[36] Nabokov's exaggeration of the elite Euro-cultured gentleman, on the other hand, sometimes limits its ability to disrupt the discourses that it implicitly critiques.

These two texts highlight some aspects of a novelistic engagement of mass culture that prove useful in the following chapters. First, in their overt and politicized incorporation of commercial cultural forms, they demonstrate how such contemporary references do not simply tie the novel to a historical context, but the objects from this context also inform the progress of the written narrative. Second, the ways in which they attempt to enact a false binary (assimilate versus preserve) enables us to look at the ways in which the next few texts enact their narratives with an understanding that the binary is already and always false.

3

What's for Sale

Consumer Fantasy, American Women, and Social Mobility in Gwendolyn Brooks's *Maud Martha* and the *I Love Lucy* Show

On the day that I first read Gwendolyn Brooks's only novel, *Maud Martha* (1953), I had finished the graphic scene of Maud's daughter's birth in a tenement apartment when I decided to take a break. That day, I watched a broadcast of the *I Love Lucy* episode in which Lucy enters the hospital to give birth.[1] I was struck by the difference between these two birth scenes created within the same year: Maud Martha's like something out of the tradition of blood-and-tears literary Naturalism; Lucy's an ultrasterilized birth, to the extent that Lucy disappears completely from the episode once she enters the hospital. (The remainder of the episode occurs mostly in the waiting room, to which I will return later.)

Witnessing these two birth scenes back-to-back served as a catalyst for helping me see the ways in which *Maud Martha* and *I Love Lucy* represent enlightening reverse narratives of 1950s womanhood in the ways that they play out the relationships between gender and consumer, class, and ethnic identities as described in the previous chapter.[2] The births themselves function as complementary events within larger narratives about the positioning of female identities within a consumer fantasy. Threaded throughout both the novel and the television program, the specter of consumer desire evolves in fascinating ways according to the politics of representation and participation as governed by ethnicity, gender, and socioeconomic class in midcentury America.

Gwendolyn Brooks's short novel *Maud Martha* was published at the same historical moment in which the *I Love Lucy* show was establishing the popularity of the television sit-com. In the lyrical style of Brooks's poetry, the novel presents a series of vignettes and interior monologues that comprise the life of Maud Martha from her early childhood to the advent of her second pregnancy at the end of World War II. While the on-going narrative of *I Love Lucy*'s seven-year run was one of increasing consumer desire and participation within the middle-class mainstream, *Maud Martha* offers a reverse narrative that begins with Maud Martha's sharing a desire for "the good life" similar to Lucy Ricardo's, but it slowly unfolds into a debunking of that fantasy. Ethnicity and racializing social practices will have everything to do with that debunking. While these two texts cannot represent all of the complexities and varieties of 1950s women's experience, they operate as the negative and print of the same photograph to provide very different visions of, and important insights into, the construction of American women's identity along ethnic lines in this era.

My intention here is not to argue that Gwendolyn Brooks meant her novel to be a reaction to what she saw on television. My goal is to expand its critical context beyond those literary canons in which it has already been studied and provide an alternate view of the novel's cultural significance.[3] By reading this novel and television show together, by imagining some kind of interplay within a shared national context (in which the notion of a unified national identity was fairly consistently promoted), their positions and functions within that context inform one another and contribute to the cultural work of understanding ethnic identity in relation to gender and midcentury American consumer culture.

Television Culture

As the economy progressed after the war, and consumer culture became an identifying trait for the nation, the ideological investment in consumerism played out clearly in the mass media and was vividly and powerfully brought to life upon the television screen. As television increasingly occupied the domestic space, it played an ever more influential role in identity formation. Arriving in American homes shortly after World War II, the television began to change the ways in which Americans saw the world—and themselves. As an object, it literally changed the domestic space; changes in architecture, furnishings, accessories, family dining habits, and even clothing helped the television assume its place as the central apparatus in most American homes. Perusing through widely distributed magazines like *Life* or *Look,* one sees a variety of new products related to television viewing. For example, the January 29, 1951, issue of *Life* contains a spread entitled "Clothes for TV Watching" that offered new fashion options for women and girls. The clothes reflected the changing nature of social interactions, picturing outfits that were both appropriate as evening wear for at-home entertaining and comfortable enough for the casual TV watching that was replacing after-dinner conversation. Television had displaced the radio as the central media unit in most American homes by mid-decade. Moreover, the consumption of televisual narratives literally displaced the consumption of written ones, as television historian Erik Barnuow demonstrates in his account of television's advent in major cities in 1949: "Public libraries, including the New York Public Library, reported a drop in book circulation, and many stores reported sales down." This is not to say that the shift was permanent, as the novel has continued to maintain its cultural importance apart from visual culture. What must be acknowledged, however, is the increase in and variety of influential cultural narratives beginning to be consumed by average American families at this point in the century, for purposes both educational and entertaining, within the private space of the home.[4]

The television became an increasingly important presence in the lives of most American families, and, thus, a powerful ideological apparatus. Extensive arguments have been made regarding the ideological functions of television, but for the purposes of this analysis, I want to focus on its specific role in shaping consumer identities. With many elements of consumer infrastructure already in place, television became an ideal communicative vehicle for a revitalized postwar commercial culture. George Lipsitz argues that programmers, advertisers, writers, producers, and policy makers quite deliberately made use of television as a tool within the consumer economy. Not only did it make goods visible to its viewers, but "it also provided a relentless flow of information and persuasion that placed acts of consumption at the core of everyday life." While the film industry relied less heavily on overt commercial messages than television did at the time, its production within the commercial field required maneuvering narratives within a similar set of economic and cultural politics (issues of which I will examine in the next two chapters). Lipsitz asserts that television's commercial lifeblood was so powerful as to actively influence the reformulation of "American ethnic, class, and family identities into consumer identities." Through various popular visual media—especially through television—performative whiteness and consumerism became normative signifiers of "American." Elaine Tyler May's *Homeward Bound*, a study of public policy's effect on the private sphere after World War II, emphasizes the further importance of purchasing power in creating a sense of belonging, in the nationalist sense: "Consumerism provided a means for assimilation into the American way of life: classless, homogenous, and family centered." Television became the ideal vehicle for disseminating and making habitual these new, consumer-driven cultural practices, itself the consumer product through which other consumer initiatives may occur.[5]

Many theorists of mass media rightly point out, however, that we should not regard television's cultural function as unidirectional, one that envisions mass media as a kind of sprinkler system that bathes the unwitting public with conformist ideological messages. As Lynn Spigel notes, American society was engaged in a variety of discourses regarding the role that television was to play in the United States, and people were as aware of its potential to disrupt daily life as of its ability to enhance American culture. Rather than viewing television as a "consciousness industry," Spigel argues, we should recognize the various possibilities for meanings and "contradictory ideas and values" within this medium that inherently "absorb[s] the discourses of social institutions." Similarly, John Fiske argues that no matter how much a single program may adhere to the status quo, the context in which it is viewed allows for resistant readings of television content. Like Fiske and Spigel, I generally do not subscribe to the theories of mass media that do not concede any viewer agency in the face of mass culture's power to disseminate a dominant ideology.[6] As noted in the introduction, the writing of a novel that implicitly questions the practices of mass mediated identity formation is evidence of such agency.

In the middle of the twentieth century, people generally did seem excited about television's arrival and saw little reason to doubt it as anything but innovative technology and a source for wholesome, at-home entertainment. It was new and modern and designed for leisure time—characteristics embraced by the average, upwardly mobile postwar American family. Even civil rights groups viewed television's arrival with optimism, according to J. Fred MacDonald. They hoped that it would be "the answer to a variety of social problems" and believed that it "had the potential to reverse centuries of unjust ridicule and misinformation" for the African American population. As television became an increasing presence in American life, though, its programming offered an increasingly homogenous picture of America. Many historians have shown the cycle: as more Americans moved to the suburbs and gained (or worked toward, through the convenience of buying on credit) middle-class status, the ethnic and class identifiers that they and their families possessed within the cities slowly shifted. In conjunction with these changes and other political and commercial influences, interest in television programs with working-class or ethnic characters, such as *The Goldbergs* and *Life with Luigi,* waned in popularity and left the airwaves by mid-decade. And because television, like U.S. society, followed many of the policies of Jim Crow segregation, it was susceptible to the same politics. Consequently, programs hosted by or featuring African Americans became fewer as the decade progressed, and the escalating civil rights conflicts in the South complicated politics within the representational media. For example, MacDonald recounts that increasing pressure from groups like the NAACP to increase ethnic quotas in programming caused studios to often simply exclude African American characters and extras. These exclusions became increasingly political and determined by issues of consumerism, such as the blacklisting of Paul Robeson or the cancellation of *The Nat King Cole Show* because of an inability to attract and keep a national commercial sponsor. His show was not the only one that faced sponsors who were unwilling to offend their Southern viewers by sponsoring shows featuring African Americans in nonstereotypical roles.[7]

In his study *Selling Culture,* Richard Ohmann provides an excellent model for examining the effects of a widely distributed and consumed cultural form upon identity construction. He delineates the "charting of social space" by turn-of-the-century home magazines that simultaneously reflected and helped to construct the values of the newly forming professional-managerial class—especially through their advertising pages: "They taught readers a symbolism of commodities and social life; they flattered a new class for its values while elaborating and clarifying those values." I would argue that television takes on this same function approximately fifty years later. After a generation's surviving the Depression and World War II, policy makers sought to boost the nation's economy through new lending practices. This, with the boom in suburban housing construction and the creation of new white-collar jobs, contributed to the construction of a new "social space" for the young families of the postwar generation. Television was integral to this process as what Lipsitz calls an "instrument of legitimation for transformations in values initiated by the new economic imperatives of postwar America." As he describes it, "Commercial network television emerged as the primary discursive medium in American society at the precise moment when the isolated nuclear family and its concerns eclipsed previous ethnic, class, and political forces as the crucible of personal identity. Television programs both reflected and shaped that transition, defining the good life in family-centric, asocial, and commodity-oriented ways." In this sense, television operated the way home magazines did decades earlier, solidifying "a large group of people into an audience." For this new middle class, participation was more readily available to a larger group of people, based on the kind of consumer participation that Elaine Tyler May describes. However, African American families were often inherently excluded from this process because of the segregationist practices described earlier.[8]

Since so much identity construction occurred within the domestic space, most of the consumer imperative was aimed at women. They were not often the sole bread winners, but their role in the family's consuming practices was clearly defined in both programming and advertising. Watching commercials from the postwar era, one often sees the same patterns present today: many products marketed solely to women and children, regardless of who actually finances a household's purchases or uses the products. Of course, women are often pictured enjoying the conveniences of the modern kitchen, but even 1950s automotive advertising most often places a well-dressed *woman* within a fantasy world of space-age auto technology, more prized for its design than its performance. In programming, domestic comedies often subscribe to the stereotypical marital dynamic in which the wife wants to acquire goods the family cannot afford, while the husband constantly falls victim to her spending habits. Likewise, good behavior within the family space (on the part of the wife and the children) often results in material rewards in many televisual representations of the era.

Star Power and the Consumer Ethos

Considering these sociohistorical circumstances enables us to interrogate gender dynamics, consumer practices, and cultural capital more closely within the domestic spaces of *Maud Martha* and *I Love Lucy*. These two texts make even more clear the slippery class/ethnic divide discussed in the previous chapter, the physical signifiers of which play into the levels of cultural citizenship afforded or inhibited.

I Love Lucy was almost instantly one of the most popular shows on television—number 1 in the television ratings for most of its initial seven-year run. Its popularity expanded and changed the star industry, as Lucille Ball's personal life merged with the plot of the show in a way that captivated the public and served simultaneously to make television stars seem more like "real people" that one could know. In the case of the Ricardos, the actors were married in real life, their real home was featured in photo spreads and reviews of the television program, and early in the same year of *Maud Martha*'s publication, Lucille Ball and her character Lucy Ricardo gave birth to what seemed to be the same baby boy (Desi Arnaz Jr./Ricky Ricardo Jr.), arranged so that the episode would air on the same day that Lucille Ball had her Cesarean section. Television histories never fail to note this monumental event, as it found some 14 million viewers tuning in to share in the happy occasion, winning an audience larger than that of the first-ever televised presidential inauguration the next morning (Eisenhower's). All of these factors, these lines blurred between the real actors and their fictional characters' lives, allowed for what Lori Landay calls the "bizarre public fantasy" of the ideal marriage—one that, fans later learned, was actually troubled and ended when the show did.[9] The *I Love Lucy* show clearly functions as an innovator in the construction of television viewing practices that foster intimate psychological connections to the characters on television and our tendency to conflate those characters with the people who portray them. The television manufacturing industry also followed this tactic of bringing together the fantasy world of television with the real world to construct value systems in relation to entertainment, as evidenced by General Electric's 1951 slogan, "G.E. makes you feel it's real!"

Many feminist readings of the *I Love Lucy* show center around questions of where Lucy (the character) positions herself within the domestic ideology of the 1950s. Some understandably read Lucy's life as one of containment, as she is often literally confined to the urban apartment, preparing meals for Ricky, with no financial independence apart from the housekeeping allowance that Ricky gives her. Her antics, in such a scenario, are attempts (almost always unsuccessful) to liberate herself from the domestic sphere (by getting into show business or working outside the home) and to gain some financial independence. Emily Nussbaum states, "I do reject that absolute insistence on seeing her as a provocative force for freedom. She shrieks and wheedles and whines and she's heightened in this way. And then she gets spanked and humiliated." Other interpretations posit these very antics as progressive moves away from domestic ideology. Gustavo Pérez-Firmat reads the apartment as a domain of power for Lucy, and Gina Barreca contends that a woman's *doing* something active—and not doing domestic work—can be read as a "feminist gesture" in the era. Similarly, because of the ways in which

Lucy breaks gender boundaries by, for example, cross-dressing or just being generally "un-lady-like" in her physical humor, Lori Landay argues that her performances may be read as transgressing the domestic ideals of the day.[10]

Unspoken within all such interpretations is the assumption that the feminist possibilities or impossibilities of such popular icons mattered only to those women who looked like Lucy: white and middle-class (that is, women with greater potential for upward mobility). Such is implied when, for example, Landay interprets producer Jess Oppenheimer's belief that *I Love Lucy* "held up a mirror" to the everyday life of Americans. She refers to the ways in which "viewers' social experience" played into the cultural phenomenon of the show and notes that "Because of television's place in the home and the domestic subject of the series, *I Love Lucy* speaks in and to the home life of its viewers."[11] Reading the implications within these phrases, the image of this home life and of these viewers comes directly from the visual culture of the 1950s. In short, we envision middle-class, white housewives and families. We do not immediately associate the period's consumers of television with Brooks's protagonist Maud Martha, a young struggling mother on Chicago's Southside, simply because there was no attempt to represent such an individual in the commercial culture that enabled the circulation of "various memories, myths, histories, traditions, and practices" in the postmodern era.[12] Unlike the recording industry of previous decades, which, though segregated, did recognize and market to an African American audience, the television industry offered little space for African American producer or consumer agency.

The written narrative, however, more readily affords a space for representing and offering some level of cultural power to this type of marginalized identity. As W. T. Lhamon notes, the postwar period saw a "proliferation" of new voices in the literary scene, picking up where writers of the Harlem Renaissance and the Works Progress Administration had left off before the war. *Maud Martha* is, in some ways, related to the traditions established within those movements, most notably in the genre that Michael Denning has named the "ghetto pastoral." Indeed, Brooks was involved with Left-oriented writers' groups that sought to document the lives in the margins of American society. But this novel, though set during the 1930s and '40s, possesses a rather different cultural function than the documentary-realist ghetto novels of the Depression, such as Michael Gold's *Jews without Money* (1930) or Richard Wright's *Native Son* (1940). *Maud Martha* takes the ghetto pastoral beyond the familiar documentary mode and offers a narrative that is much less overtly politicized than its predecessors. A novel like *Jews without Money*, for example, has a clear political undertone and is easily identifiable as socialist-influenced literature of the Depression era, while *Maud Martha* appears in a sociohistorical context with a less unified literary movement and a more right-wing-oriented political atmosphere.[13]

In this context, the novel offers an ambivalent, exploratory, and imagistic representation of a nonmainstream American identity. As I will demonstrate, the consumer fantasy turned upside-down within this novel does result in a politicized narrative that, at the very least, demands that the African American female subject be positioned differently than she is within her contemporary mass cultural representations. After all, *Maud Martha* examines the workings of a character virtually unrepresented in the popular media at the time, that of the individualized black woman. Black women did appear occasionally on television in the postwar period, but usually as well-known stereotypes—such as Beulah, the always happy domestic for a white family, or the domineering, money-grubbing Sapphire on *Amos 'n' Andy*—or as glamorous entertainers on variety shows (e.g., Lena Horne, Ella Fitzgerald). *Maud Martha* engages the representational politics within this context, and, as a book, complicates the messages within mass visual culture in ways not usually possible for women of color in early television.[14]

In the comparative analysis that follows, I offer first my interpretation of the narrative of consumer fantasy in the *I Love Lucy* show because it establishes the type of narrative against which I read the role of consumer fantasy within the novel *Maud Martha*. A large number of Lucy and Ricky's marital struggles center around the accumulation of commodities, so the issues of consumption and economics become central to the narrative of the show. At the show's outset, Lucille Ball intentionally reworked her own star image to portray Lucy Ricardo as an ordinary housewife. As Landay observes, the marketing of the show relied upon this image to sell the program to America's housewives; Lucy's claim of being "just a typical housewife" was essential to the show's success as a commercial venture: "Because television was broadcast into people's homes at a time when domesticity was a central tenet of the dominant value system, the more the Ricardos mirrored ordinary people (and Ball and Arnaz were represented as typical, not glamorous stars), the more appealing they were."[15]

Ironically, though, Lucy Ricardo ultimately functions as a woman who is anything but content to simply be a housewife, as every episode does center on her attempts to break out of the daily routine.[16] The instigator for conflicts within the home (or, sometimes, between the Ricardos and the Mertzes) is almost always a consumer product: a new hat, the latest designer dress, a new appliance, new furniture. Like *The Flower Drum Song* and *Lolita*, the program maintains its narrative momentum by keeping Lucy fixated on constant desire, in this case, for acquisition of perpetually obsolescent consumer products.

As the show's narrative progresses, so does Ricky's career, and, consequently, Lucy's consumer appetite. Her requests progress from a new washing machine and dryer, to make her housework easier, to more luxury items, such as minks and French *haute couture*. Likewise, the family's shared acquisitions fall into line with those desired and experienced by the general public over the course of the decade: the Ricardos contribute to the Baby Boom, leave the urban center for the suburbs of Connecticut, buy a car, and become increasingly mobile—both literally and socially. Lucy's activities while in the suburbs shift and recenter around the pursuit of social acceptance and "keeping up with the Joneses." For example, she wants new furniture for the new house (partly motivated by envy of a wealthier neighbor); she joins the PTA, the Garden Club, the country club, and the local historical preservation society. In their increasing travels, the Ricardos pursue every imaginable type of voyage, from road trips, to taking trains to Hollywood to live in full-service hotels while Ricky pursues his career, to going on cruises and flying to Europe with Ricky's band.

Like many arenas of leisure culture that were previously available only to the wealthy, travel became more accessible to a larger segment of the population in the prosperous postwar era because of the active economy, improved means of long-distance travel, and the creation of more long-distance tourist vacation destinations, like Disneyland. Engaging in a variety of travels and family vacations became another form of participating in the vibrant consumer culture. The travel motif within *I Love Lucy*, however, signifies more than just a reflection of contemporary social trends or a clever plot device—it functions as a significant element within the show's consumer narrative that exposes how travel as consumption also serves to reinforce the constructed boundaries of "whiteness." Bell hooks notes the importance of rethinking the notion of travel, "to expose the extent to which holding on to the concept of 'travel' as we know it is also a way to hold on to imperialism." On the television show, this "imperialist nostalgia" becomes clearest in two episodes.[17] The first takes place in a working-class neighborhood in Florence, Italy, which would still have been recuperating economically from World War II. In the Italian episode Lucy befriends a local shoeshine boy because she is lonely for her son (who is still at home in New York) on his birthday. The shoeshine boy is a stereotypical Italian street urchin who only befriends the American tourist in hopes of taking advantage of her. Giuseppe's individuality is unimportant, as his role in the episode is to fulfill a surrogate emotional need in Lucy's life. Giuseppe pretends that it is his birthday to have an in with Lucy, and she's so excited that she throws the birthday party she would have thrown for little Ricky for Giuseppe and his friends instead. With the conartistry of the children at the center of the episode, the poverty of postwar, urban Italian children effectively becomes the source of comedy.

The second such episode, "Lucy Goes to Mexico," portrays the characters on an excursion to a border town, where they have gone to find bargains on jewelry and baskets in the Mexican markets. That their sole interest is shopping underlines travel as a form of consumerism. Similar to the Italian episode, Lucy again finds herself the target of an impoverished child street vendor when a Mexican boy uses the Ricardos (who have brought a roomy convertible with a large trunk) to sneak over the border into the United States, causing the subsequent comedy of errors with the border guard. Lucy and Ethel's innocent shopping trip sets the stage for a slapstick treatment of illegal immigration, not an unimportant issue in California during the era of "Operation Wetback" (1954), in which thousands of legal and illegal Mexican residents of the United States were deported, and the border was fortified on the grounds that immigrants were hurting the economy and possibly enabling Communist infiltration of the American border. This plot complication also highlights, ironically, the major differences between Ricky and the illegal migrants, reasserting his middle-class status, his legal American residency, and his "whiteness." As tourists in the sites of recent fascist oppression and imperialistically driven poverty, the couples are able to enjoy the quaintness of the locals as tourists without acknowledging the role that tourism plays in a kind of continued colonization.[18]

This kind of traveling, though for comedic purposes, reinforces imperialist tropes of travel as consumption. As such, the episodes serve as what Herman Gray terms "frames of containment that constitute and reproduce many of the class, gender, and racial discourses of American society." In contrast, the character Maud Martha's minor experiences with travel work like those described by bell hooks in her own life during segregation. "From certain standpoints," hooks notes, "to travel is to encounter the terrorizing force of white supremacy." Maud Martha's "hikes" take her into unfamiliar territory in her city, which, as a child, she experiences only as a subtle difference in cultural expression: "East of Cottage Grove you saw fewer people, and those you did see had, all of them (how strange, thought Maud Martha), white faces. Over there that matter of mystery and hunchedness was thicker, a hundredfold."[19] As I will examine later, however, rather than functioning as a mode of consumerism, Maud's excursions increasingly expose her to the complexities of discrimination within American society.

Considering the Ricardos again in the domestic space of the average American home, the travel episodes also enable Lucy to do what no "typical housewife" was able to, for example, to interact frequently with the likes of John Wayne, Maurice Chevalier, Alan Ladd, and Milton Berle. This is hardly "holding up the mirror" to everyday life. On the surface, the appeal is one of letting everyday people enjoy vicariously the sensation of "a typical housewife" meeting a star. Over the course of the series, the line between the actors and the characters became further obscured as the number of celebrity appearances greatly increased, making it obvious that these were Ball's and Arnaz's real-life friends. The crumbling away of the "everyday" veneer of Ball and Arnaz served a different market-oriented function in the overall narrative, for, while the U.S. economy took off, and the average American family acquired more material goods, the show did indeed "hold up the mirror," with Lucy and Ricky sharing in the postwar prosperity. What would keep people watching, though, would be the continued promise of more material gain; as the Ricardos started to look more like upwardly mobile Mr. and Mrs. Suburban American, they had to keep the audience desire alive by staying one step ahead of the "real Joneses," keeping always slightly ahead of the limitations of a real family. In other words, the program itself made the desires of its contemporary viewers continually obsolete by offering more fantasies of consumer and celebrity encounter to which the average family had little or no access. Moreover, consumer desire not only functioned as a prime motivator in the narrative, but also became a driving force in maintaining the upward mobility of the show-as-product. Even as Lucy's performances transgress the behavioral boundaries of the ideal feminine, Landay notes, the program reinserts her performances within a commercially motivated (and, consequently, status quo) space: "The series seems to offer consumption as the solution to Lucy's dissatisfaction, an example of the consumerist-therapeutic ethos that presented private solutions to public problems. Week after week, *I Love Lucy* endorsed the processes of mass consumer culture. From Lucille Ball and Desi Arnaz clothing, furniture, and nursery items to Lucy and Ricky dolls, record albums, and comic books, *I Love Lucy* spawned a widening circle of commodification."[20] Lucille Ball also engaged in overt endorsements on the show by, for example, smoking (as Lucy Ricardo) the cigarettes of the show's commercial sponsor Philip Morris or driving the 1955 Pontiac that was a product-placement deal with General Motors. What results, then, from the series is a complicated set of identities, the lines between the public and private ones blurred, but both identified by a common role in constantly reproducing consumer desire.

What does it mean, then, that the monetary provider for this consumer fantasy is not a conventional Anglo-Saxon television father? Ricky's character constantly shifts among several representative identities: the good husband (according to American standards), the clown, and the exotic. In his more "serious" role as husband, Ricky enacts a patriarchal rule that serves to contain Lucy's urges to be other than a housewife. His role is to counteract her showbiz ventures by attempting to enforce her obedience within the domestic space. This is especially true after she becomes a mother, when Ricky often comments that he thinks she should be content with a baby and no longer care about fame. Her desire to be involved in the public world of show business remains both during pregnancy and after the baby's arrival. For example, she works her way into a Gay '90s review by wearing a barrel to hide her swollen belly and works her way into an "Indian" show by carrying Little Ricky on her back as a papoose.[21] What makes Ricky a "good American husband," though, is not just his patriarchal rule, but also the material kindnesses with which he rewards or forgives Lucy. By the end of most episodes, Ricky relents and buys her the fur stole or the new washing machine she wanted anyway. In this sense, he functions as an ideal material provider, rewarding Lucy each time she reinserts herself into the domestic space.

Ricky's ethnicity is many times rendered of secondary importance to his role as a good husband. When, however, he is able to perform his ethnicity, he literally *performs* it in isolated moments of an episode, either as the exotic (a romantic Latin balladeer at his fashionable nightclub, Don Juan on a Hollywood movie set); or as a clown, when Lucy's antics push his temper to the point that he is only able to roll his eyes and scream incoherently in Spanish. These moments are often his most comedic, his native language a joke to both audience and cast members. Ironically, these stereotypical moments also reveal the marketability of Ricky's ethnicity, because his character is unique within the television landscape. Karen Christian describes Desi Arnaz's career as a type of "media invention" that allowed Americans to view Cubans as racially white (disregarding the varieties of ethnicity in Cuba and the Afro-Cuban bandleaders who came before Arnaz). Arnaz's popularity in the United States, Christian continues, "is evidence of the commodification of the exotic, of the ethnic Other," and with this commodification grew Americans' appetite for the "spectacle" of ethnicity performed in easily identifiable excesses. Yet his performances also serve to expand the notion of whiteness as, according to Arlene Dávila, the "spin" of a Latino performance helps to "consolidate polarities between Latinos and other minorities—most specifically with blacks, who are the unnamed reference against which these representations are made."[22]

That Ricky Ricardo's episodes of anger are usually played out in a language other than English is telling, as this behavior contradicts the level-headed father figure embodied in such television husbands as Ward Cleaver (*Leave It to Beaver*) and Jim Anderson (*Father Knows Best*). In the end, though, the influence of Ricky's gender certainly outweighs the influence of his ethnicity within the home. After all, Lucy is never expected to "learn" the Other culture in the household, but rather learns to tolerate Ricky's "Cubanness" as one would learn to overlook an idiosyncrasy. The issue of language exemplifies this, as Lucy never learns to speak Spanish in their years of marriage, while often mimicking his accent and mocking his temperament for comic effect. For example, in "Lucy's Mother-in-Law," Lucy convinces a Spanish speaker to feed her lines through a transmitter while conversing with Ricky's mother because she has not learned Spanish before the visit. Of course, the plan falls through halfway into the visit, and Lucy ends up bumbling through the visit with made-up Spanish and amusing pantomime. While Lucy looks the fool in this episode, the comedy comes from mocking her husband's native language. Conversely, in "Lucy Hires an English Tutor," she brings in an elocution expert to tutor Ricky so that his imperfect English will not be a "bad influence" on the expected baby, an act that essentially disregards the mixed ethnicity of the household and of the baby.

But readings of Ricky's performances of ethnicity also have to be acknowledged as possibly self-aware. Gustavo Pérez-Firmat sees this same episode as one of triumph for Ricky, because, by the end, "the tutor adopts a Cuban accent and launches into a spirited rendition of Babalù." While Lucy learns almost no Spanish, she also "just gives in" and stops trying to change Ricky. In fact, Pérez-Firmat argues, Ricky's ethnicity is part of what she loves about him, evidenced in her sincere appellation, "my Cuban dreamboat." Consequently, his ethnicity is significant to Lucy's characterization on the show. In an article on the performances of Carmen Miranda, Shari Roberts identifies a "stereotypical persona as manipulated by the star herself": "She understands both her own body, along with the viewer, as well as her words; she is, moreover, in on the joke. Miranda's aural and visual presentation of herself as out-of-control excess is in fact a demonstration of her hypercontrol over her own voice and image." We might argue the same for Desi Arnaz, who, Pérez-Firmat notes, said some things in Spanish that would never have passed a censor—only Spanish-speaking viewers would be in on the joke.[23]

In the end, though, Ricky's ethnicity functions in this fictional household in much the same way that Gray describes African American ethnicity on television, working within "boundaries of middle-class patriarchal discourse about 'whiteness.'" His ethnicity and his voice may knowingly disrupt the white, nuclear family narratives of the era, but does so in ways that often compartmentalize ethnicity in the marketable roles of the exotic or the clown. Ricky's "Cubanness," then, basically serves as an entertaining tangent in a narrative that is ultimately about the rise and entrenchment of the white, middle-class American family.[24]

The Politics of Window Shopping

If we were to take the product-filled, ultimately happy image of the *I Love Lucy* series back to the lab where it was processed and edited, we might find a photo negative on the floor, one that reveals only the vaguest resemblance to what appears on television. That vague impression is the dream of eighteen-year-old Maud Martha, about to head out on her own in the world carrying a symbol of what she wants to pursue: "Maud Martha loved it when her magazines said 'New York,' described 'good' objects there, recalled fine talk, the bristling or the creamy or the tactfully shimmering ways of life. They showed pictures of rooms with wood paneling, softly glowing. . . . There were ferns in these rooms, and Chinese boxes; bits of dreamlike crystal; a taste of leather. . . . Her whole body became a hunger, she would pore over these pages."[25] In these magazine-inspired daydreams, she defines her entry into adulthood by the acquisition of luxurious material goods. The desire for these objects—this lifestyle—is termed "a hunger," implying not only the desire to possess, but a desire that, if fulfilled, could sustain one completely.

This desire for living "high culture" is one that the Lucy Ricardo of the show's early years also shares, as she occasionally attempts to emulate the WASP echelon of New York society by, for example, taking etiquette lessons. Richard Polenberg notes that the rhetoric of upward mobility permeated the social fabric, as we saw earlier in the character of Charlotte Haze, touted as an innate characteristic of democracy. Books like *Social Class in America* (1949) and magazine essays on the issue argued that, while class did exist in America, the categories were not static. Unlike in Russia's classless society, these texts argued, Americans were always afforded the opportunity to fulfill their dreams, redefine their lives, and climb the social ladder.[26] What these optimistic views overlooked, of course, was that the social forces surrounding ethnicity had a lot to do with the enactment of that "climb," despite one's personal goals and formal training. While Lucy does slowly fulfill that goal of social climbing, Maud Martha's experiences run the opposite direction, both by her own doing and for reasons determined by her socioeconomic class.

The novel utilizes this situation as a blatant discourse on the effects of ethnicity on the couple's limitations for upward mobility, just as there is an avoidance of serious issues of ethnicity in the apparent upward mobility of Lucy and Ricky Ricardo. Maud Martha and Paul begin the marriage optimistically, finding a kitchenette apartment that is supposed to be temporary until they save some money. There are few opportunities for Paul, a young African American man with no college education living on Chicago's Southside, however. He continues to struggle in the low-paying service industry and the family's prospects worsen until Maud Martha is finally forced to seek employment as a domestic. In having to fill this stereotypical role, she feels she has reached bottom, not because of her poverty, but because of her economically motivated subservience to a wealthy Anglo woman who represents the very lifestyle Maud Martha once aspired to: "There is a pear in my icebox, and one end of rye bread. Except for three Irish potatoes and a cup of flour and the empty Christmas boxes, there is absolutely nothing on my shelf. My husband is laid off. There is newspaper on my kitchen table instead of oilcloth. I can't find a job filing in a hurry. I'll smile at Mrs. Burns-Cooper and hate her just some."[27] Beyond the economic conditions that keep Paul and Maud Martha from moving out of the kitchenette, Maud's fantasies are gradually challenged over the course of the narrative by encounters with other white women who represent aspects of the same upwardly mobile lifestyle.

The first of these encounters involves a makeup saleswoman who stops at Maud's neighborhood beauty parlor to sell "Black Beauty" lipstick. While looking through an old *Vogue* magazine, Maud Martha overhears the conversation between the saleswoman (Miss Ingram) and Sonia Johnson, the shop's African American proprietor. Miss Ingram, wearing a new fur, chats with Sonia after making her sale, candidly remarking, "People . . . think this is a snap job. It ain't. I work like a nigger to make a few pennies. A few lousy pennies." Maud Martha tries to decide whether or not she has heard correctly and seems to not want to have heard the epithet. After Miss Ingram leaves, Maud Martha discusses the situation with Sonia and discovers that Miss Ingram had in fact used the expression "work like a nigger." She is as offended by the white woman's racism as she is by Sonia's silence.[28]

More than just hearing the word "nigger" used so lightly, the insult also cuts deeply because of what the woman represents to Maud Martha at this stage in the novel. Valerie Frazier argues that Maud Martha intentionally does not react: "As a commanding general would, Maud Martha weighs the benefits and risks involved in asserting her voice and selectively decides the battles she will enter." However, her psychological grappling with what she wants not to have heard indicates that her thinking on this episode is not entirely strategic. Not only does she find the remark offensive, but she wants to believe that the classy Miss Ingram is incapable of saying it. Choosing to obliterate the statement altogether, Maud Martha resolves, "'I'm glad, though, that she didn't say it. She's pretty and pleasant.'"[29] She is glamorous, a representative of the feminine beauty standard, available for purchase in the form of cosmetics. To hear such racism coming from her cuts that much deeper into the "self-solace" that Maud Martha has come to the beauty parlor seeking. In order for her to maintain her old fantasy, then, Maud's only choice is denial.

Not coincidentally, the narrative later posits Maud Martha in another site of female economy especially significant to the postwar period: the millinery. In an odd narrative shift, the scene utilizes the shop manager's perspective. On this particular day, the white milliner cannot bring herself to flatter customers, as she is preoccupied with her family crisis, and is thinking about "her daughter . . . gallivanting about with a Greek—a Greek!—not even a Jew, which, though revolting enough, was at least becoming fashionable."[30] She is especially annoyed to have to wait on Maud Martha, whom, she imagines, will leave hair oil on all the hats she tries on. The two women haggle over the price of a hat, and after getting the annoyed manager to lower the price, Maud Martha calmly decides against buying it. As Maud Martha exits and leaves the shopkeeper in a rage, one cannot help but see this moment as a small triumph for the protagonist—especially in comparison with the silence and denial of the previous scene. This triumph, though, is not a simple one, as the contemporary social significance of women's hats complicates the reading of this chapter.

Karal Ann Marling notes that, in the early years of the decade, when Mamie Eisenhower was the barometer for mid-American fashion sense, "the hat was the ultimate mark of feminine empowerment." The fashionable hat was a mark of status, since it served no practical function, "too small and delicate to shield the head from the elements, but visually obtrusive and subject to radical seasonal change." It also became a sign of willing participation in "America's vibrant new consumer culture" after the war because the possession of a hat signified participation within a market that offered an increased number of seemingly high-fashion items through the technology of mass production.[31]

Indeed, more than one episode of *I Love Lucy* centers on the social functions of hats, as hats are one of Lucy's notorious weaknesses. Ricky often ridicules Lucy's new hats or scolds her for spending more money on hats when she already has dozens. Her defense is always that her other hats are old and "out of style." For example, "Ricky Loses His Temper" centers around Lucy's desire for a small spring hat that Ricky will not let her buy.[32] The conflict of the episode develops on a bet to see whether Lucy can go longer without buying a hat than Ricky can go without losing his temper. If she wins, she gets the hat, so she spends the next days purposely trying to make Ricky angry by throwing the domestic routine into chaos. Of course, she gets the hat by the end of the episode.

In such a context, where hats signify social standing and a willingness to participate in a unified consumerist notion of the feminine, what does Maud Martha's decision to *not* buy the hat mean? Is her small triumph displaced by the fact that she is ultimately hatless and, therefore, "disempowered"? Her behavior has allowed the milliner to embrace and enhance her own racist assumptions about "these nigger women who [try] on every hat." On the other hand, Maud Martha's choosing not to buy serves as a direct critique of conspicuous consumption. This scene marks a turning point in the narrative because it signals the protagonist's willing abandonment of her previous fantasy of "the creamy or tactfully shimmering" life achievable through the acquisition of material goods. Moreover, in a world where "a woman becomes what her hat means to the world and to herself," Maud Martha is deliberately denying this mark of "femininity" as one that can signify what she "means to the world and to herself."[33]

The small awakenings that occur within these episodes of *Maud Martha* are what allow her to spend no more than one day as a well-paid employee of Mrs. Burns-Cooper, for whose lifestyle she has lost all admiration. To prove that she is "not a snob," Mrs. Burns-Cooper chats "at" Maud Martha while she works: "In my college days. At the time of my debut. The imported lace on my lingerie. My brother's rich wife's Stradivarius. When I was in Madrid. The charm of the Nile. Cost fifty dollars. Cost one hundred dollars. Cost one thousand dollars." In the face of this inventory, Maud Martha realizes how useless it would be to try to explain to Mrs. Burns-Cooper the significance of "my own social triumphs, my own education, my travels to Gary and Milwaukee and Columbus, Ohio" because they are not the kinds of mobility (like Lucy's) validated within the culture.[34] Moreover, she realizes that her being there allows Mrs. Burns-Cooper to use Maud Martha as a signifier of her own social status. Her interaction with Mrs. Burns-Cooper forces Maud Martha to acknowledge the ideological accessories and classist attitudes that almost always accompany such ownership. While embracing these attitudes, for Lucy, would signify an improvement in social status, Maud Martha realizes that to do so would further devalue her own experience. She can own some of the signifiers of status, but she can never occupy the status itself because she lacks the white privilege that Lucy was born with in American society. Ethnic signifiers keep Maud Martha from occupying the arena in which such status symbols are assigned their value.

She knows there is no point in trying to explain to Mrs. Burns-Cooper the reasoning behind her quitting. The only way she can articulate it to herself is as a metaphorical escape from execution: "One walked out from that almost perfect wall, spitting at the firing squad. What difference did it make whether the firing squad understood or did not understand the manner of one's retaliation or why one had to retaliate? Why, one was a human being. One wore clean nightgowns. One loved one's baby. One drank cocoa by the fire—or the gas range—come the evening in wintertime." In these small moments of triumph, it is important to note that Maud Martha still does not speak out her anger or her pride. Though many critics have shown disappointment in the character's silence, Mary Helen Washington defends this silence: "[T]hat disappointment ignores the novel's insistence that we read Maud's life in tone, in images, and in gestures." Frazier sees the silence as part of a tactical "holding pattern," one that reserves fighting back in order to find "an outlet in guerrilla-type tactics in which the attack is not direct but covert."[35] Similarly, Maud Martha's rationale for quitting her job could be seen as "disappointing" not only because it remains interior, but because she does not use the pronoun "I," weakening the self-empowerment of her decision by not stating "*I* am a human being." Yet, if we read the "gestures" in her rationale, she places the insistence on dignity beyond herself alone. Maud Martha's semantic weight could translate into something like, "Why, a black woman is a human being. A black woman loves her own baby—more than she loves the babies of the white woman she works for." In the evolution of her character and the expansiveness of her rationale lies a potential for a larger reading of the novel to see beyond the exterior of any seemingly two-dimensional "Beulah" figure.

It is Maud Martha's love for her child that finally does cause her to speak out publicly against an act of racism. Where she may have remained silent for herself, suppressing her anger when personally insulted, she cannot do so when she sees her daughter being conditioned for self-hatred. Notably, the scene occurs at Macy's, the famous temple of consumerism at the most consumerist time of year. While the department store Santa Claus delights in the white children, "push[ing] out plump ho-ho-ho's!" and patting their cheeks, Maud Martha's daughter, Paulette. elicits an obviously different response. At her appearance, "Santa Claus rubbed his palms together and looked vaguely out across the Toy Department. He was unable to see either mother or child." When he does not acknowledge Paulette's requests for toys, Maud Martha calmly states, "'Mister . . . my little girl is talking to you.'" She then forces him to go through with the routine, if only minimally. Of course, the damage has been done, and Paulette is convinced that Santa does not like her. Maud Martha finds herself wanting revenge against the fake Santa, "to jerk trimming scissors from purse and jab jab jab that evading eye."[36] This desire for violent retribution functions as the climax to these various encounters with discrimination in a culture that, along the lines of Lisa Lowe's thinking, validates consumer identities for everyone while simultaneously denigrating ethnic difference within the abstract body of consumers. Elizabeth Wheeler aptly describes how the very structure of the novella mirrors Maud's psychological strategies for not acting on that violent impulse: the "vignettes segregate her experiences from one another so they won't add up to an explosion."[37]

The episodes that constitute the gradual debunking of Maud Martha's consumer fantasy, and her coming into self-awareness, make up the backbone of what is really a rather nonplot-driven narrative. It would be a mistake, however, to attribute this process of self-awareness entirely to negative encounters with white people. The politics of skin color within the African American community in Chicago—and within her marriage—serve to reinforce the novel's subtle critique of the beauty standards that circulate within American culture. As the narrative progresses, Maud's husband, Paul, appears less often, and her sense of self becomes tied less to her marriage as it also loosens itself from her fantasies of upward mobility. This fact is largely attributed to Paul's participation in the "Foxy Cats Club," a social set that stages galas for light-complexioned members of the community. When he receives his first invitation, he "considers himself one of the blessed." Because Maud Martha is much darker than her husband, her early reactions to this event are self-effacing, thinking, "There will only be beautiful girls. . . . There won't be more than a handful like me." To contribute to his standing, she plans her attire, seeing herself beautified for the event through white imagery, in a "plain white princess-style thing," and smelling "of lily of the valley."[38] Mary Helen Washington suggests that this "white washing" of her own image signifies her attempts to comply with white beauty standards even when isolated within the black community: "[S]he prepares for the evening in language we know will defeat her. . . . The words she uses to refashion herself—*white, princess, wavy, lily*—all suggest how complete a transformation she imagines she needs in order to be accepted."[39] As in the Ricardo marriage, whiteness becomes a normative force in attempts to define the couple's social status.

After being snubbed at the ball by her own husband for someone "red-haired and curved, and white as a white," Maud Martha acknowledges how shallow Paul really is. She also perceives the role the Negro press plays in validating and perpetuating beauty standards based upon whiteness, with "the usual representations of womanly Beauty, pale and pompadoured."[40] Paul continues his quest for upward mobility within the black community solely by the advantage of his skin color, while Maud Martha proceeds to purposefully forfeit her active desire for upward mobility. Acting on this desire really does boil down to the set of conscious decisions highlighted in the earlier monologue of material desires, and Maud Martha chooses not to participate further. She implicitly acknowledges that any aspirations for success or beauty as represented by the likes of Miss Ingram, Mrs. Burns-Cooper, or the Foxy Cats requires her to capitulate to self-hatred.

In the novel's closing scene, we find Maud Martha on a spring day, outside with her daughter after learning of the end of World War II and of her second pregnancy. She seems newly free of her anger after sloughing off her previous desires. As she takes in the landscape and activities of her neighborhood, she works to find the same satisfaction in the mundane that she had as a child, when she thought dandelions were the best flowers to be found, "their demure prettiness second only to their everydayness; for in that latter quality she thought she saw a picture of herself, and it was comforting to find that what was common could also be a flower." Here, she does allow an object to signify her, because, unlike with the hat, to do so requires no purchase—nothing but validation of the self. Here again we see an overt engagement with the notion of identity as a response to a culture of exclusion, in which a discourse of "identity counter[s] with a rhetoric of 'liberation.'"[41]

Also in the conclusion, Maud Martha for the first time overtly acknowledges the current events outside of her own domestic space and unfulfilled desires: lynchings, wars, divorces, evictions, and taxes. She seems to find a certain satisfaction in acknowledging these unhappy events, as they make up the real texture of human experience. In the everyday world she finds perhaps what Cornel West defines as "joy," that which encompasses "those non-market values—love, care, kindness, service, solidarity, the struggle for justice."[42] The last line of the novel, "The weather was bidding her bon voyage," indicates that the end of the book is the real beginning of her life, as, like the protagonist of *Invisible Man* getting ready to come out of hibernation in the novel's epilogue, she has understood the costs of performing cultural citizenship and will now opt to live by her own codes, as he does: "I'm shaking off the old skin and I'll leave it here in the hole. I'm coming out, no less invisible without it, but coming out nevertheless. And I suppose it's damn well time. Even hibernations can be overdone, come to think of it. Perhaps that's my greatest social crime, I've overstayed my hibernation, since there's a possibility that even an invisible man has a socially responsible role to play."[43] Maud Martha's "bon voyage" signals a metaphorical journey, one that is no longer defined by her previous desires; it is a voyage that is nonphysical, noncommercial, nonexploitative. The travel here is really the beginning of her revised fantasy.

While this ghetto novel does not end with a small people's revolution or a political manifesto, as do some of its Depression-era forbearers, *Maud Martha* is no less political than its 1930s counterparts. As John Fiske argues about television narratives, the "interiority" or covertness of a narrative does not necessarily render it powerless. Instead, "fantasy" can become a realm of agency for those who are not able to engage in active public resistance.[44] In the case of a novel, the lyrical use of language and narrative contemplations serve the same purpose as subversive fantasy. Maud Martha decides at a very early age that her great contribution to the world is simply herself: "What she wanted was to donate to the world a good Maud Martha. That was the offering, the bit of art, that could not come from any other." She cannot understand the desire for public attention, which causes people to "exhibit their precious private identities; shake themselves about; be very foolish for a thousand eyes."[45] What she realizes is that, on a smaller level, engaging in the cultural citizenship defined within this context is a kind of forfeit of her "precious private identity." The narrative, then, portrays Maud in the process of "polishing and honing" herself in a very private way. The actual book allows that private process to become public before a contemporaneous audience that might be, like the Macy's Santa, "unable to see either mother or child."

Displaying private identities is what the public medium of television is all about, and in the 1950s it made private family identities much more public. The public personae served in reshaping the private lives of millions of viewers according to status quo values. Lucille Ball and Desi Arnaz certainly did "shake themselves about" for money. Despite the value systems *I Love Lucy* endorsed, however, the history of the series does reveal progressive elements for the representations of postwar women. Most notably, Lucille Ball was one

Figure 3. Ricky Ricardo as Voodoo Witchdoctor. Courtesy of Photofest.

of the most powerful women in Hollywood, the co-owner of Desi-Lu Productions, and the first woman to ever appear pregnant on television—after a good deal of controversy and threatened censorship.

Despite the potential for scandal, Lucy's baby's birth is represented in a way that celebrates her own "production" within the postwar feminine economy. Unfortunately, to do so, "Lucy Goes to the Hospital" employs a problematic representation of ethnicity in order to deflect from the "impropriety" that would have been going on in the delivery room. Indeed, the scandalous suggestion of a woman's labor is "censored" by racist play within the hospital waiting room while Lucy is hidden from sight. Ricky, in the middle of rehearsing a new "voodoo-themed" show for his nightclub, rushes back to the hospital dressed as a witch doctor. He is, essentially, in blackface, with huge barred teeth painted across his mouth, wearing a grass skirt and a fright wig. What proceeds is a comedy of errors in which Ricky scares the nurse, who calls the police, and so on. The uproar keeps Ricky in trouble and at the center of attention to distract the audience from the act of labor that is occurring somewhere out of frame. On another level, this clowning within the spectacle of another ethnicity also serves to deflect Ricky's own ethnicity and, perhaps, the mixed ethnicity of the baby. Eventually, Ricky's identity is verified for the police by the Mertzes, and the episode ends with Ricky fainting at the sight of his son through the nursery window. What one remembers of this episode, though, is not the joy of birth or the progressive act of representing a birth on television, but the dominating image of Ricky clowning in blackface. Robert Thompson reminds us that many states still had antimiscegenation laws in this period, and Lucy and Ricky's marriage would have been seen by many as "interracial." Ricky was, in Oscar Hijuelos's words, "not threatening, kind of cartoony," however.[46] Ricky's performance of another ethnicity—in hyperbolic fashion—contributes to the sense of uproarious joy accompanying the birth of Little Ricky/Desi Jr., deflects attention from the "mixed" marriage, and essentially results in a sort of validation of the ethnically homogenizing forces at work within the Ricardo/Arnaz family.

Unlike Ricky's prime-time moment, Paul's first meeting with his newborn child is not accompanied by a group "coo" from a studio audience, but by a fear that the child is stillborn. When he first sees the newborn child, it appears "gray and greasy," and the first words out of his mouth are, "It's dead, isn't it?" Juxtaposing Lucy's sanitized birth are the grim details of Maud Martha's labor: "Presently she felt as though her whole body were having a bowel movement. The head came. Then, with a little difficulty, the wide shoulders. Then, easily, with a soft and slippery smoothness, out slipped the rest of the body and the baby was born."[47] This graphic, naturalistically represented birth occurs within the tenement building, where "gray" pervades the imagery, where Maud Martha's "bloodcurdling scream[s]" are heard throughout the building and on the street below. The scene is stressful, chaotic, and Maud Martha's own mother is nauseated by the episode. In the act of birth, Maud Martha's and Lucy's bodies become the sites of cultural reproduction, and each body works as a signifier of womanhood and how womanhood is being deployed within the larger American culture. As Lauren Berlant argues, the body functions as the most basic vehicle or obstacle within the social order, and how the body is ethnicized and gendered has everything to do with one's "cultural legitimacy."[48] While the production of Lucy's child instigates celebration, Maud's labor goes uncelebrated. Maud's labor—the production of an African American girl into the postwar cultural economy—seems truly devalued by everyone but herself.

But what does it mean that during birth, Lucy's body is rendered invisible, while Maud Martha's stays firmly in frame? Perhaps, in the end, Maud Martha's presence—and her conscious labor without medical intervention, her assertion of her voice in the pains of labor—provides her some measure of agency within her cultural production. While Lucy is off-screen, Maud Martha asserts herself and her labor through her screams and a birth that seeks to hide nothing from the witnesses present; while other characters dominate the narrative of Lucy's labor, Maud Martha's perspective dominates her own labor. These contemporaneous birth scenes function as the pivots around which the larger questions of female identity are explored within the two texts. Ultimately, the narrative within Maud Martha complicates the homogenizing aspects of television performances. Because of the very different decency codes at work within the different narrative industries, this type of graphic exploration and agency remains possible in the small literary novel.

Maud Martha the novel (and also the character, whose name defines the cultural object of the book) protectively asserts a private identity into the public space of cultural narratives, challenging and contributing a different definition of ethnicity and identity occurring within those narratives. While the interior "fantasy" does possess cultural power, the next two chapters examine the responses of subjects who do try to negotiate identities publicly, who do "shake themselves about" to some extent in front of audiences. The following chapter takes up again a subject like Desi Arnaz, who pursues the performance of cultural citizenship in the form of celebrity, for an analysis of the role of ethnicity when one crosses over from consumer status to participate in the production of mass culture narratives.

4

The Celluloid Fantasy

Negotiating the Ethnic Male Star Image in William Saroyan's *Rock Wagram*

"Is identity itself, then, a fraudulence?"

—William Saroyan, *Sons Come and Go, Mothers Hang in Forever*

Like many novels about Hollywood, William Saroyan's *Rock Wagram* (1951) tells a story of the deal making and social life in movieland. What moves the narrative, however, is not an exposé-style focus on the workings of the place itself, but a complicated exploration of the title character, an Armenian American from Fresno, California, who becomes a movie star just before World War II. A character who embodies complicated images of self, he demonstrates that the inclusion afforded by ethnicity (vs. race) is more complicated than it seems. The ways in which the title character's images of self play out within the novel provide for a useful reassessment of the roles of ethnic actors at midcentury, and the novel helps to provide a history of the convoluted route by which ethnic actors both capitulated and contributed to mainstream notions of American masculinity.

Through two different narrative strands, Saroyan's novel explores the contradictions inherent within Hollywood image-making practices as these forces establish a similar pattern within the ethnic star-as-subject. Combining nonchronological scenes and actions from Rock's life with frequent italicized, stream-of-consciousness sections, the narrative presents the star's search for personal identity and meaning within his life. This italicized narrative strand appears intermittently throughout the novel, revealing the abstract internal monologues that represent Rock's struggle for identity. The other, more traditional narrative strand contains nonchronological, plot-based interactions between Rock and various characters and settings that serve as catalysts for the musings of the italicized sections. These two strands are juxtaposed at the outset of the novel: "*But there is meaning to a man. There is meaning to the life every man lives. It is a secret meaning, and pathetic if it weren't for the lies of art.* One day in September he found he was in Amarillo, Texas, on his way to San Francisco in his new Cadillac, a man named Rock Wagram, thirty-three years old. It was seven o'clock in the morning."[1] The italicized sections grow longer, more frequent, and more complicated (containing, for example, long lists of abstract philosophical questions) as the plot drives Rock's personal life further into difficulty. While the plot-centered sections provide impetus for the "deeper" parts of the narrative, the plot-focused sections actually become the more fruitful for interrogating the complexities of ethnic male celebrity and the configurations of identity within postwar American culture.

By the time *Rock Wagram* was published, Saroyan was a well-established literary figure. However, this novel did not receive the critical acclaim garnered by his prewar works: a Pulitzer prize-winning play *The Time of Your Life* (1940), the nostalgic autobiographical short stories in *My Name Is Aram* (1940), and a sentimental Book-of-the-Month Club hit about small-town America, *The Human Comedy* (1943), which was based on the script of the feel-good wartime picture starring Mickey Rooney. Despite the relative lack of attention by contemporaneous and current critics, *Rock Wagram* proves one of Saroyan's most intriguing works because of the very complicated ways in which the novel (by the man who once called himself the "best American propagandist this country ever had,") frames and problematizes the significance of ethnicity and the meaning of American identity within the context of America's own factory of representation.[2] The narrative *seems* to present a dichotomy of superficial celebrity versus "authentic" ethnicity, both forces at work upon the protagonist in his search for a concrete sense of identity; the result, however, is a much more complex dialectic that places celebrity and ethnicity as part of a larger, shifting aggregate of identities that does not allow for a simple resolution to the contradictory forces at work within the ethnic male celebrity.

Ethnic Male Star Images

A 1946 *Colliers* magazine feature on the then up-and-coming comedic actor Danny Thomas bears the playful title "Wailing Syrian." Based on the name of one of Thomas's stand-up characters, the title evokes the familiar image of the actor, especially in the situation comedy *Make Room for Daddy*, yelling in short-tempered fury, but giving way to the funny "nice guy" performer aspect of his character (in essence, "The Toothless Lion," as he was described by a writer for *Coronet* television magazine several years later).[3] The stage persona of Danny Thomas embodied several contradictory images: a fierce temper and a soft heart, the dark complexion of a Middle Eastern heritage combined with a WASP name, a traditionally handsome face overshadowed by the trademark "schnozz" that became the source of many gags.

The contradictions represented within this portrayal of Danny Thomas reflect some of the larger contradictions present within midcentury Hollywood, the locus of star identities. When I refer to Hollywood, I want to invoke not just the place and the styles associated with it, but the idea of Hollywood as a site of both filmic and cultural production, a material and metaphorical place defined by its unique foothold within American culture and imbued with its own value systems and politics—especially in the years immediately following World War II. Victor Navasky characterizes it in the early Cold War years as "a company town, but a fragile one, which had earned its coherence by holding violently contradictory tendencies in balance: culture vs. commerce, message vs. entertainment, formula vs. originality." The notion of the "company" here remains somewhat open to interpretation, as Navasky implies that Hollywood was as influenced by the ideologies of the U.S. government (positively and negatively so) as it was controlled by major studios like Metro-Goldwyn-Mayer and the powerful professional guilds during the years of the HUAC hearings.[4] These years, it seems, saw Hollywood keeping its contradictory elements in an even more tenuous hold as it negotiated its ideological role, fluctuating between concurrent tendencies toward cultural liberalism and postwar conservatism.

These contradictory elements are also clearly at work within the practices of the image making and marketing of individual celebrities who represent "the company." Star images are inherently constructs, beginning with the artifice of stage names. Name changes were a common part of the process of packaging stars, with hundreds of actors reformulating bland names into the glamorous or unusual, or awkward names into the smooth and understandable, and of course, ethnic names into Anglo-American ones. The renaming process has always been deeply connected to the extensive processes of marketing star identities, as Richard deCordova explains:

> The spectator's relation to [star] identity . . . is a relation to an intertextual field of association, not merely a formal marker. These associations are organized in part through the name, which supports the actor's identity in language. The name not only appears outside of the image, but it also refers to an identity that extends beyond the single films—into other films, into advertising preceding the film, into other extrafilmic practices.
>
> In fact, as the actor is increasingly individualized, the name supports an expansion of the actor's identity through writing that reveals what she or he is "really like" behind the screen. The actor is assigned a personality, a love life, and perhaps even a political persuasion.[5]

As Rock Wagram's story demonstrates, the common practice of such renaming and its accompanying identity reconstruction set in motion a complicated set of subject negotiations for actors of ethnic backgrounds because of a required capitulation to homogenizing cultural forces *and* a simultaneous concession that one's ethnicity could also be used as a marketing tool. I do not want to assert that all ethnic actors necessarily felt these adjustments in ways that caused some sort of psychic rift; instead, my goal is to tease out the cultural implications, to investigate the meanings drawn out of these practices, which are not always consciously held. A novel such as *Rock Wagram*, through its investigation of the subject and the construction of "Armenianness" within an aesthetically inscribed cultural form, provides an ideal space for such exploration into the larger project of reexamining postwar ethnicity.

In this fictional narrative, the act of identity transformation is shown as a simple act of producer whimsy. The producer, Paul Key, has decided that the actor's given name is not suited for a Hollywood star and has created a new name before Arak Vagramian even arrives in his office: "Your name is Rock Wagram. The pronunciation and accent is that of your own language. That is, Vah-GRAM."[6] Presumably, Paul Key offers the new name because the original is "too ethnic," difficult to pronounce, and not appropriate for star marketing. The new nomenclature reveals the protagonist at the hands of two motivations, the one that wants to anglicize him and reconfigure him as hard, masculine, and all-American ("Rock"), the other that, though not using his real last name, recognizes the exotic selling quality of a surname of unidentifiable ethnicity ("Wagram").

There are various factors at work in this kind of scenario, not the least of which is complicity. Notably, Arak Vagramian does not challenge this renaming process. The choice of working in/for Hollywood requires participation in an understood set of politics in exchange for the privileges of fame. Gina Marchetti argues, however, that regardless of what doors may open for ethnic actors, there are always larger cultural ramifications: "Positive or negative, intended or accidental, real or imagined, the image Hollywood creates of race and ethnicity points to something far more fundamentally pernicious about the relationship between American society and the mass media. Hollywood has the power to define difference, to reinforce boundaries, to reproduce an ideology which maintains a certain status quo. . . . Alternative media exist, but appear marginal and far-removed from a popular audience. Access to the industry also exists, but entrance demands a tacit agreement to assimilate."[7] While "assimilation," as I discussed in chapter 2, is perhaps too simple a blanket term for this process, Marchetti's argument does imply that the participation of the ethnic actor results in an important set of messages on the other side of the lens, messages, she goes on to argue, that must be sorted through in order to see where even seemingly progressive portrayals of otherness are complicated by the politics of representation in Hollywood. What Marchetti overlooks is that, while the mass media have "the power to define difference," the presence of the ethnic subject inflects that definition, as well. Likewise, we must work to decode seemingly stagnant portrayals of ethnicity that may provide room for alternate interpretations (as in David Henry Hwang's reclaiming of Asian types in the revival of *Flower Drum Song* or Carmen Miranda's knowing exaggeration of *latinidad*).

Some of midcentury's biggest motion picture and television stars were self-identified "ethnic" males: Danny Thomas, Desi Arnaz, Dean Martin, Sid Caesar, Frank Sinatra, Sidney Poitier, Tony Curtis, Mario Lanza, Sammy Davis Jr., Anthony Quinn. With the exception of Frank Sinatra, whose career as a romantic crooner predates his movies, few of these men made names as romantic male leads. Many times, the scripted roles and accompanying media images for ethnic males were either villainous or desexualized, relying on comedy and the image of a man either tamed through domesticity or a foiled would-be lover. A perfect example of this can be found in the earlier film *Orchestra Wives* (1942), starring Cesar Romero. His character is established as a womanizer, a man who has had many conquests and wives, while during the film's action, the female characters will have nothing to do with him. His reputation and actual potential seem at odds with one another, pivoting around both the mythical sexuality *and* the taboo of the Latin lover. Such casting and promotional trends call into question the function of gender within the construction, and public interpretation, of ethnic star images. As Marchetti argues, "Ethnicity is never neuter; rather, images of ethnicity and race always conjure up images of masculinity and femininity."[8] Ethnicity often worked as a cachet for women (such as Zsa Zsa Gabor, Sophia Loren, Anna Magnani, Gina Lollobrigida, Katy Jurado) whose "exotic" sex appeal was a powerful selling point, while the sexuality of male leads was kept in check, often through comic relief or stereotyping. This could be attributed to various, now familiar, myths about ethnic males as overly sexualized and largely responsible for the "mongrelization" of American generations through marriage to Anglo-American women. Such sentiment found voice at various periods in U.S. history, in, for instance, antimiscegenation legislation or the various nineteenth- and twentieth-century nativist movements that publicly discouraged the mixing of ethnicities and religions in marriage.

While ethnic women were often depicted as animalistic enough to be sexy but ultimately containable, ethnic male sexuality, if commodified, was typically relegated to the role of villainy (think of the Mexican gangsters attacking Janet Leigh in her negligée in *A Touch of Evil* (1958)) or strategically tempered with the seemingly emasculating forces of comedy and/or banal domesticity (as in the case of Ricky Ricardo's character). Compare, for example, the opening lines of *Look* magazine's feature on new starlet Sophia Loren, describing her "startling animal beauty and physical endowments," with the always innocent portrayals of Cesar Romero, living at home with his parents, imbued with tones of wonder that this handsome man has never married. An interesting exception to this trend lies within the career of Harry Belafonte. Michelle Stephens argues,

> Harry Belafonte became a key cultural figure for a racialized vision of American ethnicity, one that was compatible with the needs of an internationally expanding American state. The development of the tourist industry and the military expansion of the United States into the Caribbean during the period provide important contexts for understanding the racialized sexual politics of ethnic performances such as Belafonte's. Essentially, the 1950s saw Belafonte's black, ethnic, working-class consciousness, forged in both Caribbean and American radicalism, transformed to fit a quintessentially liberal story of American, interracial integration.

Belafonte's sexuality in film (especially in the 1957 film *Island in the Sun*), Stephens argues, was a source of distraction from the prolabor identities articulated in his folk songs. This type of integrationist packaging of ethnicity for the purposes of supporting transnational foreign policy rhetorics falls into the same patterns described by Klein in relation to Asian narratives of the Cold War era.[9]

Considering gender and ethnicity during this period in Hollywood also brings to light another intriguing feature: that of the "import" versus the "homegrown" ethnic star, a factor that may also account for variations in identifying "nationalities." The distinctions fall along clearly gendered lines, with the majority of significant ethnic male stars in the United States having been American-born to immigrant families, while many major ethnic female stars were "imports." Of the American-born stars of ethnic descent in this period, very few women appear before the 1960s. Apart from the featured ethnic actresses like Sophia Loren and Katy Jurado, most female leads were designed for Anglo-American actresses. For women, a clear binary existed: either All-American or exotic import. As Patricia Ovalle argues, the Latina entertainer served an important function in nation building "a familiar Other, an embodiment of the promise and fulfillment of national and sexual conquest." Her body illustrates racial boundaries within national contexts, and "[a]lthough her presence appears to diversify the media landscape, the traditions of her representation as a dancing and temporary love interest of white men in fact reinforce and reify the status quo of Hollywood representation and cultural citizenship within the United States."[10] The situation for African American actresses must be considered separately, since the politics of Jim Crow segregation required a different set of representations. African American women fell into a parallel, but differently defined, binary: to be all-American was to be subservient, segregated on screen as in life (e.g., Juanita Moore in *An Imitation of Life*), and to be "exotic" required a level of glamour that adhered to white beauty standards (e.g., opera singer Marian Anderson).

Ethnic male stars maintained various (sometimes simultaneous) identities between these two poles, their image marketers drawing upon a variety of signifiers for both Americanness *and* ethnicity. Vivian Sobchack touches on this in her assessment that "being ethnic meant having a cultural identity structured and regulated by the constraints of *descent*—whereas being American (unethnic, assimilated) meant having a cultural identity structured and transformed by the freedoms of *consent*."[11] Drawing on the work of Werner Sollors, Sobchack thus examines the effects of early twentieth-century performances of the melting pot ideology, in which new Americans (recent immigrants) shifted from one national identifier to the other. Americans of the late 1940s and early 1950s, I would argue, found themselves not so much torn between a simple dichotomous choice of descent *or* consent, but wedged within the postmodern process, which variously privileged assimilation and conformity while also celebrating levels of difference, allowing individuals multiply influenced identities rather than the options of "ethnic" or "assimilated."

Examining popular magazines of the era, we see this complex process reconciled and working itself out within the image-construction of ethnic male stars. Here, the contiguous acts of "descent" and "consent" become clear in feature articles about celebrities' personal lives. The stories play up the sentimental aspects of ethnicity, repeatedly mentioning, for example, Dino Crocetti's simple working-class background as a trouble-making Italian barber's son, and Muzyad Jacobs's effusively affectionate, large Lebanese family. These backgrounds are relegated to nostalgic history, however, as the articles continually reassert the adult Dean Martin and Danny Thomas into the upper middle-class success story. The narratives follow a predictable rags-to-riches formula, highlighting the fortunes found in Hollywood careers; young, pretty WASP wives; luxurious Los Angeles homes; and broods of happy, suburbanized children. Contained within the domestic space, the men are portrayed as happy pushover dads and participants in the everyday domestic comedies of error (as in the *Photoplay* feature "How I Trained My Husband, by Mrs. Dean Martin"), the opposite of the temperamental, drunken, or womanizing characters they may play in film and television. Predictably, these features play up what Sobchack terms a "construction of social being," a "'re-presentation' of self" that is "ultimately theatrical," playing the part of middle-American home life. Artie Shaw, in describing Saroyan's own marriage, recalls the "game called 'masks'" that everyone in Hollywood played, trying to pass oneself off as the ideal.[12] The idea of "masks" offers a useful metaphor, as it implies that individuals did not simply attempt to cover an ethnic face with one "white" mask; instead, the identities were multiple, malleable, some performed by the individual, some assigned by larger cultural forces as the notion of "the ideal" constantly shifted. This same idea plays out in other gendered ways through the concept of "imitation" in the next chapter.

Viewed in combination with filmic representations, the above types of magazine features constitute a public, nationally distributed narrative about the cultural capital of the ethnic male. Richard deCordova notes how the star system links "discursive and economic practices," and the star becomes "the point of an economic exchange only by virtue of its identity as constructed in discourse." Journalism serves as "the institutional setting for much, if not most, of the discourse on stars. The trade press, fan magazines, the popular press, and newspapers all constituted specific positions from which to speak the star." As Wendy Kozol demonstrates in her study of *Life*, the power of the magazine's on-going visual and written narrative "hails the reader into the signifying spaces of national identity, a space severely circumscribed by the patriarchal and racist ideals of domesticity," helping to formulate a notion of "'the kind[s] of people who make good Americans.'" While *Life* was at the forefront of this "dialogic process" of articulating national and family ideals, many popular magazines of the postwar era were engaged in the same processes, "speaking the [ethnic] star" in ways that translated these personae into cultural capital. In some ways, the privileging of the domestic arena in postwar visual narratives was so strong as to reinscribe the social world around them. As Nina C. Leibman argues, the American nuclear family became the locus for working out almost all other larger social issues and problems, reconfiguring issues of ethnicity, gender, drugs, etc. into parent-child conflicts with tidy family-based solutions. All controversies and problematic identities were censored or best contained within "family melodramas." Applying these notions to ethnicity, Leibman notes that ethnic distinctions were often conveniently converted into class distinctions and that narrative strategies required "the ethnic other [to] learn not only the rudiments of the American language, but the basic principles of American decorum" (familial responsibility, patriotism, the Protestant work ethic). In any case, these forms of "education" are rooted within the WASP family.[13] The specific configuration of ethnic male celebrities within the Anglo-American domestic space, then, demonstrates an appeal to status quo values and a strategic repositioning of oneself in relation to the white picket fence. It is also worth noting that, as mentioned in the earlier discussion of Ricky Ricardo's character, in these scenarios the ethnic male serves as the main provider in the American domestic space, the very marketability of ethnicity bankrolling the construction of the white picket fence.

These types of magazine features depict one set of identity reformulations, but others existed in tandem, in forms equally desirable to audiences. In contrast to the perky domestic scenarios are gossip-laden features about Frank Sinatra, someone whose ethnic identity always remained less "contained" in how he was marketed and cast, and whose ethnicity seemed to lend itself to exploitative and stereotypical speculations about his mob connections, his unhappy marriage with his first wife, Nancy, and his "tempestuous romance" with Ava Gardner. Articles like "Why They Are the Battling Sinatras" and "A Stranger to Happiness" depict Sinatra as a man washed up at an early age and plagued by trouble because he cannot succeed as a domesticated American family man. Ironically, this persona was as marketable as the family man image, because the lure of scandal sold magazines. Karen McNally credits this mixed image of Sinatra as one that, unlike other Italian American stars of his day, "consistently challenges postwar notions of American identity through its engagement with debates in contemporary Hollywood and the wider culture and by exposing limitations on the ways in which American masculinity is defined." He refused to Anglicize his name, and the fact that his Italianness mattered to his sense of identity made him marketable to ethnic audiences—those most responsible for the "come-back" phase of his postwar career when he was on the outs with the Hollywood status quo.[14] What the Sinatra-as-celebrity-image demonstrates is another version of the complexity of ethnic male identity in the postwar era: at the same time that his success (and that of other up-and-coming Italian American stars) provided for the incorporation of Italian American culture into the mainstream and a deracialization of the term "Italian," his image also helped to perpetuate the stereotype of the tempestuous Italian man. Both the stereotype and the demystified Italian American remained desirable for producers and consumers of mass culture.

Surrounding these variations of ethnic representation was the specter of the Red Scare and its penetrating effects on Hollywood. Blacklisting publications had implicated the original Hollywood Ten who were called before Congress in 1947. Hundreds of subsequent witnesses and accused actors, screenwriters, and producers were subpoenaed through the early 1950s. Saroyan never was accused or called before the House Committee on Un-American Activities (HUAC), but many of his contemporaries were. Notably, many of these people were also ethnic Americans, and most of them under suspicion for reformist beliefs or civil rights activism (Paul Robeson, Canada Lee, Lena Horne, Budd Schulberg, etc.), or, in the case of Sinatra, questioned in the Kefauver Hearings (1950–51) because of suspected "un-American" criminal ties (to the mafia). While there may not be official documentation of suspicion *based* on ethnicity, there is a clear pattern wherein cultural identifiers inherently highlighted one as suspect. Individual behaviors and identities were politicized. Historically, many public figures of ethnic backgrounds were involved with the cultural Left before the war, as ethnic groups were some of the most impoverished and politically underrepresented in the early part of the century. The cultural agencies of the New Deal, in many ways, also helped to highlight and preserve ethnicity as an important aspect of Americana. Period studies indicate that the HUAC hearings, while rather short-lived, created a grim and somewhat pessimistic atmosphere in Hollywood in those years, with production cuts and a general anxiety about who might be implicated, which actors might present a political risk, and which stories might be perceived as Red propaganda. And, as Erik Barnuow demonstrates, the real effects of the blacklists were nationally pervasive, trickling down to everyday consumers when grocery store chains threatened to sabotage the products by sponsors of television programs with politically "questionable" actors, such as *The Goldbergs*.[15]

Budd Schulberg's account of one episode gives the sense that potential red baiting became a part of the very texture of Hollywood relationships. Saroyan himself, whom biographers describe as "unpolitical," was working as a screenwriter for MGM and had an unpleasant, public falling out with Louis B. Mayer. Schulberg recalls, "Mayer's power was so great it went beyond M-G-M. . . . If Mayer called one of the others and said of Bill, 'He's a troublemaker, he's no good, he's a Communist,' or whatever, Bill was pretty much washed up." In addition to the renewal of HUAC hearings in 1951, the year of *Rock Wagram*'s publication also saw political and media attention to the fight against Communism through the Korean War and the conviction of the Rosenbergs for espionage. That year balanced postwar optimism with an anxiety in which identities and loyalties were called into question. The surrounding political factors no doubt influenced how people employed within the commercial media represented themselves. However, not only did some refuse to submit to the political scapegoating; some actively defied it. Chon Noriega documents how several of the period's "social problem" films, specifically working against gang and "greaser" stereotypes of Chicanos in mainstream media, intentionally "hired blacklisted personnel under pseudonyms."[16] Rock's interior struggles and actions in the popular and official spheres, though not overtly about "politics," resonate on levels other than just the fictional. The protagonist's internal monologues reveal an active, conscious, and often pessimistic negotiation of identity during a time when the safest pursuit in Hollywood was to embrace an identity of Anglo-American patriotism above any other.

When ethnicity functioned as a significant part of an actor's persona, the performance of that ethnicity was often excessive, as in the case of a barely intelligible Chinese waiter in a movie, or the out-of-her-blouse sexuality of Sophia Loren. This type of performance, ironically, often provided for the acceptance of ethnicity into American culture, as noted in the discussion of Desi Arnaz in the previous chapter. Similarly, a figure like Sinatra satisfies an "appetite for ethnic excess." Leibman elaborates on this in her assessment of Asian "exotics" in television and film: "[T]hey reinforce the notion that the melting pot is a myth and that ethnic heritage is too distinct to be subsumed into WASP culture," while their cultures can be "appreciated from the same safe distance that a tourist would appreciate [them] from." This idea fits somewhat with Klein's notion of the integrationist rhetoric of the era, when narratives provide instruction on how multiethnic subjects might fit into larger national ideologies more so than how they fit into local social roles.[17]

All these examples together demonstrate that the public appetite for ethnic performance in the postwar era was characterized by a complicated set of ideologies. Gaylyn Studlar explores the beginnings of this phenomenon in her work on the first major ethnic male film star, Rudolph Valentino. Valentino was a contested figure, simultaneously admired by female fans for his overt sensuality and despised by male audiences for being too "effeminate" and too foreign. Studlar assesses the intersection of ethnicity and gender within Valentino's star persona and explores its function within the context of the post–World War I nativist movement in the United States. Then, too, the star image is filled with contradictions, both within its representation and reception, "simultaneously privileged and disavowed by the Hollywood film industry." The end result of this ethnic "vogue" is a complicated one: "[T]his apparent subversion of cultural norms was actually not unique to the cinema but part of a wider web of popular discourses that linked the exotic to the erotic in forging a contradictory sexual spectacle of male ethnic otherness within a xenophobic and nativist culture." Valentino the actor would have maintained a variety of conflicting identities all at once. His stage persona, like those of his later counterparts, allowed for a positive portrayal of ethnicity within mass culture against a sociopolitical backdrop that prescribed the marginalization of ethnicity in practice. This is seen, for example, in the attempts of men involved in nativist politics to censure the white female desire for the exoticized male—despite the fact that the early cinema was largely defined by its relationship with immigrant audiences. Studlar's assessment of Valentino elucidates the ways in which all these patterns of contradiction have surrounded the ethnic male star image from the beginning of the film industry.[18]

Novelistic Interrogation

Like Valentino, the fictional character Rock Wagram is cast as a romantic lead at a significant moment in the history of national identity structuring, and his performances of gender and ethnicity are called into question by himself and others around him. Rock's story seems at first to be another enviable

California story, a modern version of the "American Dream": a handsome and charming nobody gets discovered by a Hollywood producer, is whisked away to LA, and made into a star overnight. In fact, this was the marketing strategy employed for Valentino, who was presented as the embodiment of the American Dream, an immigrant nobody who made it big Horatio Alger style.[19] *Rock Wagram* demonstrates the ways in which novelistic discourse permits an enlightening ambivalence about the process of supposed assimilation and American success. Stylistically replicating those "violently contradictory tendencies" of Hollywood itself, the novel is characterized by disjointedness, movement, and fragmentation.

Because of the shifting definitions of race and ethnicity at this moment, Rock can enact the social mobility not available to a character like Maud Martha, as "Armenian" becomes a gradually less racialized identifier, a hazy middle-ground "exotic whiteness" that is marketable to the mainstream.[20] The narrative begins with a major signifier of success in American postwar culture, as Rock speeds toward California in his new Cadillac. Travel in this car functions as the spine along which various flashbacks reveal the significant moments in Rock's adult life. This constant motion emphasizes the irony of Rock's situation, as the entire book reads as his quest to fix himself in relation to something (at various moments: family, ethnicity, nation, art). Also ironic is the fact that, while he is shown participating in ideals of American consumer culture, he uses this vehicle in a constant attempt to escape from the commercial success that has been created for him. In the year of the book's publication, the naming of a Cadillac would certainly invoke in readers an immediate understanding of the exchange value of this status symbol. The postwar years saw automotive production and its accompanying print and television advertisement almost double, solidifying the cult of the car.[21] Rock avidly participates in this cult, protecting his car throughout the book to the extent that it is the only thing he has left by the novel's end. The Cadillac should signify only material success and prosperity within postwar America, but the car comes to function as the last thread in his identity in an unraveling celebrity image.

As a Californian and a movie star, his role is even more important; more than participant, he is a trendsetter. These first years of the new decade after the war signaled the upswing in economic progress and consumerism that would set the tone for the rest of the decade. California was seen as the locus for establishing the desired lifestyle across generations. Karal Ann Marling describes a receptiveness to all things new and West Coast in the visual media: "Perpetually sunny, easy and perfect, the new West Coast way of life soon became the American ideal." The years Rock spends in Hollywood contain all the ingredients of that new ideal: financial wealth, mobility, celebrity, leisure, and blonde beauties, all at his disposal. This idealized vision of West Coast life and its certain nationwide impact is reinforced by a photo-essay in a January 1951 issue of *Life* magazine. Inaugurating the new year is a collection of photos of bronzed and blond youths frolicking on beaches, skiing, camping, and attending "parties of Hollywood scale," accompanied by an essay that argues the superior health, size, and schooling of California's children, "A Bright Asset for the U.S. Future." Such examples from popular culture extol not only the desirable lifestyle of the West Coast's white inhabitants, but their genetic superiority as well. The privileging of whites in this scenario is further accentuated by a *Life* feature a few months later focusing on the "Mexican wetback" problem and its disruption of California's economy. One photo captures a group of men being deported after a "night raid" with the caption "Back to Mexico goes a group of serape-clad wetbacks."[22] Like the latter article, the novel's pages reveal a California story that is anything but "sunny, easy and perfect." What follows is the result of a clash between mass culture, embodied in Hollywood, and the protagonist's struggle with his own identity as a person both adored by and marginalized from the mainstream.

Although the novel contains many autobiographical elements, I do not intend to read Rock Wagram's search for identity as Saroyan's own. In fact, many of his biographers and critics do interpret Rock as Saroyan's alter-ego, especially when analyzing the role of ethnicity in Saroyan's writing. I find this conflation of author and protagonist problematic, even more so when applied to "ethnic writers" because it tends toward an oversimplification of an artist's subjectivity and often implies the artist as representative of an entire ethnic group's experience. For example, studies like Walter Shear's "Saroyan's Study of Ethnicity" and Margaret Bedrosian's book-length study of Armenian American artists offer useful insights into Saroyan's works, but also problematically imply that all of his works that deal overtly with ethnic subject matter remain entirely representative of what Shear describes as Saroyan's personal "emotional record of what it means to be a member of the Armenian subculture." These same critics privilege those of his works that romanticize the "immortal quality in his ethnic heritage," namely, his somewhat sentimental collection of short stories, *My Name Is Aram* (1940). Furthermore, devoting all critical energy to exploring the author's reconciliation with and utilization of the historical Armenian past (as Bedrosian does) offers only a limited view of ethnic identity—one that seeks an "authentic."[23] According to Stephanie Brown, "By the 1950s, questions of what constituted the authentic, not merely in the racialized subject but in a far more inclusive sense, had gained new resonance. A constellation of factors, some if not most of them unique to the decade immediately following the Second World War, combined to make the period one which clung desperately to notions of the real."[24] While Saroyan did romanticize his heritage at times in pursuit of "real" Armenianness, that critics romanticize his work overlooks the important balance that Saroyan established, concurrently celebrating and problematizing ethnic identity. Shear interprets this problematization of identity as a "negative" view of ethnicity and therefore not as worthy of study as the happier nostalgic works. Another limitation of these critical approaches is that they offer a problematically unified understanding of "what it means" to belong to a particular marginalized culture, which must look only to history and essentialized notions of ethnicity to legitimate itself—a somewhat outdated notion in ethnic studies. These critical works have been useful in initiating further inquiry into Saroyan's writing, but no significant work has been done since to examine Saroyan's treatment of ethnicity in more complex ways. *Rock Wagram*—and its exploration of the concept of "Armenianness"—examined carefully within its contemporary context and not viewed simply as the "grown up" (read "bitter") sequel to *My Name Is Aram*—again points to the various forces at work within identity formation at a crucial point in American history.

As a literary character in the postwar era Rock was a "terrific disappointment," argued critic George Freedley in 1951, "perhaps because he is unpredictable, egocentric to a high degree and much given to sentimental whimsicality."[25] Although Freedley articulates disappointment in terms of what he sees as the novel's character development and general aesthetic qualities, his noting the protagonist's "unpredictability" speaks symbolically of a larger cultural desire. After all, a careful reading of the novel reveals Rock's actions to be, perhaps, unpredictable to others, but always consistent with the character Saroyan has developed. Rather, the "unpredictability" lies within those abstract, somewhat self-indulgent, introspective moments (e.g., *"What is a man? A man is his mother's son"*) that contrast with the more concrete strands of the book. Freedley seems to speak for a general audience that desired consistency in its cultural products, the predictable Rock with the veneer of the Hollywood romantic lead. To exist solely in this image, his connection to ethnicity would exist in uncomplicated, sentimental terms, like those in the magazine features discussed earlier. Such predictability and homogeneity, as many period cultural studies have so effectively argued, offer comfort for a society in crisis—a society not unified by crisis, as it seemed to be during World War II. *Rock Wagram* does not offer a quaint view into the idealized ethnic enclave as *My Name Is Aram* did. And although Saroyan wrote many works with "nonethnic" protagonists, it is within a context of relative national anxiety that the author created a narrative that does nothing less than question the meaning of nationality and American identity.

The novel immediately posits the notion of ethnic identity with the influences of mass culture by relating the story of Rock's discovery by the Hollywood producer Paul Key, "Vice-President in Charge of Production at U.S. Pictures," a character clearly modeled on Louis Mayer of M-G-M. A stereotypically powerful and self-important producer, "[t]his man only noticed those who didn't notice him."[26] Key happens to be in Fresno on business and stops into a local bar, Fat Aram's, where Rock (still Arak) works as a bartender. He listens to Arak telling jokes—half in English, half in Armenian—to a captivated group of men. After a drink, Key leaves his business card, assuming that the young bartender will come to Hollywood as requested. When he does not, Paul Key sends his assistant to physically transport Arak to Los Angeles. Their first conversation, like many of the novel's long dialogues, reveals the young man's awareness of the fluidity and manipulations of identity:

> "What are you?" Paul Key said.
> "I'm a bartender," Rock said.
> "What nationality?"
> "American Indian."
> "Are you a Turk?"
> "I'm an Armenian," Rock said. "I hate the Turks."
> "How much do you hate them?" Paul Key said.
> "Not enough," Rock said. "I was born in Fresno. To hate them enough you've got to be born where my father and mother were born, in Armenia. All the Armenian hoodlums of Fresno call themselves American Indians."

The conversation takes place the day before Rock's screen test. In his fascination with Rock, Paul Key engages in this quiz-show approach to understanding ethnicity. His question, "What are you?" assumes that Rock only understands himself in terms of ethnicity. Rock's answer that he is a bartender subverts this assumption. "What nationality?" then implies that Key cannot see Rock as first an American, indicating an assumed affiliation with some other nation before the one in which he was raised. Rock's response that he is American Indian again subverts Key's assumptions, as he offers an ethnicity that is the only truly American one. Key's persistent questions reveal an unwillingness to accept any of Rock's responses as truthful ones. Rock's "play" in this scene is reminiscent of Danny Thomas's own assertion of ethnic agency when, in his stand-up comedy act, he would play with elements from various cultures, including a "Mohammedan call to prayer" and a mournful Lebanese madrigal, after which he would quip, "Oh, you poor English-speaking people."[27]

This conversation is not intended solely for us to see how clever Arak is in response to Paul Key's ignorance, though. Rather, the identities that he invokes on this page—bartender, hoodlum, American Indian, Armenian, American—reveal the constant negotiations of the man's identity. This is not to say that Arak is confused about his identity, but he is aware of the mass-mediated forces that enable the metamorphoses of ethnic identities, that change and compartmentalize them, often seeking to place them within understandable categories and hierarchies. By playing with identities, by performing multiple ethnicities as a direct reaction to that cultural dominant as represented by Key, Arak asserts not his ethnic identity, but an identity that at this moment refuses to be defined by an essential or stereotypically perceived ethnic signifier.

The fact that "All the Armenian hoodlums call themselves American Indians" may also be read as a kind of subversion of the roles of "ethnics." True, this practice began as a joke because Arak and his friends recognize people of Armenian descent who have been cast as Indians in several films. Still, the joke also works on other levels. In one sense, it demonstrates a critique of the dominant culture's willingness to conflate all "Browns" and to use them interchangeably, to its own advantage. In this case, Armenians apparently work better as Native American characters for visual representations in Hollywood Westerns because Armenian "noses stand out better." Rock points out that the local Tule Indians do not possess the physical features of the plains Indians, in whom mass culture sought the normative Indian type. The practice of casting ethnically marked actors across ethnicities was quite common before the 1970s. For example, Ovalle describes how Anthony Quinn "was able to play other brown men such as Native Americans, Arabs, Greeks, and Italians but was often restricted from playing a nonraced or nonethnic white role." Likewise, Ken Nolley documents how Westerns like John Ford's, despite the director's desire to cast Native American actors, offered Sal Mineo, Ricardo Montalban, and Gilbert Roland as Cheyennes.[28] Rock's invocation of American Indians in particular hints at the paradox at work, one that both offers an Armenian American more cultural privilege than natives are afforded and also constrains the extent to which he can assume cultural whiteness because he is recast as a racialized subject within the visual media. On another level, Rock's comments speak of a sympathetic affiliation with those very Indians whom the Armenian actors are intended to replace, acknowledging the shared experience of ethnic erasure/genocide as well as the manipulations and constructions of stereotypical "exotics" and "savages" in movies that reify the boundaries of identity. Paul Key's question, "What are you?" incongruously seeks an identity based on difference at the same time that it initiates a reinvention of that ethnicity.

A scene from Rock's youth sets up the kind of conditioning at the hands of "official" culture that has evolved his method of ethnic "play":

> [H]e had gone to an employment agency to get a job during summer vacation. He had filled out the application.
>
> "Here under nationality," the woman said, "you have written American."
>
> "Of course."
>
> "Aren't you—? Isn't the name, Vagramian—?"
>
> "Armenian?" he said. "Of course. I was born in Fresno. I was born on Winery Street."
>
> "Hadn't I better put down Armenian?"
>
> "No," he said. "I'll tell you what you do. Change the name from Vagramian to Basoglu, change the religion from Christian to Mohammedan, change the nationality from American to Turk. . . . If you're going to change my nationality, let's have some fun. I don't want the job anyway."[29]

At the age of fifteen, the protagonist has already begun to recognize the shortsightedness of official culture in regard to ethnicity. Gestures such as this last one ("let's have some fun with it") complicate a simple reading of the novel that interprets its agenda as one of trying to rediscover and preserve Armenian culture. Regardless of what Rock wants to call himself or to what extent he wants Armenianness to matter on the personal level, his experience in this instance reveals his understanding that identity will almost always be mediated by racializing hegemonic forces. After all, he is not trying to "pass"; he is only stating what he believes himself to be in terms of employability—American. Rock comes to view Hollywood as an extension of such official culture, though he realizes that the performance of identities is less strictly mediated, "passing" for something else almost a requirement of participation (at least passing as an understandable identity—an unspecified "exotic," for example).

Hollywood as the purveyor of media products and illicit affairs is evoked within characters and conversations, but very little of the novel's action actually occurs in Los Angeles. Once Rock's screen test has taken place, once the pertinent intersection between ethnicity and mass culture has been established early in the novel, few scenes take place there. Rock's seven years and fourteen films are mentioned in passing as the narrative skips forward again to Rock's cross-country road trip from New York to California. Tired of Hollywood, he has accepted his draft notice and is making the trip to see his family before going off to war. Despite Paul Key's attempts at intervention, Rock refuses to use his notoriety to gain an officer's commission or to join the forces as an entertainer.[30]

His visit home represents the portion of the novel that most critics read as "reaching out for his lost past."[31] There are, in fact, many elements in Rock's return to Fresno that could be read as such. He surrounds himself with relatives, speaks Armenian for the first time in years, and he and his cousin Haig take a nostalgic tour of the Armenian neighborhood, driving past vineyards, visiting the Armenian church, and stopping by the office of the Armenian-language newspaper (*Asbarez*) where Rock's father used to work. Though Rock speaks Armenian, he has never learned to read it. Notably, at various times he seeks a reconnection with his ethnic heritage through Armenian-language media. In moments of personal crisis he turns to the newspapers for which his father wrote articles and poetry—as both an attempt to know his father and to know his father's understanding of ethnic identity through language. Like many Americans, Rock here buys into the assumption that fluency in language and cultural practices equates with a complete coalescence of one's ethnic identity—a notion that is itself problematized from the outset of the novel. Abandoning those practices epitomized in language—and adopting others (such as speaking English and participating in conspicuous consumption)—would mean greater participation in cultural citizenship, still popularly characterized by the symbol of the melting pot during this period. This notion recalls the advice given to young Yiddish-speaking Mikey in Michael Gold's *Jews without Money* (1930): "One can make much money here, but first one must learn to speak English."[32] Interestingly, Rock attempts to reconnect with ethnicity by a means similar to that by which he moved away from it: through commercial media. However, he is never as successful in these attempts as he is in his participation in Hollywood culture.

During this same visit home, other fascinating intersections between mass culture and ethnicity are played out in the context of the ethnic enclave. Rock's return raises questions and reveals assumptions about what happens to ethnicity and traditional morality in Hollywood. The narrative in this section is composed of pieces of overheard conversation and slips into the minds of undeveloped characters to illustrate the community's perceptions of Rock. Most noteworthy are the thoughts of an Armenian American with whom Rock and Haig play poker. The perspective systematically shifts around the table to reveal each player's thoughts, including "a man of twenty-seven with black bushy eyebrows called Aslan" who "never believed Fresno would ever see Rock Wagram, or he himself would ever speak to him in Armenian, and hear Rock speak to him in Armenian."[33] Of course, his thoughts reveal amazement at interacting with a famous person, but, more importantly, they express the assumption that Rock's participation in mass culture would require complete assimilation into mainstream (white) culture and the abandonment of any ties to an ethnic identity. In other words, the poker player is as surprised at Rock's willingness and ability to speak Armenian as he is at Rock's presence there at the table. This man mistakenly sees Rock's identity in either/or terms, while Rock is in a constant process of negotiating his presentation of self in terms of both/and *and* either/or at various points throughout the narrative, with some of his permutations of identity self-appointed, some not.

Rock's presence also instigates all kinds of gossip among the relatives who have come to Rock's grandmother's house while the star is in town. The gossip centers not only on Rock's activities, but also on what Hollywood does to individuals who work there. For example, one aunt wants to ask him if all actors and actresses are "immoral," while two young cousins contemplate the existence of lesbianism in Hollywood. Meanwhile, an uncle's discussion with his wife reveals the assumption that perfecting assimilation and gaining cultural power guarantees institutional power: "Of course he knows Roosevelt. Everybody famous knows Roosevelt." The uncle, unable to conflate the celebrity and his nephew as one person, needs constant reminding that this person is his "own dead brother's son."[34]

Finally, one of Rock's conversations with his grandmother Lulu shows how she is unable to reconcile his performance of gender and ethnicity in terms consistent with her own values: "Having your picture taken as you kiss one girl after another? What kind of work is that?" These bits of conversation are all meant to be humorous, perhaps to show how charmingly naïve these relatives are. But these examples also reveal how Rock's identity becomes confused for others once he has entered the world of media representation. As in the real-life example of Lucille Ball and Desi Arnaz, the lines blur between the real people, their star personae, and their characters because of the system in which they work. DeCordova describes this system as a set of "discursive practices {that} produce the star's identity, an identity that does not exist within the individual star . . . , but rather in the connections between and associations among a wide variety of texts—films, interviews, publicity photos, etc. The star's identity is intertextual, and the star system is made up in part of those ingoing practices that produce the intertextual field within which that identity may be seized by curious fans." Rock's grandmother, someone who does not usually consume mass media products, comments only on his films as a strange kind of work to do. She ignores the intertextually constructed star, demonstrating that the idealized qualities of exotic manhood embraced by Hollywood are not perceived the same way by all audience members. His peers, however, are avid consumers of mass culture and immediately after the release of his first film, "his pals in Fresno saw Rock in *To Remember Harry* and began to remember him as if he had died."[35] Acting in films removes him from what his relatives understand as "real life": physical labor or service work, heterosexual marriage with children, an understood system of moral codes. This is a restricted and normed view of life, yet it is coded as ethnic here. Ironically, these moments at home reveal the amount of negotiating that Rock must do: in Hollywood he is inscribing himself in one set of normative identities (mass media), while at home he must inscribe himself in another; simultaneously, each location (both literally and symbolically) provides a certain level of escape from the normative limitations set up by the other. In this instance, Rock's grandmother cannot reconcile his idealized masculine star image with her understanding of masculinity, specifically because he does not have a mustache. His performance of masculinity within mass culture does not meet her understanding of masculine performance, which is based on her interpretations of gender strictly defined by traditional notions of ethnicity. These interactions should not be read so much as Rock's simple alienation from the community as they need to be seen as relationships *complicated* by the mass mediation of his identity.

Lulu's hassling Rock to grow a mustache further signals the novel's work on ethnicity in relation to the performance of gender. In fact, the moments when Rock struggles for some kind of "authentic" ethnic identity occur in relation to a traditional and patriarchal notion of gender, which he suddenly equates with an authentic performance of ethnicity. When playing the dark, strong-but-silent leading man on screen, he is performing Hollywood's visual ideal of masculinity, as his grandmother's challenge demonstrates. She comes to embody the traditional understanding of gender roles and admonishes him to "look like a man. Look like your father, the way you were meant to look," and to not wait for a wife because "[a] man creates his woman. She is not found standing somewhere." From both perspectives, the performance of an ideal is not just signaled by the physical attributes of the man but seems to have its very foundation in the physical.[36]

Interestingly enough, Lulu's advice implies that to be a "true" Armenian man, one does not necessarily have to have an Armenian wife. In fact, Rock cannot fathom marrying a "nice Armenian girl," as he regards them as "sisters, everyone of them." Nor does monogamy seem to be an issue for Lulu, as long as one wears the signifiers of masculinity. She describes watching him in the movies: "I have been to the ones in which you have stood there and kissed them. . . . I sit there and marvel at their delicate white beauty, a new one in every picture, sometimes two or three, or three or four, and yourself forever a false man, with no mustache, a man with a naked lip, kissing them."[37] A traditional performance of virility (mustache, heterosexuality, and children) seems to be enough to restore ethnicity, regardless of the wife's ethnic identity or the husband's allegiance to her.

In fact, the woman that Rock wants to marry represents the ideal of "delicate white beauty." Ann Ford, whose monosyllabic name presents a distinct symbolic contrast to Arak Vagramian's ethnically marked, syllable-heavy name, is a seventeen-year-old WASP from New York, whom he meets in a posh Hollywood nightclub. Her name calls to mind industrialist Henry Ford and his associated dabblings in the restructuring of capitalist economy and commodity production, and in pageants of patriotism and "melting pot" ideology. A point is made of emphasizing Ann's background: "'Scotch-Irish on her father's side. Russian-French on her mother's. All well-to-do and well-mannered.'" In this, Rock's ultimate motivation for marrying Ann is self-serving, which is revealed in a conversation with Paul Key:

> "Why are you going to marry her?"
>
> "For my kids," Rock said. "I was a father the minute I was born. No sense being a father without kids. I want to see them now. I'd like to see them looking at least half like her."[38]

Here, though half joking, he reveals that she will become for him another vehicle through which he can achieve some just-out-of-reach sense of identity and a particular version of manhood—and one that, ironically, brings him closer to whiteness than back to ethnicity, as the children would likely not be raised in Fresno. When trying to decide whether or not to marry her, Rock engages in several conversations in which he explores the significance of ethnicity as it relates to marriage, revealing his understanding of an excessive performance of ethnicity and gender. He explores these notions further in a series of bizarre late-night phone calls and lengthy dialogues with Ann's (annoyed) mother:

> "Do you think she could learn Armenian?"
>
> "I don't know," the mother said. "It's a rather difficult language, isn't it?"
>
> "Not after you get the hang of it," Rock said. "Do you think she could learn to be the wife of an Armenian?"
>
> "I don't know," the mother said. "Is an Armenian very different?"
>
> "Very," Rock said. "They order their women around and expect them to have a lot of children, keep house, cook, sew, sing, dance, and manage money. Do you think Ann ought to marry an Armenian?"[39]

Rock's description here reveals a complicated negotiation: on one hand, he articulates a belief in the extreme, traditional gender roles as the key to ethnic identity; meanwhile, Rock's use of "they" (Armenian husbands) indicates that gendered ethnicity is another kind of performance he can learn, but he does not yet see himself as possessing. One could argue that this desire to be an *Armenian* husband functions as a resistance to assimilation into the dominant culture, or marrying Ann could be seen as a means of completing assimilation (like the domesticated ethnic fathers with white wives and children portrayed in the movie magazines).

However, that Rock wants to incorporate "all that dazzling white" into his identity, on terms that he establishes, further complicates the situation. Artie Shaw, one of Saroyan's contemporaries and friends, recalls Saroyan's own marriage to his wife, Carol Marcus, in a way that renders a biographical element helpful to this discussion. He characterizes the relationship as a kind of interracial display: "Bill wanted to *own* Carol. Carol was a thing, a status thing to him. Blonde, beautiful little girl. He was a black [*sic*], minority Armenian—a despised minority. . . . She represented a big step up in the world. A little immigrant, second-generation Armenian boy marries this society girl." This was all part of that "game called 'masks,'" basically, an identity performance. In fact, R. L Friedman's centennial retrospective of Saroyan hints that Carol Marcus may have been Jewish and passed for WASP. Part of Rock's motivation to marry Ann does seem to be the "appearances" factor. Nevertheless, his inability to see Armenian women as anything but "sisters" and his desire to make Ann into an "Armenian wife" further highlights the complex negotiation of identity in which Rock is engaged. He even goes so far as to examine the question with a lawyer cousin, hoping to find a succinct understanding through the same official institutions against which he bristled as a youth. He frames the question to his cousin (who also happens to be a completely "assimilated" and seemingly "white" man): "'The girl says she wishes to learn Armenian, so she can speak to me, to my mother, to my grandmother. If she learns to do so, will she *become* Armenian?'" Here, Rock articulates again the notion that ethnic identity can be accomplished through a set of linguistic, gendered, and legal practices. The lawyer then responds, "'Legally . . . A wife accepts or acquires the various identifying cultural or religious labels of her husband, insofar as he himself is aware of them or has employed or accepted them.'"[40] This answer clinches Rock's decision to propose, maybe more so because—bolstered by a legally defined ethnicity—it allows him to determine the course of their relationship along traditional gender lines and to enact the power to *create* ethnicity where there seemingly is none (i.e. disrupting "whiteness").

At this same important juncture in the narrative, Rock and his cousin/close friend Haig engage in several philosophical conversations about ethnicity, nationality, and personal subjectivity. This, again, is a section biographical critics read as a yearning to reconnect with his Armenian past simply because he is musing on ethnicity. Haig is useful in understanding Rock's self-contradictory character because he overtly voices the contradictory impulses to both identify with and reject ethnicity. Haig jokes, with the same awkward pain we hear in Louis Armstrong's "What Did I Do to Be So Black and Blue?" that he is as "white as the next man underneath. Whiter. . . . When did you ever see me peddling rugs?" He says that Armenians literally make him "sick to [his] stomach." In the same conversation he argues that no one should have to be any nationality at all, just "his own lousy self," then ends at the other extreme, confessing that he "loves the Armenians so much it's stupid." Rock reconciles these contradictory impulses by responding to Haig's idea of one's "own lousy self" with an elucidation that "self" is always, inevitably multiply determined:

> "A man wants to do anything he does because he himself wants to do them. He wants to do them *as* himself, not as his father's son, not as a member of a family, a nation, a religion, a society, a class. All

the same, it turns out that even if he does what he does as himself, he also does them as other things."

"So you're a Christian," Haig said.

"I'm an Armenian," Rock said.

"What's your class?"

"The proud poor."

"What nation?"

"American."

"What race?"

"Human."

"What family?"

"Vagramian."

"Yes you are," the younger cousin said. "All you are is a human being, and you know what phonies they are."

At the moment that Rock names "Human" as his race, asserting that always-problematic universal, Haig undermines that romantic universality by noting, like his contemporary literary counterpart Holden Caulfield, that all people are "phonies."[41] This reflects Saroyan's statement (in this chapter's epigraph) that perhaps all forms of identity are artificial constructs or theatrical performances—even those that seem to be "authentic." The lies and phoniness are about all any of the novel's characters have in common, as each seeks to negotiate identities in an atmosphere destabilized by the mass mediation of identities.

Rereading Nostalgia

The novel, upon first reading, seems to mourn the entry of Hollywood upon the scene of a seemingly secure and happy ethnic enclave. In a sense, it does. At one point, after spending seven years in Hollywood, Rock even says to Paul Key that had he never been discovered, he would probably be living a safely mundane and happy life in Fresno with a wife, kids, and a vineyard. However, I am not forwarding a reading of the novel's ultimate lesson as a "what if": "if that Hollywood producer had stayed out of that neighborhood, had never discovered Rock, everything would be all right." By the novel's end, it becomes clear that the "what if" scenario glosses over the novel's conclusion far too simply. Hollywood does not rob Rock of his identity. Rather, his active participation within the production of mass culture further complicates a process that is always already in motion, regardless of Rock's levels of capitulation or resistance. The novel cannot be easily categorized as the quest of "an Armenian man reaching out for his lost past"; seeing the quest in terms of success or failure in this pursuit results in an oversimplification of the issue.[42] As a multiply determined subject, Rock necessarily embodies variable, inflecting, and mutually influencing versions of identity. His visits to the Armenian community do matter, but returning is not an option, for there is no "authentic" *there*. By novel's end, after all, there is no actual or idealized community to return to: his siblings are dispersed or dead, his parents have died, the *Asbarez* is going out of print because there are so few readers of Armenian, and, divorced, Rock is alone. (This dispersion of community is a perhaps intentional echo of the genocide that historically dispersed Armenians in the first place.) The mother's bread dough, sitting unbaked while she dies in the hospital, functions as the final symbol of an idealized ethnicity. Rock believes that if his mother can simply get well enough to bake the bread, everything will fall into place for him and his family, the return to community will be successful because her recovery will reactivate domesticity for the extended family. In the end, she dies, and Rock has to throw away the dough. He will not transgress the boundary of his understood gender role to bake the bread himself, and his sister is seemingly not an adequate replacement matriarch, as "inauthentic" as he is because she also no longer lives in the ethnic enclave. Within the span of his Hollywood career, Armenian ethnicity remains, but it has been translated into something else, perhaps something less intelligible as "ethnic" to its own participants—at the same time that his persona further ethnicizes whiteness.

Though seemingly disjointed, the protagonist's abstract internal struggles (those revealed through the italicized sections) are intimately tied with those sections of the book that depict Rock's mobility within the contemporary, material world. While Rock seems to search for universal meanings, the former sections are so revealing precisely because they offer an acknowledgment of the specific ways in which ethnicity is manipulated by popular and official cultures—through real practices that simultaneously render ethnicities fluid while trying to compartmentalize (sometimes homogenize) them into something understandable and predictable. That they are sometimes not understandable or predictable to the ethnic subjects themselves reveals that ethnicity matters, but it is also a perpetually slippery concept. This convoluted relationship between ethnicity and dominant culture allows an "unpredictable" subject like Rock to make perfect sense: at the same time that he is adored by thousands of fans for his "exotic" good looks, his identity is subject to machinations that simply cannot be avoided in the postmodern, mass-mediated world. Defined by contradiction, he fits in well in Hollywood. He acts out, to various degrees, the disparate facets of identity: being completely socially constructed *and* working to construct one's own sense of identity along simple, essential lines—in addition to every permutation in between these extremes. Engaging all of these variables becomes the only real option, for he consciously acknowledges that he possesses a multiply-determined and never-fixed subjectivity. Ethnicity can and must be a part of that subjectivity, but as he has always known, ethnicity cannot be stablized or all-defining. The psychic division, represented stylistically by the two kinds of typeface throughout the book, parallels these various impulses within the negotiation of identity. This is why, by the novel's end, Rock has not made a successful retreat into a traditional ethnic lifestyle, and why he has also not persisted within the status quo ideals of Hollywood success.

Perhaps it is his inability to accept the truth he realizes about identity in American culture that leads to the existential pessimism in the novel's conclusion. Here, he is driving through the night in his run-down Cadillac, en route to Tijuana, realizing that he has truly lost his wife, children, and all hope: "All his life a man knows, he knows, he knows, forever and forever, but all he knows is, I am alone, I am unhappy, but I've still got my car."[43] The star image, constructed, remains in celluloid, while the actual self behind the image never fixes itself permanently in relation to anything but continued movement in a now dilapidated icon of American success.

5

Leaving the Dark Room in a Lighter Mood

Narrating Invisibility in Douglas Sirk's *Imitation of Life* and Ralph Ellison's *Invisible Man*

Like Rock Wagram, the protagonists discussed within this chapter strive for identities in public celebrity that will provide them with greater cultural legitimacy as defined within their visual culture contexts. While Rock's shifting relationship to ethnic categories ultimately allows him a large measure of social mobility and participation within mass culture (albeit a complicated one), the character Sarah Jane Johnson of *Imitation of Life* and the protagonist of *Invisible Man* find themselves in situations similar to that of Maud Martha because of the historically racializing determinants at work within American culture. Unlike Maud's interior, relatively private fantasy of social mobility, however, both of these characters attempt to enact notably public fantasies, the outcomes of which are compounded by their attempts to reconfigure the social spaces and material conditions of "blackness" in such public fora. While public performances provide settings for these attempts, the narratives themselves plumb those experiences of performance.

Early in his New York City adventures, the protagonist of Ralph Ellison's *Invisible Man* (1952) finds himself killing time and fantasizing about his future success while waiting to hear about a potential job. Many significant scenes occur in this portion of the book when he has first moved to New York after leaving college in the South: his first encounter with black nationalist Ras the Exhorter, the "enlightenment" offered by the privileged young Emerson, a first encounter with the folk wisdom of Pete Wheatstraw. These encounters and others weave together in a continued thread of episodes in *Invisible Man* that evolve into an acute awareness that he outlines in the book's retrospective prologue—the complexities of his "invisibility." Among these scenes lies a brief but significant trip to the movies—one that serves as an avenue through which to examine the placement of the novel within its mass-cultured milieu. In this scene, a narrative of American national identity serves as a palliative to his anxieties: "I went out to a movie, a picture of frontier life with heroic Indian fighting and struggles against flood, storm and forest fire, with the out-numbered settlers winning each engagement; an epic of wagon trains rolling ever westward. I forgot myself (although there was no one like me taking part in the adventures) and I left the dark room in a lighter mood." Just before this trip to the cinema, he has realized a feeling of being unmoored from the clear-cut—albeit problematic—codes of conduct in the South, resulting in a greater anxiety than ever in his life, "and all the more, because here [in the North] there was nothing concrete to lay it to." Here, the rhetoric of Manifest Destiny and westward expansion of nation displaces the particularities of region, drawing the viewers into a world in which the "small" cultures like those of Native Americans ("them") are portrayed as mere obstacles within a larger heroic conquest ("us"). Alan Nadel analyzes these kinds of narratives as "rampant performances' of national history "in such a variety of sites and forms as to create the illusion that national narratives were knowable and unquestionable realities." Through mass culture, the protagonist is able to set aside the uneasiness he feels when he is newly away from the predictable, socially conditioned framework of race relations in the South and "forget himself" in the larger mythic American story.[1]

The substance of the protagonist's fantasy is one that I will delve into later, for it is within this fantasy—and the destruction of it within the narrative—that we gain a further understanding of what *Invisible Man* means as an ethnic novel of the 1950s. Like other early scenes in the novel, the Western movie metaphorically alludes to and critiques a larger national culture in which periodic participation in brief mythic, national narratives functions to restore one's sense of belonging in the postwar American Dream—even if, as he notes, one finds "no one like me taking part in the adventures."

Using an analogy from the popular context of *Invisible Man*'s writing, William Lyne appropriately characterizes the novel as "the Jackie Robinson of literature—the first novel to make a successful transition from the marginal Negro leagues to the mainstream, the unhyphenated 'American' literature."[2] The successful film *Imitation of Life* (1959), appearing seven years after the novel, again takes up issues of ethnicity, identity, and the American Dream from its "major league" position in the myth-making center of Hollywood. On the other side of the screen from *Invisible Man* is the character Sarah Jane Johnson, acting out another version of invisibility. The light-complexioned daughter of an African American domestic worker, she lives in the home of a glamorous white actress and struggles to identify herself from childhood as "white." Like Ellison's protagonist, she is rendered invisible by the limitations within American history and law, but it is her lack of visible "blackness" that results in her negotiating a kind of double invisibility.

Much has been written about both the film and the novel, yet these two well-known texts of the 1950s have seldom been examined in relation to one another. As it happened, both narratives found great popular success within their respective media while taking on issues of identity and invisibility. With its bestseller status and the receipt of the National Book Award in 1952, the novel gained instant authority and has consistently remained one of the most respected literary works of the twentieth century. *Imitation of Life* was immensely popular with its contemporary audiences, as well, and was one of the top ten grossing films of 1959—perhaps in part because of its director and star, as well as the story's previous success in Fannie Hurst's 1933 novel and John Stahl's 1934 film adaptation. While several other postwar films took on "social problems" involving ethnicity—Elia Kazan's *Pinky* (1949), Daniel Petrie's adaptation of *A Raisin in the Sun* (1961), John Cassavetes's arthouse film *Shadows* (1959)—few have had the staying power that *Imitation of Life* has, both as a popular and influential mainstream "classic" and as an intriguing case study for cultural critics. Almost as canonical as *Invisible Man*, "*Imitation* compels us because it marks the intersection of numerous powerful cultural forces that define the postwar era and the place of cinema within it."[3] In terms of assessing issues of African American identity in popular narrative, these two texts read together prove especially insightful because of the ways in which they engage the notion of the social "place" for African Americans within the particularities of their respective genres.

I place Sarah Jane's narrative figuratively within the space of Ellison's novel. In some ways, she allows us to further assess his project by following up on the interstices of the book, absent of well-developed women characters marked by the complicated history specific to miscegenation. The Invisible Man and Sarah Jane can be read as complementary characters, each enlightening our readings of the other in ways that help us to further understand the possibilities for articulating ethnic identities within the postwar public space. Furthermore, as this chapter concludes the larger project, these two texts provide a means of finally evaluating written and visual texts in conversation with one another, to use them to explore the politics and possibilities of various types of narrative to inflect national discourses of identity.

Because *Imitation of Life* and *Invisible Man* are both rich and complex texts, my reading of them here is by no means comprehensive. There are many important aspects that I leave untouched simply because much critical work on those areas has been done already. As much extant criticism as there is, though, discussing these two texts together reveals that there is actually quite a bit more to say about them. Comparatively, we can explore the ways in which they teach us more deeply about the newly mass-mediated world in which they appeared, the ways they work with and against one another, and, ultimately, the ways that examining them outside of their respective media categories actually enhances the ways we understand the narratives within their own generic contexts. To do so, I will examine parallel motifs within these two works: the characters' attempts to negotiate new identities through public performances, and the complications of gender and ethnicity within such attempts in the 1950s.

Whose Imitation of Life Is It, Anyway?

> To go back, though, to *Imitation of Life* I think this picture also shows up one of the big differences between the media of the novel and the movies. The novel has never been subjected to something like Hollywood, to the pressure of time and big money, to sales people, producers, exhibitors—or at least not to such a degree—saying you've got to have a happy end even in the most goddam awful situations. With a novel you are more independent—at least as long as you are working. Until you have finished you are only answerable to your own artistic conscience.
>
> —Douglas Sirk, 1972 interview[4]

Though his view of the novel is somewhat romanticized in the above excerpt (and his version of filmmaking perhaps overly deterministic) Douglas Sirk's awareness of the parameters of each genre—the film and the novel—highlights the politics of narrative making in mass culture: despite a filmmaker's intentions, film is always more restricted by capital, time, marketing politics, and censors than its narrative counterpart. (At least, this was the case in the postwar era, when books and films occupied more distinct commercial spheres than they do in today's world of integrated marketing.) In the same interview, Sirk also maintains that his choices about how to portray ethnic elements in the film were influenced by the contemporary atmosphere. He seems to have wanted to take liberty with the earlier versions of *Imitation of Life* to make a point about inequality in the context of the growing national discussion on civil rights. But what exactly was the point he was trying to make in the film? While Sirk's direction reveals unmitigated sympathy for the African American character, Annie Johnson (Juanita Moore), and, conversely, pity for the shallowness of Lora Meredith's (Lana Turner) glamorous life, the seemingly simple comparison of the two women's lives and maternal struggles contains layers of meaning when considered more deeply within its contemporary segregated context. Many aspects of the film read as socially progressive, such as the focus on single-mother protagonists establishing a nontraditional, multiethnic household. In adapting the story, though, Sirk made other choices in characterization that have nothing to do with the theme of inequality and women's lives, in that he converted all the professional ambitions toward visual culture and the entertainment industries. For example, the "Aunt Delilah" pancake company created by both women in earlier versions becomes Lora's stage and movie career, with Annie in a supporting role rather than as a partner in developing a business; Lora's love interest Steve Archer is converted from scientist to photographer; and Peola, who tries to pass as cashier in a white-owned business, becomes Sarah Jane, the cabaret performer. All these characters desire to work in the performance or creation of visual media, a narrative motif that demonstrates a perhaps less-self-aware attention to other aspects of the contemporary cultural atmosphere that Sirk had in mind. The ambivalences within the film's narrative—and its attention to the space of performance as a site for working out identity—provide for a complicated set of interpretive possibilities that ultimately seem to affirm the notion of identity as it is based in segregationist ideology.

The fact of mainstream success aside, the issues broached within Sirk's film and Ellison's novel remained marginal in the real world of a United States still in Jim Crow's grip. Despite President Truman's desegregation of the U.S. military in 1948, segregationist thinking remained entrenched in much of American culture, from the extreme, sanctioned violence of the Deep South to the nuanced modes of exclusion from middle-class life in other regions of the United States. The subsuming of various issues of ethnic equality to other issues in mainstream American media (like the economy, the family and juvenile delinquency, Cold War fears) finds an echo in *Imitation of Life*, as we see the conflicts in African American identity/family within the film form a secondary plot to Lora Meredith's rise to fame, romantic tribulations, and parenting challenges. Marina Heung concedes that Sirk's version of the tale enters more deeply into territory (race, class, gender) not broached in the earlier versions, but adds that a "scrutiny of his film also reveals a systematic suppression and displacement of these issues through recourse to the ready-made ideology of the maternal melodrama." Despite Sirk's interest in what he calls "the Negro angle," this aspect is briefly summarized and buried within the production notes, while the energy of the film's promotional rhetoric concentrates on detailing the extravagances accompanying Lana Turner's performance: a $78,000 dollar designer wardrobe of thirty-four outfits and "$1,000,000 worth of jewels" described in gem-by-gem detail and requiring "two armed guards [to stay] near Lana every minute that the fabulous gem collection was in use." This focus on the material opulence of the movie clearly functions as part of the marketing of the film, drawing people in to see the largest costuming budget to date in the history of Universal-International Studios, but it also speaks to the entrenchment of reading successful cultural citizenship through the material signifiers of class status, celebrity, and gendered beauty.[5]

In the politics of the production on and off screen, Lana Turner is unquestionably deemed a personality worthy of sporting treasure, while the "blackness" worn by Sarah Jane's character becomes an issue of balanced material concern. In describing the hunt for an actress, the notes read, "Producer Hunter and Director Sirk interviewed almost 100 Negro actresses and tested five non-Negro thespians before deciding on Susan [Kohner], the talented daughter of film agent Paul Kohner and Mexican film star Lupita Tovar. Susan, of German-Mexican heritage, is an ideal choice, but it was her superb talent as an actress, coupled with her physical appearance, that won her the role." This description is fascinatingly conflicted. On one hand appears the subtext that defends, "We tried to find a 'real' Negro to play the part, but none of them was nearly so believable in the role of a hypothetically white person as a 'white' girl was." One may also suppose that Kohner's film industry family gave her some assistance that others did not have. In Stahl's 1934 version, the passing daughter was played by African American actress Fredi Washington, who drew adoring crowds in the African American urban South, despite African American intellectuals of the era deriding the film as rehashing literary tropes of mammy and "tragic octoroon." Sirk and company, it seems, in searching for someone "convincing," chose a non-African American, implying that acting talent is the priority. Still, they justify their choice by noting that Kohner's "heritage" makes her particularly suited for the part, suggesting the need for some kind of "ethnic" element within the actress to lend "authenticity" to the part. Film critic Hiram Perez finds all this play with identity ultimately ironic and entertaining:

> While Stahl's adaptation, plagued by a censorship battle over the representation of miscegenation, averts its look from the notoriously seductive beauty of its tragic mulatto [*sic*], Sirk's lavishes its attention on her, creating spectacle from her racialized sexuality—as it is safely performed by a presumably white actor. The dominant culture's eye rests more easily on Kohner because it perceives a white actress playing exotic. But here is the delicious secret about the 1959 adaptation's racial spectacle and masquerades: the film presents an exotic playing white playing brown passing for white.[6]

The issue of material signifiers, whether in the appearance of ethnicity or in the things one owns, comes to bear again here—in both the casting and characterization. Such evidence of cultural participation has proven important to some extent within each of the texts I have examined in this project, such as Chi-yang's inability to buy and wear an American suit, Humbert's willingness to shop and play the American tourist in order to fulfill his desire for the one aspect of American culture he really wants to consume (Lolita), Maud Martha's deciding what a hat means to her and what she means to Mrs. Burns-Cooper, and how Rock's Cadillac and face (whether mustached or not) perform masculine success. Here, too, is a pair of narratives that grapple with a question of particular weight for Americans of color in the postwar era: how can one change the values of the things through which he or she is seen? Joseph Urgo argues that Ellison views American culture as affected by a "tragic materialism" when it comes to hanging onto outdated notions of race and ethnicity, as the culture seeks out (sometimes arbitrarily) signifiers of material, bodily, visual connection to the artificially succinct categories "black" and "white" or "Asian." What Invisible Man discovers is that there are also external material signifiers that inflect identity on other levels. Valerie Smith notes that this occurs most obviously when he puts on the sunglasses and "becomes" Rinehart: "[T]he invisible man is compelled by the hustler because he is able to change identities at will, thereby turning the ephemeral nature of the world to his advantage." Sarah Jane, too, attempts to take advantage of what the Invisible Man calls the "seething, hot world of fluidity" by manipulating the material elements that affect readings of identity.[7] Such acts within each text forefront those same questions of identity and authenticity that form the basis of my contemplations on ethnicity in other cultural texts of the 1950s, but, as the previous chapter demonstrates, the ability to hustle and "change identities at will" is fraught with qualifiers because of the social forces that frequently reassert limits upon ethnic bodies no matter what levels of "fluidity" they may find for the moment.

To whom does the notion of "imitation" apply in *Imitation of Life*? Most critics have examined the ways in which the title applies primarily to Turner's Lora Meredith, whose career as an actress trains her to only play-act when it comes to the real crises in her life. But the "imitation" also applies to Sarah Jane, who, some argue, seeks to imitate Lora in being both a glamorous performer and a white woman. Overlooked, however, is the title's implication that both these characters are denying a more "authentic" life. Presumably, Lora's authentic self should have been found in being a wife to her on-and-off boyfriend Steve Archer and an at-home mother to her daughter, Susie (Sandra Dee)—a realization that is melodramatically driven home after it is too late to salvage her relationship with the child. Sarah Jane's supposed authentic self clearly sits in, if not an embracing of, at least an admission of "blackness." We are reminded of this persistently throughout the narrative, with Sarah Jane constantly being "outted" and punished for her attempts to alter the material conditions supposedly connected to her ethnic identity. This is a fairly common anthem in mainstream film: if you try to be something you are not, you will be miserable. The theme resonates on deeper and more ideological levels, however, when that "true self" is "Negro" in the segregated United States. With hundreds of years of evading the role of miscegenation in American history and one-drop legal maneuvers preceding the 1950s, the belief in arbitrarily clear-cut racial definitions was entrenched within American culture upon Sarah Jane's appearance. While Sirk admittedly wants to draw attention to a relatively "invisible" and complex type of American identity in the way he plays out the subplot of racial passing, the script's structuring also does not fail to remind Sarah Jane and audiences that there are only two identity choices—and only one *right* one. This is made especially clear in the way she and the character of her mother are played up as foils to one another. Annie is a classic angelic martyr who happily and unquestioningly accepts the social order as part of God's plan—a trait of the role, Donald Bogle argues, set in stone by the Loretta Beavers performance of Delilah in the 1934 version.[8] She earnestly sells these qualities to Lora Meredith on their first meeting, offering herself as a maid and "Someone to take care of your little girl? A strong, healthy, settled-down woman who eats like a bird—and doesn't care if she gets no time off—and will work real cheap?" Sarah Jane, in contrast, plays the vamp, a typical postwar bad-seed character who disrupts the domestic order and must climactically and miserably "reform" before the film's end.

The film's narrative structure, costuming, and *mise-en-scène* serve as replication of the second-class status of its African American characters—and not always in ways that can be read as social commentary on Sirk's part. Most obviously, Lana Turner upstages all other characters and story lines in the film. Lora Meredith's suitor, Steve Archer, tells her early in the film, "My camera could easily have a love affair with you," and this is exactly what occurs, with Lana Turner dominating the cinematographer's viewfinder through most of the two hours. Sarah Jane and Annie are sent to the back of the bus for the majority of the film, and when their storylines are developed, they are kept rather simplified by the film's structural constraints. For example, near the end of the film, after the women have been living together for ten years, Annie refers to "all the friends" she would like to have at her funeral. Lora responds with surprise, and the conversation proceeds:

> Lora: It never occurred to me that you had many friends. You never have any visit you.
>
> Annie: I know lots of people! Oh, hundreds!
>
> Lora: Really?
>
> Annie: I belong to the Baptist church, and I belong to several lodges, too.
>
> Lora: I didn't know.
>
> Annie: Miss Lora, you never asked.[9]

The moment reads as a small triumph, Annie having exposed Lora's blinding self-involvement to both Lora and the viewing audience. Yet the audience has been kept out of Annie's life as much as Lora has kept herself out, since the film demands that we remain intimately linked to Lana Turner's artificial emotional world. In this structure, the African American characters' constant attempts to render themselves more complex are side-swiped by the final editing of the film, rendering them basically underdeveloped, subplot characters.

Likewise, the staging and *mise-en-scène* reflect racial privileging, with Lana Turner and Sandra Dee always brightly lit and costumed and glamorously framed, while Juanita Moore appears often neatly but drably dressed, and Susan Kohner is dimly lit and shot at skewed angles that convey a world out of sync. Sandy Flitterman-Lewis also points out the ways in which Sirk uses colors to "articulate [the] social fact" of racial division, utilizing "a wide

Figures 4 and 5. Examples of racialized semiotics within the images of *Imitation of Life*. The dim lighting, tense blocking, faces averted from the lens, and dark colors surrounding Annie and Sarah Jane reinforce the sense of familial discontent that results from an unwillingness to conform to public constructions of racial identity. In contrast, Lora and Susie are centrally framed. Even when in conflict with one another, they face forward, eyes focused upward, brightly clad and lit, reifying white privilege. Courtesy of Photofest.

and vibrant spectrum throughout—from the pastel reds, whites, and blues of familial ideology" (Lora's and Susie's outfitting and home décor) "to the scandalous yellows, peaches, and aquas of sexual transgression" (colors often surrounding Sarah Jane). All of these colors are reduced, Flitterman-Lewis notes, to the simple blacks and whites that dominate the final funeral scene, clearly reiterating the color line.[10] All in all, then, the attempts to portray the lives of African Americans are filtered through the lives of the white characters within the setting of their home in, presumably, all-white communities.

Within the world of the narrative, Sarah Jane attempts to reinvent the materials at hand so as to challenge the "place" deemed proper for her, both in the household and in the larger social order. The idea of what "her place" is varies from definer to definer, but none of them are places Sarah Jane herself wants to occupy: a domestic of sorts, who uses the back staircase and stays in back rooms, a proponent of racial uplift at a Negro teacher's college, or, more generally, a woman who will "accept what she is" (which seems to be something only the maternal figures in the film are qualified to determine).

We first see Sarah Jane attempting to challenge her place in the social order as a grade-schooler (played by Karin Dicker). The stage is set when Annie and Lora first meet, by accident. Having lost Susie at the beach, Lora finds her with Annie, who waits with the two young girls until a police officer can locate Susie's mother. Lora at first assumes Sarah Jane to be the white child of Annie's employer, but she quickly learns that Sarah Jane is her daughter, whose father was "practically white." The two have nowhere to stay, so Lora offers them a room for the night at her coldwater flat. The understanding is that Annie will stay there until she gets on her feet financially, and though she offers to work for Lora, the offer is refused because Lora is too poor, her modeling/acting career not yet off the ground. Regardless, Annie continues to care for Susie and to do laundry without pay ("I like taking care of pretty things," she defends), while Lora leaves the apartment to pursue her career. The relationship proceeds throughout the film as one of employer/domestic.

In these early phases of the relationship between the two families, there are several brief scenes featuring Sarah Jane as a generally unhappy child. When shown to the spare bedroom behind the kitchen, she whines, "Why do we always have to live in the back?" Again, when offered one of Susie's dolls—a dark-skinned one—Sarah Jane refuses to play with it and snatches away Susie's favorite doll, which happens to be a blonde-haired, blue-eyed baby. Her mother is embarrassed by these and other episodes, culminating in an emotional family crisis when she discovers that Sarah Jane has not challenged at school the assumption that she is white. Overall, the child is presented as complaining, duplicitous, and ungrateful. However, similar traits in Lora—a dissatisfaction with her socioeconomic status and a willingness to use trickery to get ahead—are depicted in such a light as to seem comic, charming, and sympathetic.

As the film jumps forward ten years, we see the two families moving into a newly constructed and glamorous suburban home. The material divide based on class and segregationist assumptions becomes even clearer here, as Lora's success on Broadway has garnered her considerable wealth and fame. While Annie appears consistently matronly, slightly grayer, and now frequently wearing a domestic's uniform, Lora has only become more glamorous, more tightly corseted, poised, and glittering in center-frame. The daughters remain dichotomous, as well: Susie blonde, perky, and innocent (even when poutingly depressed over her crush on her mother's suitor Steve); and Sarah Jane brooding, dissatisfied, and, at the age of eighteen, highly sexualized.

The sexualization of Sarah Jane's character is one of the most fascinating elements of the Sirk adaptation, for in it are intertwined issues of ethnicity and gender and many possibilities for interpretation. We gradually learn that she is sneaking out, at first, to hang out in Greenwich Village with her white boyfriend (Troy Donahue), and, later, to work as a cabaret performer while her mother thinks she is shelving books after hours at the library. The sexual element also complicates the possible readings of Sarah Jane's character, indicative of many of the film's ambiguities. On one hand, we could read her actions in tandem with Flitterman-Lewis's assertion that "although Sarah Jane desires legitimation as a white woman, her only currency in this transaction is her sexuality." This is a representation that takes various forms in several of the narratives in this study, as well: in order to succeed within the white patriarchy, one must translate his or her self into a usable commodity that fulfills the desires of those in power. Marina Heung adds that "Sarah Jane's nightclub act is obviously a pathetic imitation of Lora's theatrical success," which, she argues, "compels us to understand, if not condone, her smoldering frustration with the constraints relegating her to such demeaning means for satisfying her aspirations."

On the other hand, I am not entirely convinced that Sarah Jane's actions are "pathetic"—imitation or not. Yes, she uses her body as a commodity, but does that always require a negative reading? A third-wave feminist approach, one that sees the knowing deployment of sexuality as a strategy and not always as demeaning, offers another potential reading. Her decision to be a "white" cabaret performer rather than a Negro teacher could be read as a powerful cultural move on her part: she has placed a supposedly black body into view as a means of disrupting the definitions of whiteness and blackness. She gets what she wants (whiteness, a paycheck, a venue for performance) while denying the patrons' knowledge of what they are "really" paying for. Quite obviously (in contrast with Heung's characterization of this performance as "demeaning"), Sarah Jane does not act as though she feels demeaned during the first major performance sequence; she seems to be enjoying herself. However, as much as Sarah Jane tries to enact sexuality on its own, the plot announces the inextricable cultural link of ethnicity and gender when Annie shows up after Sarah Jane's performance to remind her—and notify the club owners—that the body Sarah Jane is performing with is "black." Both Marianne Conroy and Lauren Berlant note that her second performance in the movie renders her more anonymous.[11] Where in the first performance she is solo, singing directly to members of the audience of a small nightclub, the second performance at a fancier club offers her less agency, as she is one of many chorus girls. This is an important point, because it again highlights the differences in cultural capital for her and Lora, who grows more autonomous as her career progresses. Nonetheless, the critical focus on Sarah Jane's second performance often overrides the first one—one which occupies more space within the film and offers important possibilities for transgressive readings. Furthermore, one could argue that Sarah Jane's second performance, while more anonymous, also affords her reinvented ethnicity more security, as, visually, she appears to be one "white" girl among many.

We can read Sarah Jane's performance along the lines described by Judith Butler in her analysis of Lana Turner's gender performative in the film. While Butler does touch on racial issues within her theorization of Lana Turner's performance, it is within her laying out of the gender performative that perhaps we can find a more distilled form of her theory to extend to considerations of ethnicity.[12] She sets up the theory of gender performance for this analysis as a series of repetitions that reveal a nonexistent, unattainable ideal: "The repetitive practice of gender, then, can be understood as the vain and persistent conjuring and displacement of an idealized original, one which no one at any time has been able to approximate. As a result, there is no ideal standard or recoverable origin against which that imitative structure might be measured except the one that is performatively and repeatedly produced by the imitation itself. The site in which the "ideal" or the "original" might be located is in the performed *effects* which try—and fail—to approximate it." Butler's work on gender offers an effective model for exposing the ways in which our general notions of ethnicity also have undergone manipulations and contain assumptions that need further working through. Thinking about the performativity of ethnicity helps us to more clearly link the cultural practices and ideologies surrounding the concept of ethnicity and the practices of racialization to the historical moments in which they occur, and this, consequently, enables us to further interrogate the narratives that have been constructed about and within American history. Her work offers, to borrow David Leiwei Li's formulation, not just an "illumination of the performative aspects of identity" but a more important "insistent inquiry into the very material conditions of identity's emergence and operation."[13]

To return to the above formulation, and to apply it to the more culturally specific context, ethnic identities in the United States can be read as series of performances that approximate some ideal or "authentic" that is most often itself only a cultural construct. For example, Sarah Jane's attempts to perform "whiteness" are based on a nonexistent original, since whiteness itself is a series of historical "gestures" based on the exclusionary practices of particular factions within a citizenry, as discussed in the book's introduction. Extending Butler's discussion of drag as a metaphor, Sarah Jane's "drag" performance of Lora's showbiz "whiteness" acts as "the production of 'identity' through an imitation that seeks to approximate an ideal that is always already expropriated and elsewhere. Hence, 'women' who perform femininity are as much 'in drag' as 'men,'" and Lana's performance of whiteness is as constructed and inauthentic as Sarah Jane's.[14] The same could be said of Annie's performance of an idealized "blackness."

This ethnic "drag" is further pronounced by Sarah Jane's alternate performance: the oft-cited scene in which she embarrasses Lora in front of her guests by carrying a serving tray on her head and affecting a Creole slave persona. Moments before, Lora has asked Sarah Jane to help her mother serve hors d'oeuvres to the guests, to which Sarah Jane responds that she cannot because she is on her way out for a date. Angered by Lora's request to serve her, and by her assumption that her date must be with the neighbor's Negro chauffeur, Sarah Jane turns to the kitchen to throw these assumptions back in Lora's face. Entering the living room, where an intense discussion of a European film project is in the works, she prances in and announces, "Fetched you-all a mess o' crawdads, Miss Lora, for you an' your friends." While Lora tries to laugh off the awkward scene as a cute "trick," Sarah Jane quips, "Oh, no trick to totin', Miss Lora. Ah, l'arned it from my mammy . . . and she l'arned if from old Massa . . . 'fo she belonged to you!" Sarah Jane is subsequently treated as most teen rebels are in postwar films, with a stern talking-to that drives her to tears—and out of the house. She defends her actions, saying, "You and my mother are so anxious for me to be colored . . . I was going to show you I could be." In this scene, Flitterman-Lewis astutely notes, through "self-conscious mimicry" the text exposes that "what makes Sarah Jane black or white is in fact socially defined, and in this sense, race is seen to be an effect of discourse."[15]

But the discourse of the text also reiterates that those constructs seem to work best when unchallenged, for the sympathetic Annie adopts the rhetoric of the civil rights era's gradual integrationists, telling Sarah Jane to "be patient. Things'll work out." This is the same passive rhetoric that Martin Luther King Jr. later criticized for its utter appeal to inaction. Indeed, Sarah Jane is punished for her awareness of the socially constructed discourse of race and place—and for acting upon that knowledge—when, in the next scene, she is violently beaten and left in an alley by her boyfriend, Frankie, who has found out that she has been "lying" and that her "mother's a nigger." Medovoi notes how Sarah Jane's rebellion is not just against her racialization, nor against racism, but against the signifiers of postwar success as embodied in Lora's home: "Sarah Jane literally flees from the false utopia of the new suburban home into the arms of a youthful bohemian world. The 'white' world into which she tries to pass, paradoxically, . . . resembles the whiteness borne by Norman Mailer's 'white negro,' a racialized hipster whose self-definition as a rebellious free spirit leans upon his uses of blackness for the purpose of counter-culture self-fashioning."[16] Unlike the youthful rebellion that might have taken form in, say, a sit-in at a lunch counter, Sarah Jane's is neither collective nor clearly aware of its target. The script ultimately renders her pathetic—and a bit foolish—in her attempts to rebel.

While the notion of performance could apply in various ways to any of the characters I have discussed in these chapters, the character who is trying to "pass" affords an ideal opportunity for examining the ways in which performativity informs and erodes our notions of the constructions of identities within American culture, precisely because she is able to act out these constructs in the invisible middle ground she occupies between races. At various moments, Desi Arnaz, Rock Wagram, Lucy Ricardo, Maud Martha, Wang Ta, Lolita, and Humbert Humbert are all trying to "pass" for an ideal version of something or someone, be it a willingly assimilationist immigrant, an all-American teen, a "feminine" woman, an "Armenian Man." Medovoi reminds us that identity is not simply a construct born of historical moments and practices but a concept that must be understood through a historicization of its origin as a concept. With this in mind, we must consider ethnic identities as both performative and as expressions of the period's new interest in identity and questions of "authenticity" itself.

While Butler's argument about the movie lends a helpful perspective to Sarah Jane's performances of ethnicity, she says little about the character's sexuality other than that it imitates and contributes to the exposure of Lana's own imitations of the gender ideal. As such, Butler's theories lend insight into Sarah Jane's gender performative, too, but also leave some room to explore other cultural readings of her sexuality and the ways in which ethnicity and sexuality converge in this character. The field of cultural studies has contributed to a great understanding of the ways in which sexuality and gender, race and ethnicity are inextricably linked. But I also wonder if this is always a productive assumption, because it often leads to negative readings of portrayals that contain a sexualized component—an a priori sexualization of a cultural Other within a white hegemony—and perhaps cannot recognize the possibility for more active agency within ethnic performance. In many ways, performative ideals are hegemonically constructed, but that does not mean that there is no room for interpretation or "play" with those ideals. Butler's brief comments on Sarah Jane's character, along with her concept of "drag," reveal that there is more to the young woman's performance career than the aforementioned interpretation. However, many people do read her burlesque in this way, and Flitterman-Lewis goes so far as to assert that passing reveals a "racial self-hatred that emerges with sexuality."[17] It seems that we are not as quick to characterize, say, Josephine Baker in this way. Her move to France to do cabaret performances is often characterized as a clever move away from the racist ideology of the United States and a celebration of her own sexuality. Is not Sarah Jane doing something similar? While Sarah Jane's sexual "exhibitionism" (as Butler calls it) derives not from *négritude*, her cultural maneuvering is not unlike Josephine Baker's unabashed cabaret. The issue for both seems to be one of moving beyond the established parameters of race to explore and utilize sexuality on its own terms. Instead of a "racial self-hatred" emerging with sexuality, Sarah Jane seems to want to separate out the various factors in all aspects of her life, to find a "self-love" that has been severely limited by racialized social discourses and practices.

After all, she could have chosen to pass as white in another occupation, as in the Hurst novel and 1934 film version, in a white service industry job. Sirk's alteration of Sarah Jane's job is certainly intended as an updating that hints at some of the sexual tensions of the era, and maybe even pokes fun at them. Butler hints at this when she assesses Sarah Jane's catalytic function in the film: "This performance is also an imitation of Lana, but one which releases the exhibitionism that remains inchoate within Lana's stilted, photographic poses. The look-don't-touch quality of Lana's performance . . . is fully displaced by Sara Jane's [*sic*] exaggeration of Lana's exaggeration." In so doing, she argues, Sarah Jane works to "expose the power differential of race and to refuse it" and, through her sexual "demands," outs Lana's sexuality as "the gestures of suggestion."[18] In other words, by exposing the seemingly overt sexuality of Lana as one that is actually contained and repressed, Sarah Jane exposes the arbitrary values and empty categories of "sexy," "feminine," and "white." In these ways, we may read agency into Sarah Jane's actions.

On the surface, it seems that the contemporary audience was supposed to view *Imitation* moralistically, though there are significant elements of irony within the melodrama. Ultimately, by implication, Sarah Jane's refusal to accept her "real," racialized identity is presented as a moral issue, one that causes a laxity of morals in all areas of her life. The climactic scene firmly reiterates the film's message, as Sarah Jane relinquishes her secret identity to return to her mother's funeral, where she throws herself upon Annie's coffin sobbing. In front of the crowd in Harlem's streets, she implicitly proclaims her blackness, sobbing, "It's my mother!" The lesson: you cannot be truly happy unless you accept who you *really* are (according to hegemonic definitions). Ryan DeRosa notes how the scene "retract[s] social rebellion": "We not only witness her ask for pardon, we witness integration itself, happening before our eyes, as the music brings black and white together inside and outside the church. In other words, 'integration' coincides with clear delineation of racial identity along lines of cultural separations and class hierarchy."[19] Lora's and Susie's embraces of her at the funeral indicates that she is also "reformed" of her desire to be a burlesque performer, implying Sarah Jane's willingness to participate in normative gender.

But Sarah Jane's very public display of grief and "blackness" at this moment (she allows her mother's body to be the evidence of her identity) is also, at root, a performance. As critics, it seems we fall too easily into the moralistic reading, safely viewing Sarah Jane as demeaningly "relegated" by some larger external forces. Yes, her identity is often determined for her by the cultural politics of a segregated nation, but her *choices* to remove herself from that system are not. This seems to be the point of fracture between Richard Wright and Ralph Ellison, Wright unable to imagine Bigger Thomas outside of larger determining forces, Ellison unwilling to believe that the African American subject need necessarily be unable to escape such determinism.[20] If the light-complexioned African American character provides the real texture and substance of the film, as more recent critics agree, why must we often return to reading her character as flawed and demeaned? I find myself wanting to champion Sarah Jane's cause as critics continually refer to her identity as simply "black" and her performances as "demeaning." This is not to condone what some see as her "hatred" of blackness. Perhaps that notion is too extreme, for her character exhibits an awareness of racial categories as a social construct and seems to levy hatred not just at the idea of blackness, but at the discourse that perpetuates the succinct racialized categories—the *limitation* of life inherent within the construct of race. Culturally specific gender and racial constructs affect the amount of control she has over her own body, as Lauren Berlant argues, because "American cultural legitimacy" has always "deriv[ed] from the privilege to suppress and protect" the bodies of citizens. In the film, as in the larger culture, "a woman who lives with difference . . . enjoys no prophylactic private sphere, no space safe from performance or imitation."[21] In 1959, Sarah Jane had to be one race or the other, but we should also allow for the possibility that her performance seeks a subversive use of this compulsory performative space, a subversive reading of Sirk's intentions with her and the didactic "Negro angle."

Heung offers a convincing "subversive reading" of the passing character that the film provides in spite of itself. Sarah Jane, she argues, "presents the threat of chaos because she has the catalytic ability to activate the themes that are otherwise suppressed in the film." Heung notes with irony, too, that it is Sarah Jane's practice of imitation and mimicry that often motivates her power within the narrative: "So, while the film falls short of consciously commenting on its own limitations, it does, through Sarah Jane, allow for a reading that goes against the grain of its basic ideological formulations." As Rainer Werner Fassbinder describes the film, it "starts as a film about Lana Turner's character and turns quite imperceptibly into a film about Annie, the black woman." Fassbinder overlooks the fact that functioning as the catalyst for this is Sarah Jane, her role clearly depicted in the framing of Annie's deathbed scene toward the end of the film—a visual metaphor for the very subversion that Heung argues the character supplies. Annie lies in bed, describing her last wishes of a grandiose funeral for which she has been saving her whole life, while Lora sits at her bedside sobbing. On the nightstand, between the two women, is a portrait of Sarah Jane. This framing seems metaphorical for a larger historical narrative that any relationship between white and black moves on the hinge of shared, miscegenated history, one in which race is not so clearly defined as some would like to believe. Like the hidden black element necessary to make Ellison's Optic White Paint so white, Sarah Jane's photo reminds us of the perpetuated narratives that obliterate that shared history, of the "blackness" in white and vice versa. And this is part of the film's fascinating texture: just as it seeks to detract from larger, serious issues through visuals and melodramatic techniques, it also constantly reminds us of those issues it attempts *not* to deal with in full. The figure of Sarah Jane, as Heung reminds us, cues us to the reality of what is going on this film: that domestic narratives of family strife trump deeper discussion of the interethnic relations that are very much present.[22]

In a sense, Sarah Jane functions as a postwar version of the "tragic mulatta." Like the nineteenth-century versions, she seems simply to be a character to whom white audiences can relate, the whitish buffer through which to broach issues of ethnicity and racialization. Sarah Jane does possess many of the characteristics of the classic tragic mulatta figure in American literature: she is a social misfit, unable to fit into either white or black communities comfortably; she is made to suffer more than other characters because her identity—which is viewed only in terms of race—is unfixed; she is given both to extreme emotionalism because of this and to wiliness (as is seen especially in some of the more racist representations, such as the "yellow vampire" of Thomas Dixon's *The Clansman*); she is perpetually dissatisfied because she is "marked" by her African heritage. Werner Sollors argues that simply "unmasking" the stereotype of the tragic mulatta is no longer a productive critical goal. My goal here, though, is not simply to "out" another fictional stereotype, but to ask what that relatively outdated stereotype is doing in this particular context. By the postwar period, African American magazines were reporting that "passing" had "passed out" of fashion because of increased possibilities for social, geographical, and occupational mobility—especially in the North and in urban centers.[23] So what does the fictional tragic mulatta mean in postwar America?

Bogle notes that this stock character saw resurgence in early 1950s movies, with actresses like Yvonne De Carlo and Natalie Wood taking on mixed-race roles. He does not, however, speculate why this renewed interest in the tragic mulatta might have taken place. Likewise, Susan Gilman notes that the nineteenth-century "race melodrama" of passing found new forms within twentieth-century genres. Though she does not attempt to analyze postwar versions, her examination of the race melodrama in nineteenth-century contexts can shed light on how the tragic mulatta might function in the post-World War II era. She notes that there seem to have been two major tropes: the "tragic" (mostly generated by white writers) and the "romance" of pan-African narratives like those of Pauline Hopkins and W. E. B. Du Bois. The tragic mode was almost always tied to larger cultural anxieties: "[W]hen race is represented as a sole, determining social formation, the one determinant of individual identity, then tragedy is inevitably the result, both formally and socially. . . . The individual, not the community, is the fundamental social unit of the race melodrama in its tragic mode. The national and, indeed, global scope of racial conflict at the turn of the century is thus contained in the tragic race melodrama, which defines race as a problem primarily limited to the individual." While the white characters in the film negotiate identities based on various influences of love and career, all of these concerns are boiled down into issues of "Negro" identity for Sarah Jane and Annie. Within the postwar context, then, we can imagine the same intersections of fiction and social condition in which questions of ethnicity, identity, and nation came to the forefront and became contained in the way that Gilman describes above. In Lucy Fischer's estimation, *Imitation of Life* has been viewed as a film whose "formal and narrative structure have been favored at the expense of its links to the social terrain." The complexities of identity within Sarah Jane, consequently, have been contained as a tragic problem of the individual more than related to larger cultural concerns about identity in the era.[24]

The simplification of the issue within the narrative is linked to the medium and genre in which it exists: film and melodrama, respectively. As noted earlier, Sirk himself acknowledged the constraints placed upon telling a story within a text that is highly commercially influenced. The melodrama, too, has its traditional parameters often involving formulaic plot lines, high emotionality, relatively flat characters, and what Fischer calls "exaggerated generic codes." While this is often the case, critics like Fischer, Gilman, and DeRosa have worked to expand possibilities for interpreting melodrama. Gilman argues that melodrama does not necessarily limit the power of a story, because everything depends on who is telling the story and how. Her work on the nineteenth-century sentimental "race" narrative echoes that of scholars who have revisited the popular romance to challenge dismissive attitudes about "low-brow" narrative forms. When ethnicity becomes a central element in melodrama, she claims, the genre can "acknowledge, even embrace, everything that is most unsettling about [the] period and its cultural expression," to defy formulaic elements and offer "different resolutions to different conceptions of racial tensions and conflict." DeRosa, building on the work of Thomas Elsaesser, identifies a form of "radical" melodrama that, in its reliance on the "repetitive (circular) experience of suffering" can be made "specific to the current social arrangement of power." He argues that the melodramatic form "*articulates* Sarah Jane's return [to her mother's funeral and Lora's family], however foreseen in the narrative, as going against her interests, against her freedom," so it posits this return as a not-so-formulaic "emotional dissonance." In this and other scenes DeRosa identifies how the very elements of the melodrama reveal an "ambivalent relation of white liberals" to the black freedom movement.[25]

Gilman joins Hazel Carby and Werner Sollors in making a similar case for the literary device of the tragic mulatto. The mulatto character, according to Carby, "should be understood and analyzed as a narrative device of mediation" rather than as a limited stereotype. She sees the character type as a "response" to the real-world social segregation following the Reconstruction, "a more frequently used literary convention for an exploration and expression of what was increasingly socially proscribed."[26] Perhaps the occasional postwar mulatto character serves a similar metaphorical purpose of mediation in the ways explored above. The potential that Carby sees, however, applies particularly to African American writers. Sarah Jane is, in both her literary and filmic forms, a construction of "white" imaginations, whatever that might mean, and whatever mediating force she may possess, they, too are negotiated by the temporal realm of the white household in which she lives.

Such views on these somewhat formulaic subgenres are important to keep in mind, because no genre provides for only one kind of reading. Indeed, *Imitation of Life* does broach complicated issues of identity in a historical moment of tension and inquiry about ethnicity and national identity. In the case of this film, the creators and controllers of the narrative—on and off screen—have access to cultural power and work within the well-established genre of melodrama to promote, more than anything, the careers of Douglas Sirk and Lana Turner. Still, Sarah Jane's presence and the questions she raises allow us at times to wipe the romantic haze away from the lens.

Over the course of the film's narrative, then, we see Sarah Jane act out the reverse of Invisible Man's experience at the cinema: "I forgot myself (although there was no one like me taking part in the adventures) and I left the dark room in a lighter mood." Reprimanded for "forgetting herself," she, instead, leaves the light room of the "American Dream" suburban home in a darker mood, both literally and metaphorically. Allowed a space in the glamorous fantasy, she can exist but not participate. Though Lora claims that Sarah Jane has never been treated "as if she were different," Sarah Jane acts out a realization in scene after scene that "there is no one like her taking part in the adventures," and the place she is expected to be is that which fits most comfortably with the assumptions of her white patrons: in the kitchen with her mother, dating the neighbor's Negro chauffeur, and leaving through the back door.

At her mother's funeral, Sarah Jane finds herself in the darkest mood yet, convulsively sobbing upon the casket and proclaiming her love for her mother in the midst of a crowded street in Harlem. Lora comes to her side and, physically supporting the grieving young woman, pulls her into the limousine within the funeral procession. Marianne Conroy and Flitterman-Lewis interpret this scene as a full-circle enactment of the role of the African American woman in the social order, that Sarah Jane's going "home" means that she will replace her mother as the maid in the household.[27] This climactic, tear-jerking scene proves, if nothing else, that the film maintains a consistent ambiguity until the last moment. Leaving with Lora, Susie, and Steve as she does, it is difficult to tell what will become of Sarah Jane, for here it becomes clear that the only way for her to alter the material signifiers through which she is seen is through the death of her mother (the "evidence" of her blackness). She has admitted her faults and reformed. Consequently, the white family embraces this admission of "blackness," but, ironically, they also bring her into the limousine, symbolically incorporating her into the white nuclear family-in-process. Admitting "blackness," now the materiality of her apparent whiteness (absent of family to prove otherwise) can conduct the relationships from this point forward. This is clearly stated through the visual elements of the final scene: Sarah Jane sits in the back seat of the car, Susie and Lora on either side of her, embracing her, while Steve looks back and smiles paternally and approvingly from the front seat. Sarah Jane's face is framed within the car window, an apparently white face within a car full of white people, driving away from Harlem and the visibly African American people lining the streets.

It is at this point that Sirk's lamentations over the Hollywood mandate for a happy ending come full circle. Though the film ends in melodramatic high volume, it is a seemingly happy conclusion primarily because Sarah Jane has returned "home" to the domestic space in which she was raised and seems to have accepted her "place" in society. Despite the funereal finale and the ambiguities of the characters' futures, the fade-out contains that Hollywood flare that would somehow encourage its contemporary viewers to believe they have witnessed a catharsis; the worst is over. Lora will probably marry Steve, Susie and Lora will reconcile, everyone will be happy, and . . . Sarah Jane, well, hey, she is with them, so she will probably be happy, too. With this seemingly neat resolution of the film's issues, the audience is encouraged, too, to leave the dark room in a lighter mood.

The Body, the Dollar, the Nation

> It is felt that there is something in the Negro experience which makes it not quite right for the novel. That's not true. It becomes important to the novelist because it is in this problem, as Faulkner makes us aware, that the American human conflict is at its most intense and dramatic.
>
> —Ralph Ellison, 1952

The above quotation, from a *New York Times* interview shortly after *Invisible Man*'s publication, reveals two interesting ideas relevant to the novel in its sociohistorical context: one (and this is an element at which much critical energy has been aimed) is the fact that, despite Ellison's own claims to be searching for the "human universals" in the protagonist's experiences, the novel overtly speaks with the awareness that the narrative cannot completely escape a specifically inscribed, culturally influenced history; the second factor at work in the statement is one that reinforces the cultural power of the novel, that it is a space available for articulating and working through that which has been inarticulable throughout much of American history.[28] This attitude of the possibility for the novel is one worth keeping in mind when discussing it in conjunction with a film like *Imitation of Life*. This is not to say that the media possess hierarchical relations (i.e., novels are "better" than movies for dealing with these kinds of issues), but that the creators in these various media have an inherent awareness of their potentials, limitations, social gestures, and dialogic relations with one another. Particularly in postwar American culture, they are the dominant narrative forms positioned vis-à-vis one another.

Though *Invisible Man*'s protagonist remains "invisible" within the world of the narrative itself, the published book functions as an object in circulation, articulating many of the problems of ethnic identity in the United States of the 1940s and '50s. The interpretation of the protagonist's actual power (or potential for it) remains a point of contention in the novel's criticism. Some argue he does not have much real agency because he remains invisible and underground at the story's conclusion—all his actions have led to inaction.[29] However, I would argue that he does have real *potential* for action/agency, which is found in his own defense of his "hibernation" in the epilogue: "Please, a definition: A hibernation is a covert preparation for a more overt action." Rather than simply hiding, the narrator is in the process of readying himself for action. More important, the novel—the writing of his story of understanding his invisibility—should be read as the "overt action" itself. Again, we see how an ethnic novel contributes to a larger construction of midcentury ethnicity and Americanness. This is the stance, too, of John Callahan, who describes the act of narration as "an act of profound visibility" and cites the protagonist's acknowledgment that he is "'drawn upward again.'" Hortense Spillers nicely handles the ambivalence of the issue in her description: "The book has never called itself 'revolutionary,' but it begins and ends with a revolutionary determination: If 'I' am to be victimized, why not let it be for a good reason?" The character reveals the project of writing in the epilogue, through which Valerie Smith notes, "He creates for himself a persona that develops, indeed exists, in contradistinction to the images that others projected onto him. Moreover, he inverts his relation to the figures of authority who dominated him in 'life.' As author/narrator he is able to control the identities of such people as Norton, Bledsoe, and Brother Jack." By examining the questions of the material within the novel (along the lines of what Smith here calls "images projected onto him"), I hope to further elucidate these questions of agency.[30] Consequently, this helps us to further evaluate the cultural work of the novel within its sociohistorical framework because of the ways in which the narrator takes on a project similar to Sarah Jane's: questioning the material elements through which he is seen and the place he is supposed to occupy as a young African American man in the postwar period.

This questioning is achieved through the symbolic structures within the narrative. In it we find the intersection of African American vernacular culture and American mass culture in one man's life, and the reconciling of the influences of these upon his identity. I imagine "mass" and "vernacular" elements within the novel mapped out literally, as two parallel, balanced sets of symbols. One is composed of the objects and behaviors belying identity formations circumscribed by larger national narratives articulated in mass culture; the other presents the products of black vernacular subculture as a counterbalance to the former. The second set of symbols provides the protagonist a set of figurative tools for trying to reconfigure his sense of identity. Examples of these would be jazz as an empowering cultural expression in contrast to the racist caricature "Feed Me" bank. These items are derived from within African American culture and not from the larger commercial values defining the era. While it is difficult to definitively separate out these two categories because of the ways in which cultural forms evolve and take on new meanings in new contexts (for example, jazz gradually gets popularized and distributed through mass-mediated forms outside of African American communities), the narrative sets up two relatively clear kinds of symbols: those that objectify bodies and those that do not. Ellison argues that there are no such things as "black" values and "white" values, only variations on "American values." He admits, however, that in the latter half of the century, those American values lean evermore toward the commercial, "which tends toward homogeneity." As noted in the previous chapter, the search for the "authentic" took on cultural resonance as people feared the homogeneity imagined in the Communist block. According to Stephanie Brown, that notion of the authentic was often "grounded in local and vernacular practices, overwhelmingly identified with both a racialized other and/or a working class romanticized to the point of unrecognizability."[31] Rather than romanticizing, the protagonist of *Invisible Man* has to learn to recognize African American vernacular in order to use it as a means to some other (as yet unknown) end, since the signifiers of the African American past are not sufficient in themselves to express his identity. I am not proposing that Ellison elevates the vernacular as a curative or superior influence, only that he offers it as a means through which his protagonist can learn to decode the social system. In contrast to the mass culture items that are clearly produced with a profit motive for wide circulation and widespread by other consumers, the vernacular culture of the novel derives from and continues to circulate primarily for the use of members of a subculture.

The vernacular culture thread, as I will call it, presents a series of idioms in distilled symbolic forms that gradually demonstrate a path for reclaiming racialized bodies, one that enables cultural visibility and, concomitantly, resistance to the narratives that have heretofore attempted to determine ethnic lives. This is how *Invisible Man* takes the project of *Maud Martha* one step further: realizing that participating in a system that uses and consumes some ethnic individuals as part of a material value system, Maud Martha rejects participation; *Invisible Man* offers an alternate course, an attempt to change the very material signifiers through which one is seen.

The motif of participation/exclusion in national culture is introduced in the first chapter of the novel, at the "Battle Royal." The well-known scene presents a surreal allegory of life in the midcentury South. The narrator, having been invited to give a speech at a "smoker" for "some of the most important men of the town" (the "white" modifier of "important" implied, of course) finds himself caught up in a boxing brawl with some of his schoolmates. Optimistic that the evening will work out well, the narrator goes along with all directions given to him. At this point in the narrative, it has not occurred to him to resist any instructions that seem to compromise his own best interests precisely because he believes that following along will serve this interest. He mostly embraces the ideology represented within a white patron's remark, "We mean to do right by you, but you've got to know your place at all times," and represses his own inadvertent call for "social equality." "Indeed, his remarkable innocence and gullibility regarding these matters," remarks Robert Stepto, "provide a major comic strain" throughout the book. The comic element that Stepto highlights seems to keep the story moving, the undoing of this "gullibility" the real motor of the narrative.[32]

At the smoker, however, he is willing to play along because he believes it will benefit him. Ironically, his willingness to play the brute is based in his endeavors toward a mainstream ideal of success: play the game, get into college, get a job in a major institution or corporation—success complete. Like Sarah Jane, he believes for a while that a mastery of the performance can lead to "becoming." His performance pays off for the moment, too, as he is awarded the briefcase and scholarship at the end of the evening. The importance of the briefcase as symbolic within his aspirations and within postwar American culture must not be overlooked. As Stepto notes, "the Invisible Man's briefcase is much more than a repository of cultural signs and false 'protections'; it is, most ironically and humorously, *the* trope for the strategy of self-authentification [he] values most during the tale." Indeed, throughout the story he holds protectively to the briefcase until he is finally forced to destroy its contents. After being lost and retrieved several times, the briefcase finally vanishes underground as well, and its disappearance spurs the protagonist's climactic dream that demands, "HOW DOES IT FEEL TO BE FREE OF ILLUSION?"[33] If the briefcase functions as the receptacle that perpetuates illusion, then the illusion is tied not only to those illusory items within, but to the briefcase itself. If it is "*the* trope for the strategy of self-authentification," that self-authentification within the postwar context must be read as a struggle for identity within white middle-class ideals of success represented in the now-famous icons of the briefcase-toting "Man in the Gray Flannel Suit" figure or *Mad Men* (the characters of which reveal deep discontent beneath their iconic appearance).

Andrew Hoberek offers insight into this crucial aspect of the novel's context through its engagement of a postwar "organization-man discourse": "understanding [*Invisible Man*'s] universalist narrative of threatened individuality as the product of a historically specific, class-based transformation of American culture provides us with a more complex picture of how Ellison's racial concerns relate to the rest of the book." Drawing out what seems like a subplot—the struggle for white-collar success—Hoberek demonstrates the ways in which this narrative functions as a framework that defines much of postwar American culture and, similarly, the modes of identity formation critiqued within Ellison's novel. He uses *The Man in the Gray Flannel Suit*'s

Tom Rath as a kind of racial counterpart for reading the white-collar discourse within Ellison's novel. Ultimately, Hoberek demonstrates that "by implication, the protagonist's relationship to white-collar culture shapes as it excludes him."[34]

The evocation of white-collar culture in the postwar era, I would add, contains the referent of consumer culture writ large, given that those who participate in white-collar culture on the occupational level are the ones who help to produce and perpetuate the cultural and largely consumer imperatives that were widely promoted as an important part of national pride and patriotism. This link is acknowledged in the narrative of *The Man in the Gray Flannel Suit*, as well, for Tom Rath leaves a job he likes with a small private foundation, at his wife's urging, to pursue a higher paying, but ultimately unhappy, job in the commercial television industry, the motive being more prestige, a better house, and better everything to go with the house.

For the Invisible Man, though, as noted earlier, the same system that structures his desires also excludes him from their achievement, in what Hoberek has described as a period-specific "historical paradox: a white-collar culture that simultaneously pretends to be universal while excluding a significant proportion of the postwar population." Like most other characters discussed in this work, Invisible Man is acculturated into a quest for the signifiers of the "American Dream" at the same time that the Dream is continually denied him—another dangling carrot to "Keep This Nigger-Boy Running."[35]

He begins to learn this early in the novel, through a more complex and localized metaphor involving sexuality and gender. Before the Battle Royal commences, the boys are pushed into a "sea of faces, some hostile, some amused," and are forced into place facing a "magnificent blonde—stark naked." While the scene with the stripper seems unrelated to the white-collar fantasy, it is actually closely tied to it, functioning as an allegory for the larger social dynamics shaping postwar America. The stripper is described in detached and objectifying language, both in the terms used by the narrator to describe her and in the attitude the stripper herself seems to convey: "The hair was yellow like that of a circus kewpie doll, the face heavily powdered and rouged, as though to form an abstract mask, the eyes hollow and smeared a cool blue, the color of a baboon's butt." She dances in a "slow sensuous movement" and "[flings] herself about with a detached expression on her face." The stripper scene posits the female body as objectified and subject to the "male gaze" (a notion made famous by film critic Laura Mulvey, whose work is also used by Daniel Kim in reading this scene), a reading necessitated by Ellison's language here.[36]

The descriptions of the mask-like detachment during the performance and the doll-like qualities resonate with the same language the narrator uses to describe Brother Tod Clifton's Sambo doll later in the narrative, which moves in a "shoulder-shaking infuriatingly sensuous motion, a dance that was completely detached from the black, mask-like face." The narrator grows angry and sickened by the Sambo doll "throwing itself about with the fierce defiance of someone performing a degrading act in public," but he finds himself wanting to join in the laughter of the crowd even as he spits on the doll. He experiences a similar ambivalence when facing the stripper: "I wanted at one and the same time to run from the room, to sink through the floor, or go to her and cover her from my eyes and the eyes of others with my body; to feel the soft thighs, to caress her and destroy her, to love her and murder her." Johnnie Wilcox asserts that in this scene, "[t]he repression of black male sexual desire and the provocation of white female sexual disgust are part of the maintenance of an oppressive white male sexual power, a power predicated by the transformation of the white woman and the black men into objects of desire and objects of abjection."[37]

In both the stripper and Sambo doll scenes, that which allures and sickens the narrator is the paradoxical realization that what fascinates him in its Otherness from him also implicates him on some level. That Brother Tod Clifton, the member of the Brotherhood with whom he has most identified, could play the minstrel resonates on a level deeper than betrayal or disappointment for the narrator; in it lies the knowledge that he, too, could play the Sambo—and most likely *has* unwittingly done so by smilingly working for Bledsoe, the white patrons at the College, and the Brotherhood. Lesley Larkin points out that the "lack of control over the meaning of his own speech" works as a kind of "ventriloquism." Tod is not simply "selling out," however, by replicating the bigoted ideology that generates such stereotypes as Sambo; he is manipulating the Sambo in a performance that attempts to expose the puppetry-disguised-as-liberty within the political organization of the Brotherhood. Wilcox sees this message as one offered to the narrator even earlier in the story. In the scene with the electrified rug, "when the M.C. tells the men that 'You get all you grab,' one blonde man affirming with a wink, 'That's right, Sambo." Wilcox continues, "I want to consider, now, how the blonde man's words are a slyly delivered clue to a strategy the narrator can use to subvert the dominant system, words similar to the narrator's grandfather's advice." Though he does not yet understand such subversive potential at this point in the story, the narrator works toward an understanding that the "dominant power structure cannot be opposed through direct confrontation, that the narrator will have to work from inside the system. In particular, the narrator is encouraged to embrace the abject and grotesque comic figure of the Sambo." Julia Sun-Joo Lee concurs with this notion, arguing that playing the minstrel role allows the protagonist to function as an "accidental trickster."[38]

The content and tone of Brother Tod's performance reveal, in Butler's formulation, the series of effects that typify the Sambo stereotype but also the reality of belonging in the Brotherhood. In a rhythmic and "insinuating," "out-of-the-corner-of-the-mouth" voice, he lures potential customers with: "*Shake him, stretch him by the neck and set him down/—He'll do the rest. Yes!*" and, "*he'll kill your depression/And your* dispossession, *he lives upon the sunshine of your lordly smile/And only twenty-five cents, the* brotherly *two bits of a dollar*" (emphasis mine). By borrowing the vocabulary of the Brotherhood and the protagonist's eviction-site speech, he hails him into the performance. Lee reads Tod as trickster here—the type that the protagonist himself may become—as he works the minstrel trope, "spieling conventional blackface rhetoric but injecting his lyrics with devastating irony." Probably most "devastating" in his language is the allusion to lynching, which juxtaposes their own roles in the Brotherhood with those of victims of white supremacist violence. Invisible Man does not understand at first, but he adds the doll to the collection of mass-produced objects that point him toward a knowledge that Valerie Smith describes: the dolls are not "randomly selected products to be hawked on the streets. The black caricatures dangled on a string are, instead, metaphors for the black members of the Brotherhood who are manipulated, unknowingly, by the white leadership." Taking Smith's notion one step further, though, the notion of performativity enhances our understanding of Clifton's character and his little "high-stepping joyboy." After all, Clifton reveals that the system is not one of just ideological puppetry, but also a complex network of performances on the part of all involved.[39] In other words, Clifton's Sambo performs a metaphorical "drag"—like Sarah Jane's crawdad moment—of the very role Clifton himself has played in gesturing toward an "already expropriated" identity of Brotherhood.

Daniel Kim notes that the narrator sees a similar version of himself in the stripper, as well: "What he thus seems to recognize in her body is his own experience of humiliation, the humiliation of being deprived of control over his body." Like the Sambo, however, this lack of control functions as part of a complicit performance. We see his connection to her confirmed as the stripper exits the room, tossed in the air and groped by the white men, a "look of terror and disgust in her eyes, almost like my own terror and that which I saw in some of the other boys."[40] While Kim's project is to examine the homoerotic racism within the white characters of the novel (and Ellison's own "homophobic critique" of this enactment of racism upon the black male body), his reading of the stripper scene also works on another level, historically allegorical as well as psychoanalytic. What the narrator sees as sexual power play and "castration" in both himself and the "magnificent blonde" also resonates as a cultural powerlessness that comes with the realization that, despite their intentions, in the larger social order they are both the objects rather than the subjects of consumption—*consumed* rather than consumers, because their perhaps unknowing roles as performers (unlike Sarah Jane's rather knowing first cabaret performance) ultimately relegate them to the status of commodities in the context of the smoker. His violent reactions toward the woman seem to speak to a need to destroy this aspect within himself. The motif of violence returns later in the novel, too, but takes on various forms in the process of enacting a challenge to the definitions of social place.

Despite similar commodifications of the body, however, the stripper and the protagonist are not equals. They share similar experiences in this microcosm of the larger market-driven culture, but history testifies to their ultimate inequalities. This is made most apparent by the fact that the stripper, though treated roughly, is obviously also elevated by the white men to remind the black "boys" of the socially constructed racial hierarchies at work. The representation of the stripper is paradoxical, for while she is singly objectified, she is equally sanctified as emblematic of the American nation, evidenced by the American flag tattooed on her belly. This is a cultural message not missed by many of the protagonist's "educators," such as Ras the Exhorter and the veteran from the Golden Day, who realize the cultural capital of white women and the role of sexuality in cultural power dynamics. The flag on her belly resurfaces in an unrelated episode later in the story, in the protagonist's memory "that there was a sense in me of being apart when the flag went by. It had been a reminder . . . that my star was not there yet." In these two images meet the observation of the vet: white women are invested with the symbolism of freedom.[41] "Nation" is literally inscribed into the skin of the white woman.

With Old Glory on the belly, the body of the stripper lends itself easily to a reading of body-as-nation, a relatively common trope within Anglo-American literature of imperialist or nationalist bent. Examples of this can be seen in many popular narratives in which the female Anglo protagonist's body is threatened by an "impure" force, and to save her from corruption, kidnapping, or death is to preserve the very nation. Depending on the context of a novel, this narrative relates to contemporaneous cultural anxieties, like fear of miscegenation (Thomas Dixon's *The Clansman*, 1907), fear of immigration and cultural change (*Dracula,* 1897), fear of collapsing colonial power (*A Passage to India*, 1924) or the anxiety of establishing a coherent national identity (early American Indian captivity narratives). Ellison plays with this trope, to "out" it and implicitly critique it. The narrative that centers on protection and rescue is warped in *Invisible Man*. Instead of a treasure to be protected in the interest of the nation, the stripper is portrayed as artificial, made-up, a "kewpie." The white men display her as an object of desire denied to black men, but, ironically, the white men present the real threat to her as they chase her around the room, capture her, and throw her into the air like a doll. Wilcox observes, "The differing spontaneous reactions of these men suggests that sexuality, like race, generates contradictory responses even from subjects located inside the system. In other words, the woman as sexual fetish is an ideological object that stitches the inconsistencies of the several racial sexual subject positions which come into being by the fact of her very presence."[42] Here, the idea of woman-as-nation is mocked, an artifice, since that which is supposedly revered is here commodified, a carnival prize. The real threat to her is not the mythical sexuality of African Americans, but the animal behavior and reifying practices of a corrupt white patriarchy.

Despite his baptism by violence, Invisible Man is slow to relinquish the twin fantasies of white-collar success and consumer status. This is most clearly revealed in his fantasy of success in New York, a fantasy in which he indulges despite his disappointments at college and a complete lack of response by the New York–based trustees upon whom he is relying for the enactment of this fantasy. His success is figured most notably *not* in the achievements he imagines, but in the *look* that will signify that success as configured by mass culture, like "the men you saw in magazine ads, the junior executive types in *Esquire* magazine." He places himself in an unspecified public eye, "making a speech and caught in striking poses by flashing cameras, snapped at the end of some dazzling eloquence." This fantasy is also associated with an imposing sense of public celebrity, as he compares himself to Ronald Colman and, later, when working for the Brotherhood, Paul Robeson.[43] To borrow Butler's depiction of Lana Turner, the protagonist here adopts and engages in the repetition of a similar series of photographic poses that expose the "phantasm" of iconic white-collar masculinity.

The photographic reveries, though, are as fleeting as the phantasm of national mythology found in the movie theater. As with every mass culture encounter in the novel, the protagonist furthers his "acquaint[ance] with ambivalence," and the night after he enjoys the palliative of the Western movie, he dreams again of his grandfather's cryptic message to "overcome 'em with yeses, undermine 'em with grins, agree 'em to death and destruction." The sense of contradiction and ambivalence multiplies as the narrative progresses, with a continuing series of mismatched identity messages. For example, at the same moment that he eloquently configures himself as the next Paul Robeson within the Brotherhood, he is simultaneously greeted with the request to sing a "Negro tune" for the organization members at the Chthonian reception. Here he experiences something similar to that which Rock Wagram lives: at the same moment that he is admired and "marketable," his identity also remains marginalized and open to manipulation. His sense of feeling himself a "part in some scheme" that he does not understand speaks to this very ambivalence, for as he is offered power, that power is also subject to the fact that his identity has been fabricated and handed to him in an envelope, just as Rock's has been brainstormed by a producer.[44] The only difference is that the Brotherhood is marketing an overt ideology instead of motion pictures.

The stripping away of white-collar ideals (whether in being expelled from school, being knocked out of the running for a job with the likes of Norton and Emerson, or escaping the Brotherhood organization) is juxtaposed with the symbolic idioms described earlier, serving to gradually enlighten the protagonist to the more abstract ideological underpinnings of his fantasy. More specifically, the mass cultural objects that visually display African American bodies as commodified/commodifiable objects include Bledsoe's leg shackle, Mary Rambo's "Feed Me" bank, and the dancing Sambo doll. The vernacular culture thread contains two kinds of items: 1) those material objects that represent "transitional'" struggles to liberate and reclaim those bodies and the contested identities within them, like the portrait of Frederick Douglass, the free papers of the ex-slave couple being evicted in Harlem, Brother Tarp's bent chain link, and the protagonist's high school diploma; and 2) nonmaterial cultural practices that possess empowering and creative qualities, such as the Brer Rabbit trickster tales, jazz, blues, signifying, and playing the dozens. The narrator's understanding of these progressive threads begins to shift at one hinge within the plot, the scene in the factory hospital. Medovoi points out that this scene is the first to bring the question of identity to the forefront of the narrative—introducing the word "identity" itself for the first time in the story. Locked into what seems to be an electroshock machine, answering questions about folk tales, he realizes that identity "must be nonprescriptive."[45]

The first series of material objects are the most obvious bearers of meaning to the protagonist because they represent those "images projected upon him" in a seemingly clear system of white racism enacted upon black bodies. These are the objects he needs to "unprescribe" to himself. Of course, the meanings invested within each are revealed to be more complex as the narrative progresses. The first of these material reminders, the leg shackle on Bledsoe's desk, is supposed to serve as a "symbol of our progress." In Bledsoe's possession, it initially seems like a worthy symbol, an instrument of oppression owned by an African American leader. What becomes clear, however, is that Bledsoe is not really "free," and his shackle's symbolic meaning is revealed to be shallow. In contrast to Brother Tarp's twisted chain link, one that bears "the marks of haste and violence, looking as though it had been attacked and conquered before it stubbornly yielded," Bledsoe's unbroken, polished shackle reveals the perfect craftsmanship of oppression still intact. While he does possess some power, he enacts it only within an accommodationist system, reliant on traditional white paternalism for its survival. Brother Tarp's leg iron has a "heap of signifying wrapped up in it" because it represents the struggle of an individual to reclaim his body by altering the materials that literally oppress it. In rending the leg iron to free himself, Wilcox observes, "Tarp literally frees his labor value, or capital, enabling it to circulate more widely." Though the protagonist does not want the gift of the iron at first, he quickly realizes that it has "restored [his] perspective" and he carries it in his pocket throughout the rest of his journey to hibernation. Bledsoe's shackle, on the other hand, symbolizes what it always has, and while he is at the controls, he still helps to perpetuate a system that refuses to work beyond the indoctrinated notion that one African American represents them all.[46] This is a perfect instance in the narrative when one object replaces another to create new meaning.

The Sambo doll and the "Feed Me" bank both present an intriguing extension of the Bledsoe shackle because they also represent the commodifying and objectifying force upon a black body, yet they too are symbols of oppression owned by African Americans. The protagonist, upset by "the tolerance or lack of discrimination, or whatever, that allowed" them to possess such "self-mocking" images, feels compelled to destroy them. Ironically, he cannot simply destroy them, as both icons manage to stick with him until the end. He must carry around the broken bank and all the coins until he sees them as he sees the Sambo—as emblems of his complicity. He describes the face of the bank as a grin that seems "more like strangulation," "choking, filled to the throat with coins," and, riding around in his briefcase, it also speaks to the fantasy of monetary, white-collar success at the cost of individuality. Though he believes he is fighting against bigotry in the Brotherhood, he discovers that they are feeding him full of coins to play the role they want him to play. In Hoberek's formulation, the Brotherhood is simply another "organization man" guise that, despite its rhetoric, attempts to manipulate the protagonist's identity for the benefit of its corporate greed.[47]

These two objects in themselves do not completely encourage such revelations, however. They are assisted by other material signifiers, like Tarp's leg iron and the free papers, of the commodification of African American bodies in the process of becoming free. Though the protagonist does not destroy these transitional objects as he does the previous ones, they, too, must disappear by the end of the novel because they represent a holding onto the past. History plays a role in forming identity, of course, but as we see in Rock Wagram's case, an archived ethnic history cannot be the sole signifier of the modern self. The portrait of Frederick Douglass and the free papers are strong reminders of the struggle to change the perceived value of the self, but they are fleeting images in a novel packed with various visual symbols of the complicated history of ethnic oppression in the United States. Not only do they represent the past, but these nineteenth-century objects are all left behind because they embody a means to an end that cannot be symbolized completely within them, as they still rely on white, paternal institutions for their existence. A legal document freeing a slave and Frederick Douglass's cultural significance both derive their meanings from the existence of slavery; to make progress, the protagonist must learn them, then set them aside, along with the inhumane ideology that made them possible. This is why the protagonist must also burn his diploma at the end of the narrative: the struggle for literacy has been achieved, but it is no longer an end in itself in post-Reconstruction America.

The objects that represent these struggles in black nationalist forms (the Marcus Garvey newspaper article, the Ethiopian flag) are also left behind. By finally throwing the spear that violently stops Ras's speaking, the protagonist rejects nationalism as a viable alternative for himself. In his final incarnation as an African warrior, Ras performs an imitative ideal that no longer really exists—especially for those generations raised in the United States.[48]

So what is left? It seems impossible that a narrative so infused with the material symbolic could complete itself with an absence of it. What remains are the nonmaterial, vernacular forms that offer the protagonist the power to move beyond material signifiers of identity created within mass culture and its institutions. These forms offer possibilities for negotiating identities that are, above all, creative: telling trickster tales, signifying, singing the blues. In the 1950s, these would have seemed like residual folk cultures from another generation, but this was also the period when the search for the "authentic" (discussed in the articles by Brown and Cheever referenced elsewhere) resulted in an interest in reviving and preserving folk forms. Thus, the 1950s witnessed Alan Lomax building on his father's work to record folk musicians, and young people learning the songs of Leadbelly and Appalachian banjo players in a new folk revival. C. W. E. Bigsby argues the importance of the "improvisation" inherent within such forms, as it "is made to stand for the act of self-invention that is the essence of a private and a public drive for meaning and identity."[49] This kind of self-invention was being increasingly set aside in the mass, homogenizing commercial culture of the period. One of the most significant of these improvised vernacular forms is jazz, as the music initiates the narrative at the end of the psychological journey. It is the remaining cultural form that can convey the narrator into more "overt action" as he prepares to end his hibernation.

In the prologue, Louis Armstrong's "What Did I Do to Be So Black and Blue" not only transports the protagonist into and out of his drug-induced dream conversation with the old slave woman; it serves a function parallel to that of the novel itself. Ellison affirms the cultural power of the novel—even as a commercial object—as a space available for articulating and working through that which has been inarticulable throughout much of American history. Jazz fills a similar role, what Ellison calls an "unvoicable affirmation" of African American culture—even when recorded and mass distributed. Like the novel, jazz also has the potential to circulate meanings within mainstream culture. Greg Tate argues that jazz, before "the post-nationalist present," was the manifestation of "Black intellectual and academic achievement" as a "major currency through which racial progress could be bought and sold . . . on a rarified and individual basis." Though Tate's view of the pre-megacorporate music industry is somewhat romanticized, he does help to assess the ways in which jazz gradually enabled the African American vernacular to circulate within mainstream mass culture without the necessary filter of a white narrator. DeRosa notes that in the 1950s jazz moved way from being associated with crime in media representation to becoming "America's music" as it was exported abroad with Dizzy Gillespie as jazz ambassador.[50]

Jazz has the opposite connotation in *Imitation of Life*. It arrives in association with Sarah Jane's rebellion and serves as the soundtrack of social transgression. For example, a scene that seems to exist only to build her "bad girl" characterization depicts her dancing to a jazzy record in her bedroom, wearing a short nighty and stiletto heels, kicking a stuffed animal across the room with a gleeful and pedantically symbolic farewell to her childhood innocence. Discordant jazz also accompanies the scene in which her boyfriend, Frankie, beats her. In contrast, the narrator's jazz-entwined dream at the beginning of *Invisible Man* introduces the protagonist to the imagined son of a slave woman who levies a new, positive imperative: "*{T}he next time you got questions like that, ask yourself!*" This is exactly what the protagonist ends up doing within the narrative, asking himself what "freedom" means, making "poetry out of being invisible" the way Louis Armstrong does, and "illuminat[ing] the blackness . . . of invisibility—and vice versa." At the moment of Louis Armstrong's trumpet riff, the narrative elements and generic forms converge to exhibit the potential for challenging the representations of "images projected upon" African Americans throughout the course of American history.[51] This is where we meet Invisible Man, on the verge of launching that challenge in ways not yet imagined by the other characters we have encountered in these narratives—and maybe not yet conceivable to the audience.

Epilogue

Through the cultural product of the "The Great American Novel," Ellison was able to circulate the African American vernacular in the postwar mainstream (and to examine some of the ways in which African American vernacular entered public discourse within the twentieth century) by means of the instant cultural authority that accompanied it. Hortense Spillers asserts that this is one of the major factors contributing to the novel's endurance, that "[f]ollowing a line of American fictions that had rendered 'black' an item of sociological data or the subject of exotic assumptions, or yet, the gagline of white mischief . . . *Invisible Man* addresses the issue as an exposition of modern consciousness." Among the comparative readings in this book, what a pairing of the film *Imitation of Life* and the novel *Invisible Man* illuminates is the conditional terrain for a narrative within a particular medium. Pierre Bourdieu argues that the more a work of art is tied to and reliant upon the principles of mass marketing and economy, the less "autonomy" it typically possesses within its field. As noted in the introduction, novels also rely on mass marketing for their circulation.[1] Any medium has parameters that vary with the cultural influences at work at the time it appears, and each of these narratives may end up replicating some of the very limitations that it is trying to escape. However, reading texts from different media in dialogue with one another, and considering how they work across fields of cultural production, expands their possible readings. This is generally true, but it also seems a particularly useful practice when examining constructions and articulations of ethnicity in a period when the notion of identity takes on new significance in a changing culture.

Because of the narrative structures that support racial upstaging and status quo morality, *Imitation of Life*'s attempts at forwarding a "liberal" plot end up only hinting at a critique of the social system, mirrored within the film in Lora's wish to act in a "social problem" play that, as Butler notes, has little to do with Lora's "own sense of political commitment" and mostly to do with *performing* a surface social consciousness. Similarly, *Invisible Man*'s critique of the exclusions and denigrations of African American men tends to reproduce those same gestures in its limitations, exclusions, and denigrations of women and homosexuals of all ethnicities. C. W. E. Bigsby points out that even trying to commit "the raw experience" of life to the page is a process that Ellison saw as "fraught with ambiguity" and limitations. "To deploy language as a means of inducing coherencies," Bigsby explains, "is to subordinate oneself to the constraints of that language, which is, at the very least, historically stained."[2] This same set of subordinations and constraints, one could argue, applies to the moving and print images in similar ways—"stained" by commercial concerns, perhaps, as much as by history.

While the film may have a few shortcomings in promoting the socially aware narrative that it purports, Sarah Jane's character actually enables a furthering of Ellison's project in the ways that her character progresses the discussion of invisibility, conformity, and interethnic violence in relation to women. In sorting through Ellison's construction of invisibility, Joseph Urgo formulates this set of connotations: "In one sense, then, invisibility refers to the blinding force of race, in which the individual self is obscured by the force of the racial categorization. On the other hand, invisibility refers equally to the obliteration of those same categories in the name of individual autonomy—so that historical context is denied by a blinding insistence upon the irrelevance of categorical injustices. However, to be properly understood, these two functions of invisibility must be recognized as existing and operating *simultaneously*." This scenario is set up in the novel as a system the protagonist must learn to decode, to see the "blackness of invisibility" and the invisibility of blackness. Wilcox adds that the racialization works not just between invisibility and visibility, but also among racializing practices in all directions:

> It is important to note that invisibility here is not a failure of visual perception or of psychological registration on the part of the tall blonde man [the narrator describes in the prologue]. Invisibility here is a positive substance that transforms the narrator's race into something other than black, even at the same time it is "produced"

by the blonde man's perception of the narrator's blackness. Racialization also operates in the other direction. Imbued with his own racial-desiring, the narrator identifies the source of his invisibility as an already racialized figure. In the period just following the second World War (and even today), the description of "a tall blonde man" would convey an image of Aryan (white) supremacy. In one sense, then, the narrator influences his own racialization when he identifies (racializes) the man as "a tall blonde."[3]

These same systems exert doubly upon Sarah Jane, whose invisibility is both "black" and "white," whose apparent whiteness further obscures her identity. Urgo explains further that, for Ellison, invisibility "is the result of a *failure* to conform; conformity, on the other hand, produces visibility." In a sense, this is true, as the modes through which the protagonist gains cultural visibility are those that adopt the performances of "black man" already culturally inscribed: race leader, Black Nationalist, Uncle Tom, and so on. It seems, however, that Urgo fails to completely unpack the complexities of this configuration, for if conforming produces visibility, that visibility only replicates invisibility. What makes the protagonist visible at any particular moment also renders him invisible because it succinctly obscures his individuality within the racializing practices described above. Instead of presenting an either/or scenario, Ellison has delineated a view of American society that renders this man invisible regardless of whether he conforms or not. "Becoming" Rinehart ultimately exposes this, as Rinehart represents the possibilities, fluidities, and falsities of the various conformities. In his efforts to become increasingly visible through his attempts at success, the protagonist comes to realize that the options existing for him are really just variations of invisibility. The same holds true for Rock Wagram, in constant negotiation of the *either/or* and *both/and* of ethnicity, and for Sarah Jane, who would remain culturally invisible regardless of which racial identity she were to adopt. As a "black" woman, she might be like her mother, subservient and invisible until the pageantry of her funeral. Her mother, Annie, conforms, yet she remains visible only within the confines of her role within Lora's home, just as Maud Martha's visibility is most apparent as an exchange-value commodity in Mrs. Burns-Cooper's employ. Conversely, as a "white" woman, Sarah Jane would further problematize that which Urgo describes: "obliteration of those same categories in the name of individual autonomy—so that historical context is denied by a blinding insistence upon the irrelevance of categorical injustices."[4]

This configuration is the point of rupture between the work of Richard Wright and Ralph Ellison that has been consistently examined since the appearance of *Invisible Man*. In *Native Son*, the only way for Bigger Thomas to become visible to white America is to occupy the black criminal persona, that is, conformity to one of the predominant stereotypes for African American men. In his response to Irving Howe's 1961 comparison of the two writers, Ellison takes to task this factor of Wright's creation, that Bigger Thomas is so thoroughly inscribed by racist determinant forces he can do nothing but conform to a notion that African American men cannot be imagined without an identity attached to violence. As such, Bigger has no individual agency. *Invisible Man* spurs a rethinking of this notion by inhabiting some of the same spaces and being manipulated and influenced by some of the same social forces as Bigger Thomas, but with different results. The novel's persistent motifs of sleeping/waking and blindness/sight articulate the protagonist's discovery that unthinking conformity, occupying the visible stereotypes in order to get ahead in the mainstream culture, reinscribes his own invisibility. In a way, the violence he engages in, while seemingly for survival, moves him toward epiphany, not as the means by which he is made visible, but as one vehicle for questioning the means by which African American men are afforded cultural visibility. For this reason, he invokes the idea of violence from the outset of the narrative, when he admits to viciously beating that tall, blond man who bumped into him one night. As he is about to take the man's life, he realizes, "the man had not *seen* me," revealing that his conformity to the stereotype of the black male body as "contained violence" renders him even more thoroughly invisible to the stranger. Throughout the story Invisible Man negotiates violence, either quelling it at seemingly opportune moments (his reaction to the stripper), acting it out when expected of him (boxing, fighting Ras for the Brotherhood), and finally, acting it out against the objects that have heretofore contributed to those very defining stereotypes he is trying to work around (smashing Mary's bank, spitting on the puppet, burning the contents of the briefcase). Perhaps this is why, at the end of the tale we find him in hibernation. Having recognized the catch 22 that Bigger gets caught in, he is working out the antideterminist, intellectualized strategies to "carry on a fight against [the sleeping ones] without their realizing it."[5] Perhaps this is the only place he can be in the immediate postwar era, where the "fights" were still largely rhetorical and exceedingly slow.

If the African American man's body has seldom been imagined without association to violence up until this point, the same is often true of the ethnic woman's body. Sarah Jane, in trying to escape a predetermined domestic role for herself, encounters violence in the scene of her beating by her boyfriend, Frankie, who has just discovered who her mother is. Her attempt to occupy the visible identity that seems most likely to her ("white") backfires. Not conforming to her "blackness" ends in violence, just as conforming to blackness would also mean social violence, as it does for *Invisible Man*'s protagonist. Either way, she, too, remains invisible because of her skin color—for reasons ironically reversed from Invisible Man's—though she is in as much need of escape from the social double-bind he has retreated from in his underground hideout.

Maybe violence is not always to be negatively connoted, however, when the violence is *not* being acted upon ethnic bodies. As we see in *Maud Martha*, the interior fantasy of stabbing the Macy's Santa Claus with her sewing scissors after he discriminates against her daughter is a necessary, empowering moment in the protagonist's reconfiguring of her own identity on positive, ethnic, noncommercial terms. In his discussion of violent fantasies in Chester Himes's detective fiction, Christopher Breu argues that it "may seem less genuinely transgressive, merely repeating the racist and sexist fantasies that formed the meat and potatoes of the postwar cultural imaginary. On another level, however, Himes' insistence on the violence of these encounters foregrounds, on the most intimate of intersubjective terrains, the simultaneously sexual and political libidinal aggressivity that is the inevitable product of this cultural imaginary."[6] We expect to encounter violence in crime stories, though. Not so in domestic fiction. In Breu's reasoning, however, Maud's violent fantasy makes sense as an outgrowth of the "cultural imaginary" of history that has permitted physical and psychological violence upon ethnic bodies for so long.

The texts in this study were originally organized in a way that their engagement with the increasingly public performances of ethnicity could build upon one another. The texts also progress from the most accommodationist and chaste (*Flower Drum Song*) toward narratives that introduce interethnic sexuality and violence in more overt ways. In doing so, they approach notions of ethnicity in very different—but very complementary—ways. Whether comedic or melodramatic, action-filled or quietly lyrical, the films, television shows, and print text I have discussed here work collaboratively across medium and subgenre toward a similar, panethnic cultural gesture. Forced into conversation with one another, they take on the essential questions of American identity and who is imagined as entitled to that identity. Medovoi writes, "Identity, to loosely paraphrase Stuart Hall, became the modality through which antiracist, antisexist, or antihomophobic struggles could be fought with considerable potency." The questions of identity in these texts occur always in relation to cultural citizenship, how that citizenship is pictured in the larger culture, and where ethnicity fits into it. Often, violence has accompanied or countered the moves toward greater cultural participation. Yet, in the face of potential violence, the assertion of "identity" as a concept demands inclusivity, with ethnicity representing "ways of declaring an identity in righteous rebellion against the conformities of Fordist heteronormativity and whiteness."[7] Across these texts we may interpret regressive, progressive, and noncommittal representations of ethnicity, but, collectively, they force the issue of cultural invisibility into plain sight. Somewhere between "containment" and "emergence," these midcentury ethnic narratives delineate the spaces where ethnic subjects are simultaneously "yessing" the containment to death and forcing new notions of ethnicity to emerge.

Notes

Chapter 1. Introduction

1. James Baldwin, *Notes of a Native Son* (Boston: Beacon, 1955), 4.
2. John Fiske, *Television Culture* (New York: Methuen, 1987), 108.
3. Michele Wallace, introduction to *Invisibility Blues* (New York: Verso, 1990).
4. Evan Brier, *A Novel Marketplace: Mass Culture, The Book Trade, and Postwar American Fiction* (Philadelphia: University of Pennsylvania Press, 2010), 8–9.
5. Joel Foreman, ed., *The Other Fifties: Interrogating Midcentury American Icons* (Urbana: University of Illinois Press, 1997), 16; Steven Belletto and Daniel Grausman, eds., *American Literature and Culture in an Age of Cold War: A Critical Reassessment* (Iowa City: University of Iowa Press, 2012); Joshua Lukin, ed., *Invisible Suburbs: Recovering Protest Fiction in the 1950s United States* (Jackson: University Press of Mississippi, 2008), xv.
6. Leerom Medovoi, *Rebels: Youth and the Cold War Origins of Identity* (Durham: Duke University Press, 2005), 50.
7. Ibid., 68.
8. Jinqi Ling, *Narrating Nationalisms: Ideology and Form in Asian American Literature* (New York: Oxford University Press, 1998), 8.
9. Toby Miller, *The Well-Tempered Self: Citizenship, Culture, and the Postmodern Subject* (Baltimore: Johns Hopkins University Press, 1993), xxi.

10. Ling, 30; Stuart Hall, "What Is This 'Black' in Black Popular Culture?" in *Black Popular Culture*, ed. Michele Wallace and Gina Dent (New York: The New Press, 1998), 32; Manning Marable, "We Need New and Critical Study of Race and Ethnicity," *Chronicle of Higher Education* February 25, 2000. Posted March 30, 2000, http://chronicle.com/weekly/v46/i25/25b00401.htm. I also do not claim to identify a particular movement or trend that marks the era and its ethnic minority writers, in the way that a larger literary-historical approach like Morris Dickstein's attempts, in *Leopards in the Temple: The Transformation of American Fiction, 1945–1970* (Cambridge: Harvard University Press, 2002).
11. Fredric Jameson, *The Political Unconscious: Narrative as a Socially Symbolic Act* (Ithaca: Cornell University Press, 1981), 35.
12. *A Face in the Crowd*, directed by Elia Kazan (Warner Brothers, 1957); *The Manchurian Candidate*, directed by John Frankenheimer (United Artists, 1962).
13. See, for example, Robert H. Stanley, *The Celluloid Empire: A History of the American Movie Industry* (New York: Hastings House, 1978); Robert Sklar, *Movie-Made America: A Cultural History of American Movies* (New York: Vintage, 1994); John Sedgwick, "Product Differentiation at the Movies: Hollywood 1946 to 1965," in *An Economic History of Film* (New York: Routledge, 2005): 186–217; and Wheeler Winston Dixon, *A Short History of Film* (New Brunswick, NJ: Rutgers University Press, 2008).
14. Richard Wright, *Native Son* (New York: Harper, 1940), 25–29.
15. Brier, 3, 15.
16. Lisa Lowe, *Immigrant Acts: On Asian American Cultural Politics* (Durham, NC: Duke University Press, 1996), 3; Edward Said, *Culture and Imperialism* (New York: Knopf, 1993), xiii.
17. Ellison quoted in Alfred Chester and Vilma Howard, "The Art of Fiction: An Interview," *Paris Review* (Spring 1955) reprinted in *Conversations with Ralph Ellison*, ed. Maryemma Graham and Amritjit Singh (Jackson: University Press of Mississippi, 1995), 15; Joseph R. Urgo, *Novel Frames: Literature as Guide to Race, Sex, and History in American Culture* (Jackson: University Press of Mississippi, 1991), xiv–xvi.
18. Jonathan Arac, "What Kind of History Does a Theory of the Novel Require?" *Novel: A Forum on Fiction* 42, no. 2 (2009): 193; For studies of book culture in the first half of the twentieth century, see Brier and Joan Shelley Rubin, *The Making of Middle-Brow Culture* (Chapel Hill: University of North Carolina Press, 1992); Janice Radway, *A Feeling for Books: The Book-of-the-Month Club, Literary Taste and Middle Class Desire* (Chapel

Hill: University of North Carolina Press, 1997); Amy L. Blair, *Reading Up: Middle-class Readers and The Culture of Success in the Early Twentieth-Century United States* (Philadelphia: Temple University Press, 2011).

19. Priscilla Wald, *Constituting Americans: Cultural Anxiety and Narrative Form* (Durham: Duke University Press, 1995), 10–11, 304.
20. See, for example, Josh Lukin, ed., *Invisible Suburbs*; Elizabeth A. Wheeler, *Uncontained: Urban Fiction in Postwar America* (New Brunswick, NJ: Rutgers University Press, 2001); and Bill V. Mullen and James Smethurst, eds., *Left of the Color Line: Race, Radicalism, and Twentieth-Century Literature of the United States* (Chapel Hill: University of North Carolina Press, 2003).
21. Worth noting in relation to Cold War politics and race is Mary Helen Washington's assertion that a leftist, progressive strain in the black arts has been whitewashed out of midcentury scholarship on the Cold War, so that key authors of the period have been left out of the current midcentury canon; Mary Helen Washington, "Alice Childress, Lorraine Hansberry, and Claudia Jones: Black Women Write the Popular Front," in *Left of the Color Line: Race, Radicalism, and Twentieth-Century Literature of the United States*, ed. Bill V. Mullen and James Smethurst (Chapel Hill: University of North Carolina Press, 2003), 183–204. For a study that does try to comprehensively define a specific, collective impulse in ethnic writing of the period, see Morris Dickstein, *Leopards in the Temple: The Transformation of American Fiction, 1945–1970* (Cambridge: Harvard University Press, 2002).
22. Clara E. Rodriguez, *Changing Race: Latinos, the Census, and the History of Ethnicity in the United States* (New York: New York University Press, 2000), 83–85; Michael Roediger, *Working toward Whiteness: How America's Immigrants Became White: The Strange Journey from Ellis Island to the Suburbs* (New York: Basic Books, 2005), 8–9.
23. Karen Brodkin Sacks, "How Did Jews Become White Folks?" in *Race*, ed. Steven Gregory and Roger Sanjek (New Brunswick, NJ: Rutgers University Press, 1994), 79; Arlene Dávila, *Latino Spin: Public Image and the Whitewashing of Race* (New York: New York University Press, 2008), 3–15. See also, for example, Fred Gardaphé, "We Weren't Always White: Race and Ethnicity in Italian American Literature," *LIT* 13, no. 3 (2002): 185–199; Stefano Luconi, *From Paesani to White Ethnics: The Italian Experience in Philadelphia* (Albany: State University of New York Press, 2001); and Mathew Frye Jacobson, *Whiteness of a Different Color: European Immigrants and the Alchemy of Race* (Cambridge: Harvard University Press,

1998); and Nathan Glazer, "The Emergence of an American Ethnic Pattern," in *From Different Shores; Perspectives on Race and Ethnicity in America*, edited by Ronald Takaki (New York: Oxford University Press, 1987), 13–25.

24. Rey Chow, *The Protestant Ethnic and the Spirit of Capitalism* (New York: Columbia University Press, 2002), 26.
25. Richard Polenberg, *One Nation Divisible: Class, Race, and Ethnicity in the United States since 1938* (New York: Viking, 1980), 20–23.
26. Ellison quoted in C. W. E. Bigsby, "Improvising America: Ralph Ellison and the Paradox of Form," in *Speaking for You: The Vision of Ralph Ellison*, ed. Kimberly W. Benston (Washington, DC: Howard University Press, 1987),180; Chow, 22; Roediger, 25.
27. Michael Omi and Howard Winant, *Racial Formation in the United States, from the 1960s to the 1980s* (New York: Routledge, 1986), 4–5, 3; Roger Sanjek, "The Enduring Inequalities of Race," in *Race*, ed. Steven Gregory and Roger Sanjek (New Brunswick, NJ: Rutgers University Press, 1994), 10; Chow, 23–24.
28. Etienne Balibar and Immanuel Wallerstein, *Race, Nation, Class: Ambiguous Identities*, translated by Etienne Balibar and Chris Turner (New York: Verso, 1991), 96; Werner Sollors, introduction to *The Invention of Ethnicity* (New York: Oxford University Press, 1989), xi.
29. Sollors, xv. For a more radical critique of this conceptualization of ethnicity from a Native American perspective, see Ward Churchill's "*Beyond Ethnicity*: Werner Sollors' Deepest Avatar of Racism," in *Fantasies of the Master Race: Literature, Cinema, and the Colonization of the American Indians* (Monroe, ME: Common Courage, 1992); Chow, 24.
30. Foreman, 9.
31. I use the term mass culture to differentiate any form of popular culture that is clearly commercialized and mass mediated, whereas popular culture can exist in any era, as originally defined, as a set of practices created and maintained by the populace, outside of commercial relationships.
32. See, for example, Michael French, *U.S. Economic History since 1945* (New York: Manchester University Press, 1997).
33. Polenberg, 36; Lizabeth Cohen, *A Consumer's Republic: The Politics of Mass Consumption in Postwar America* (New York: Knopf, 2003) 323–331; Alan Nadel, *Containment Culture: American Narratives, Postmodernism, and the Atomic Age* (Durham: Duke University Press, 1995), 8.
34. Lynne Spigel, "Installing the Television Set: Popular Discourses on Television and Domestic Space, 1948–1955," in *Private Screenings: Television*

and the Female Consumer, ed. Lynn Spigel and Denise Mann (Minneapolis: University Minnesota Press, 1992), 6.

35. Roediger, 230; Polenberg, 127. Some of the more well-known studies of American suburbanization and its effects on ethnic and class relations include George Lipsitz, *Time Passages: Collective Memory and American Popular Culture* (Minneapolis: University Minnesota Press, 1990); Richard Polenberg's chapter "The Suburban Nation," in *One Nation Divisible*, 127–163; Herbert Gans, *The Levittowners: Ways of Life and Politics in a New Suburban Community* (New York: Pantheon, 1967); and Kenneth T. Jackson, *Crabgrass Frontier: The Suburbanization of the United States* (New York: Oxford University Press, 1985).
36. Cohen, *Consumer's Republic*, 170 and 200–205; Meihzhu Lui, Bárbara Robles, Betsy Leondar-Wright, Rose Brewer, and Rebecca Adamson, *The Color of Wealth: The Story Behind the U.S. Racial Wealth Divide* (New York: New Press, 2006), 96–97; Cohen, "From Town Center to Shopping Center: The Reconfiguration of Community Marketplaces in Postwar America," *American Historical Review* 101, no. 4 (October 1996): 1079. See also Catherine Jurca on the way racial exclusion was built into housing development by-laws, "Tarzan, Lord of the Suburbs," *White Diaspora: The Suburb and the Twentieth-Century American Novel* (Princeton: Princeton University Press, 2001).
37. For descriptions of cultural, political, and corporate practices that actually bolstered consumer culture's strength before and during the Great Depression, see Lizabeth Cohen's *Consumer's Republic* and Gary Cross, *An All-Consuming Century: Why Commercialism Won in Modern America* (New York: Columbia University Press, 2000), 17–65; Martyn J. Lee, *Consumer Culture Reborn: The Cultural Politics of Consumption* (New York: Routledge, 1993), 73; Medovoi, 19.
38. Reproduced in the documentary *The Atomic Café*, the Archives Project, Inc. (Thorn EMI Video, 1982).
39. Foreman, 10; Hall, 32.
40. "Passing" in its original usage named the practice of light-complexioned African Americans performing themselves as white to, originally, escape slavery or, in the late nineteenth and early twentieth centuries, to leave behind segregation and discrimination to pursue occupations and status positions afforded only to white Americans. I borrow this term from its original usage because I think it makes an apt, descriptive metaphor for the larger panethnic phenomenon located within these chapters. The concept of passing in its original sense appears in the last chapter, but

"passing" also serves as a useful metaphor for understanding the various ways in which individuals of ethnic backgrounds (or sexual identities, for that matter) had to "pass" at times in order to access some measure of the social mobility promoted within the culture.

41. Medovoi, 7–10.

Chapter 2. The Land of Plenty

1. Lisa Lowe, *Immigrant Acts: On Asian American Cultural Politics* (Durham, NC: Duke University Press, 1996), 2–3; Toby Miller, *The Well-Tempered Self: Citizenship, Culture, and the Postmodern Subject* (Baltimore: Johns Hopkins University Press, 1993), xii; Pierre Bourdieu, *The Field of Cultural Production: Essays on Art and Literature* (New York: Columbia University Press, 1993).
2. For more thorough accounts of the racism and ethnocentrism present within American immigration law in the nineteenth and twentieth centuries, see Lisa Lowe, "Immigration, Citizenship, Racialization: Asian American Critique" in *Immigrant Acts*; Ronald Takaki, ed., *From Different Shores; Perspectives on Race and Ethnicity in America* (NY: Oxford University Press, 1987); Richard Polenberg, *One Nation Divisible*; Michael Omi and Howard Winant, *Racial Formation in the United States*; Thomas J. Archdeacon, *Becoming American: An Ethnic History* (New York: Free Press, 1983).
3. Christina Klein, *Cold War Orientalism: Asia in the Middlebrow Imagination, 1945–1961* (Berkley: University of California Press, 2003), 2. For critiques of the novel, see Elaine Kim, *Asian-American Literature: An Introduction to the Writings and Their Social Context* (Philadelphia: Temple University Press, 1984), and Frank Chin et al., introduction to *Aiiieeeee! An Anthology of Asian-American Writers* (New York: Doubleday, 1975). These two texts deal with the novel cursorily, mostly to posit it as the type of representation most other Asian American writers attempt to work against. Other studies of Asian American literature do not usually bother to include discussion of the novel. For a detailed discussion of the differences between the novel and staged versions, as well as discussion of professional reviews of the stage and film versions, see Christina Klein, "Asians in America: *Flower Drum Song* and *Hawaii*," in *Cold War Orientalism.*
4. Klein, 328–330; Amy Ling, "C.Y. Lee," in *Yellow Light: The Flowering of Asian American Arts* (Philadelphia: Temple University Press, 1999), 13;

C. Y. Lee, *The Flower Drum Song* (New York: Grosset and Dunlap, 1957), 106.

5. Lee, 115.
6. Ibid., 4.
7. Kathryn Edney, "'Integration through the Wide Open Back Door': African Americans respond to *Flower Drum Song* (1958)," *Studies in Musical Theatre* 4, no. 3 (2010): 265.
8. Lee, 4–5, 68–69.
9. Ibid., 33–34, 57.
10. Ibid., 63–65.
11. Ibid., 65.
12. Ibid., 20–22, 118.
13. Ibid., 105, 108–109.
14. Ibid., 7, 179.
15. Ibid., 103.
16. Ibid., 115.
17. Ibid., 197. For a more detailed discussion of the emasculation of Asian American men, see Frank Chin's rationale for a recovery of masculinist nationality in *Aiiieeeee!* as well as Jinqi Ling's challenges to that masculinist stance in *Narrating Nationalisms*.
18. Lee, 180, 172, 211.
19. For informative reviews of the revival see Misha Berson, "A Drum with a Difference: David Henry Hwang Repaves Rogers and Hammerstein's Road to Chinatown," *American Theater* 19, no. 2 (2002): 14–18; Dan Balcazo, "A Different Drum: David Henry Hwang's Musical 'Revisal' of *Flower Drum Song*," *Journal of American Drama and Theater* 15, no. 2 (2003): 71–83; and Eve Oishi, "The Asian American Fakeness Canon, 1972–2002," *Aztlán* 32, no. 1 (2007): 197–204.
20. Vladimir Nabokov, *Lolita* (1955, New York: Vintage International, 1989), 37.
21. Ibid., 32; Stephen Schiff, "Nabokov's *Lolita*," in *A New Literary History of America*, ed. Greil Marcus and Werner Sollors (Cambridge: Harvard University Press, 2009), 869.
22. Ibid., 148.
23. On postwar teenage consumerism, see Michael Barson and Steven Heller, *Teenage Confidential: An Illustrated History of the American Teen* (San Francisco: Chronicle Books, 1998); David Halberstam, *The Fifties* (New York: Villard Books 1993), 473–474; Martyn J. Lee, *Consumer Culture Reborn: The Cultural Politics of Consumption* (New York: Routledge, 1993), 93.

24. Lynne Joyrich, "All That Television Allows: TV Melodrama, Postmodernism, and Consumer Culture," in *Private Screenings: Television and the Female Consumer*, ed. Lynn Spigel and Denise Mann (Minneapolis: University of Minnesota Press, 1992), 242–243; Lynn Spigel "Installing the Television Set: Popular Discourses on Television and Domestic Space, 1948–1955," in *Private Screenings: Television and the Female Consumer*, note 33; JoAnne Meyerowitz, "Beyond the Feminine Mystique: A Reassessment of Postwar Mass Culture, 1946–1958," *Journal of American History* 79, no. 4 (March 1993): 1455–1482.
25. Lizabeth Cohen, "From Town Center to Shopping Center," 1050–1081, 1055; Marianne Conroy, "'No Sin in Lookin' Prosperous': Gender, Race, and the Class Formations of Middlebrow Taste in Douglas Sirk's *Imitation of Life*," in *The Hidden Foundation: Cinema and the Question of Class*, ed. David E. James and Rick Berg (Minneapolis: University of Minnesota Press, 1996), 121–122.
26. Here Rubin describes a pervasive view as represented in the words of Ellis Hawley in the 1920s. Joan Shelley Rubin, *The Making of Middlebrow Culture* (Chapel Hill: University of North Carolina Press, 1992), xv; John Haegert, "The Americanization of Humbert Humbert," in *Lolita*, Major Literary Characters Series, ed. Harold Bloom (New York: Chelsea House, 1993), 125.
27. Nabokov, 78.
28. Haegert, 127.
29. Nabokov, 152–153.
30. Ibid., 15, 107, 142–143.
31. Ibid., 264, 44, 30, 43.
32. Ibid., 48, 62, 299.
33. Ibid., 33.
34. Ibid., 82, 79, 117; Douglas Anderson, "Nabokov's Genocidal and Nuclear Holocausts in Lolita," *Mosaic* 29, no. 2 (1996): 73–89. See also Alfred Appel, ed., *The Annotated Lolita* (New York: Vintage, 1991); Nabokov, 80.
35. Vladimir Nabokov, "On a Book Entitled *Lolita*," reprinted in *Lolita* (New York: Vintage International, 1989), 314.
36. Erik Martiny, "The Unreachable 'Eden-Red Apple' of Nabokov's Film Technique in Versions of Lolita by Stanley Kubrick and Adrian Lyne," *Lolita: From Nabokov to Kubrick and Lyne*, ed. Erik Martiny (Paris: SEDES, 2009), 133–147. Lee qtd. in Amy Ling, 13.

Chapter 3. What's for Sale

1. "Lucy Goes to the Hospital," January 19, 1953.
2. Gwendolyn Brooks, *Maud Martha* (New York: Harper, 1953). I am reading the *I Love Lucy* series as an ongoing narrative rather than as a set of isolated episodes. The series ran from 1951 through 1957.
3. See, for example, Patricia H. Lattin and Vernon E. Lattin's study of the novel within the African American canon, "Dual Vision in Gwendolyn Brooks's *Maud Martha*," *Critique* 25, no.4 (1984), 180–188; Barbara Christian's examination of the novel within the traditions of African American women's writing, "Nuance and Novella: A Study of Gwendolyn Brooks's *Maud Martha*," in *A Life Distilled: Gwendolyn Brooks, Her Poetry and Fiction*, ed. Maria K Mootry and Gary Smith, 239–253 (Urbana: University of Illinois Press, 1987); study of the book in the *bildungsroman* tradition in Šárka Bubíková, "Maud Martha and the Tradition of the Ethnic Female Bildungsroman," *Litteraria Pragensia: Studies in Literature and Culture* 21 (July 2011) : 7–21; and Mary Helen Washington, "Plain, Black, and Decently Wild: The Heroic Possibilities of *Maud Martha*," in *The Voyage In: Fictions of Female Development*, ed. Elizabeth Abel et al, 270–286 (Hanover, NH: University Press New England, 1983); and within the cultural Left, Michael Denning, "'The Tenement Thinking': Ghetto Pastorals," in *The Cultural Front: The Laboring of American Culture in the Twentieth Century* (London: Verso, 1997): 230–253.
4. See Lynn Spigel, "Installing the Television Set: Popular Discourses on Television and Domestic Space, 1948–1955," in *Private Screenings: Television and the Female Consumer*, ed. Spigel and Denise Mann (Minneapolis: University of Minnesota Press, 1992), 3–38; Erik Barnouw, *Tube of Plenty: The Evolution of American Television*, 2nd ed. (New York: Oxford University Press, 1990), 114.
5. On the consumer infrastructure, see Lizabeth Cohen's *Consumer's Republic*; George Lipsitz, "The Meaning of Memory: Family, Class, and Ethnicity in Early Network Television," in *Time Passages: Collective Memory and the American Popular Culture* (Minneapolis: University of Minnesota Press, 1990), 47; Elaine Tyler May, *Homeward Bound: American Families in the Cold War Era* (New York: Basic Books, 1988), 172.
6. More extreme, traditionally Marxist theories, like those of Max Horkheimer and Theodor Adorno, argue that the advances of capitalism and technology have resulted in a "uniform" mass media that holds everyone

in "enthusiastic obedience to the rhythm of the iron system." "The Culture Industry: Enlightenment as Mass Deception," in *Dialectic of Enlightenment*, translated by John Cumming, 120–167 (New York: Herder and Herder, 1972), 120; Lynn Spigel, *Make Room for TV: Television and the Family Ideal in Postwar America* (Chicago: University of Chicago Press, 1992), 8; for Fiske's case studies, see "Active Audiences," 62–83, and "Conclusion: The Popular Economy," 309–326, in *Television Culture* (New York: Methuen, 1987).

7. J. Fred MacDonald, *Blacks and White TV: Afro-Americans in Television Since 1948* (Chicago: Nelson-Hall, 1983), xv, xvii; see also Marlon T. Riggs's documentary *Color Adjustment* (Signifyin' Works, 1991), Jannette L. Dates and William Barlow, eds., *Split Image: African Americans in the Mass Media*, 2nd ed. (Washington, DC: Howard University Press, 1993); and Alan Nadel, *Television in Black and White America* (Lawrence: University Press of Kansas, 2005). Jewish actors were also subject to politicized censorship via advertising sponsors, as when Sanka pulled its support from *The Goldbergs* because of actor Philip Loeb's blacklisting, and the program could not find another sponsor. James Roman, *From Daytime to Primetime: The History of American Television Programs* (Westport, CT: Greenwood, 2005), 95–96.
8. Richard Ohmann, *Selling Culture: Magazines, Markets, and Class at the Turn of the Century* (New York: Verso, 1996), 219; Lipsitz, 44, 55.
9. Kurt Andersen, "American Icons: *I Love Lucy*," transcript of *Studio 360* (WNYC/Public Radio International, aired October 8, 2010, posted August 5, 2011) http://www.studio360.org/series/american-icons/; the viewer number for the birth episode is that given by the series producer, Jess Oppenheimer, in Jess Oppenheimer and Gregg Oppenheimer, *Laughs, Luck . . . and Lucy: How I Came to Create the Most Popular Sitcom of All Time* (Syracuse: Syracuse University Press, 1996), 3; Lori Landay, *Madcaps, Screwballs, and Con Women: The Female Trickster in American Culture* (Philadelphia: University of Pennsylvania Press, 1998), 155–196; on the dissolution of The Ball-Arnaz marriage, see Gustavo Pérez-Firmat, "The-Man-Who-Loved-Lucy," in *Life on the Hyphen: The Cuban-American Way* (Austin: University of Texas Press, 1994), 48–76.
10. Emily Nussbaum, Pérez-Firmat, and Gina Barreca quoted in Andersen, "American Icons"; Landay, 155–196.
11. Landay, 179.
12. Herman Gray, *Watching Race: Television and the Struggle for "Blackness"* (Minneapolis: University of Minnesota Press, 1995), 4.

13. W. T. Lhamon Jr., *Deliberate Speed: The Origins of a Cultural Style in the American 1950s* (Washington, DC: Smithsonian, 1990), 7; Michael Denning, *The Cultural Front: The Laboring of American Culture in the Twentieth Century* (New York: Verso, 1996).
14. See MacDonald, *Blacks and White TV*, and Jannette L. Dates and William Barlow, *Split Image: African Americans in the Mass Media* (Washington, DC: Howard University Press, 1993).
15. Lucille Ball's claim of being "Just another housewife" comes from a 1953 *Cosmopolitan* interview, quoted in Landay, 166; Landay, 177; for a detailed account of Lucille Ball's post-film-career "repackaging" for television, see Alexander Doty, "The Cabinet of Lucy Ricardo: Lucille Ball's Star Image," *Cinema Journal* 29 (1990): 3–22.
16. Landay, 168.
17. "Imperialist Nostalgia" is Renato Rosaldo's term, quoted in bell hooks, *Black Looks*, 173; Brooks, *Maud Martha*, 10.
18. "Lucy Gets Homesick in Italy," April 9, 1956; "Lucy Goes to Mexico" appeared in a brief series, with the same characters, immediately after *I Love Lucy*'s run, called *The Lucy-Desi Comedy Hour*, October 6, 1958.
19. Gray, 4; hooks, 173; Brooks, *Maud Martha*, 9.
20. Landay, 176.
21. "Lucy's Show Biz Swan Song," December 22, 1952; see also Landay's analysis of "The Indian Show," 190.
22. Karen Christian, *Show and Tell: Identity as Performance in U.S. Latino/a Fiction* (Albuquerque: University of New Mexico Press, 1997), 60; Arlene Dávila, *Latino Spin: Public Image and the Whitewashing of Race* (New York: New York University Press, 2008), 3.
23. "Lucy's Mother-in-Law," November 11, 1954; "Lucy Hires an English Tutor," December 12, 1952; Gustavo Pérez-Firmat, 27–40; Shari Roberts, "The Lady in the Tutti-Frutti Hat: Carmen Miranda, A Spectacle of Ethnicity," in *The Contemporary Hollywood Reader*, ed. Toby Miller (New York: Routledge, 2009), 107–108.
24. Gray, 9.
25. Brooks, 48.
26. "Charm School," January 25, 1954; Polenberg, 103.
27. Brooks, 158.
28. Ibid., 139.
29. Valerie Frazier, "Domestic Epic Warfare in *Maud Martha*," *African American Review* 39, nos. 1–2 (2005): 138; Brooks, 140.
30. Brooks, 154.

31. Karal Ann Marling, *As Seen on Television: The Visual Culture of Everyday Life in the 1950s* (Cambridge: Harvard University Press, 1994), 23; 21.
32. "Ricky Loses His Temper," February 22, 1954.
33. Brooks, 155; Sally Victor, a midcentury milliner, quoted in Marling, 32.
34. Brooks, 161.
35. Ibid., 163; Mary Helen Washington, "'Taming All That Anger Down': Rage and Silence in Gwendolyn Brooks's *Maud Martha*," *Massachusetts Review* 24, no. 2 (1983): 465; Frazier, 135.
36. Brooks, 173, 175.
37. My thinking here parallels Lisa Lowe's ideas about capital's need for a racially differentiated labor force but, paradoxically, a homogenized "abstract citizenry" in order to function well. The same holds true for the consumerist imperative within capitalism. See Lisa Lowe, *Immigrant Acts*; Elizabeth A. Wheeler, *Uncontained: Urban Fiction in Postwar America* (New Brunswick, NJ: Rutgers University Press: 2001), 13.
38. Brooks, 81–82.
39. Washington, 457.
40. Brooks, 85, 179.
41. Ibid., 92; Medovoi, 50.
42. Cornel West, "Discussion," in *Black Popular Culture*, ed. Michele Wallace and Gina Dent (New York: New, 1998), 86.
43. Ralph Ellison, *Invisible Man* (New York: Vintage, 1990), 581.
44. Fiske, 318.
45. Brooks, 21–22.
46. Thompson and Hijuelos quoted in Andersen.
47. Brooks, 96–97.
48. Lauren Berlant, "National Brands/National Body: *Imitation of Life*," in *Comparative American Identities: Race, Sex, and Nationality in the Modern Text*, ed. Hortense Spillers (New York: Routledge, 1991), 114.

Chapter 4. The Celluloid Fantasy

1. William Saroyan, *Rock Wagram* (Garden City, NY: Doubleday, 1951), 2.
2. Quoted in Lawrence Lee and Barry Gifford, *Saroyan: A Biography* (New York: Harper & Row, 1984), 90.
3. M. Nichols, "Danny, the Toothless Lion," *Coronet*, April 1960: 15; L. Lewis, "The Wailing Syrian," *Colliers*, April 20 1946.
4. Victor Navasky, *Naming Names* (New York: Viking, 1980), 76. While the official name of the congressional body was The House Committee

on Un-American Activities, it came to be popularly known by the transposed acronym HUAC.

5. Richard deCordova, *Picture Personalities: The Emergence of the Star System in America* (Urbana: University of Illinois Press, 2001), 20–21.
6. Saroyan, *Rock Wagram*, 37.
7. Gina Marchetti, "Ethnicity, the Cinema, and Cultural Studies," in *Unspeakable Images: Ethnicity and the American Cinema*, ed. Lester D. Friedman (Urbana: University of Illinois Press, 1991), 278.
8. Ibid., 288.
9. *Look*, December 25, 1956; *Photoplay* June 1941 and May 1946; Michelle Stephens, "The First Negro Matinee Idol: Harry Belafonte and American Culture in the 1950s," in *Left of the Color Line: Race, Radicalism, and Twentieth-Century Literature of the United States*, ed. Bill V. Mullen and James Smethurst (Chapel Hill: University of North Carolina Press, 2003), 226; 232–233; Christina Klein, *Cold War Orientalism*.
10. Priscilla Peña Ovalle, *Dance and the Hollywood Latina: Race, Sex, and Stardom* (New Brunswick, NJ: Rutgers University Press, 2011), 1–4.
11. Vivian Sobchack, "Postmodern Modes of Ethnicity," in *Unspeakable Images: Ethnicity and the American Cinema*, ed. Lester D. Friedman (Urbana: University of Illinois Press, 1991), 332.
12. Mrs. Dean Martin (*sic*), "How I Trained My Husband," *Photoplay*, March 1953, 52; Maxine Arnold, "The More the Merrier," *Photoplay*, January 1954; Leo Rosten, "Extraordinary Jacobs," *Look* 17, 1953; Sobchack, 332; Artie Shaw quoted in Lee and Gifford, 155.
13. deCordova, 11–12; Wendy Kozol, *Life's America: Family and Nation in Postwar Photojournalism* (Philadelphia: Temple University Press, 1994), 92; Nina C. Leibman, *Living Room Lectures: The Fifties Family in Film and Television* (Austin: University of Texas Press, 1995), 171–172. Another useful source on the selling of the domestic ideal is Elaine Tyler May's *Homeward Bound: American Families in the Cold War Era* (New York: Basic Books, 1988).
14. Arnold, *Photoplay*, 1954, 38, Susan Clarke, "Why They Are the Battling Sinatras," *Photoplay*, June 1952, 30; see also Hedda Hopper, "The Breakup," *Photoplay*, November 1951, 42; Rosten, 51–56; Earl Wilson, "A Stranger to Happiness," *Photoplay*, April 1954, 44; Karen McNally, *When Frankie Went to Hollywood: Frank Sinatra and American Male Identity* (Urbana: University of Illinois Press: 2008), 2.
15. See William Barlow, "Commercial and Noncommercial Radio," 208–209, and Jannette L. Dates, "Commercial Television," 312–313, in *Split*

Image: African Americans in the Mass Media; Steven Whitfield, "Boxed in: Television and the Press," *The Culture of the Cold War* (Baltimore: Johns Hopkins University Press, 1996): 153–178; a discussion of Sinatra's encounters with the Kefauver Commission appear in McNally, 50–52; Barnouw, 127–130.

16. Schulberg quoted in Lee and Gifford, 85; Chon Noriega, "Citizen Chicano: The Trials and Titillations of Ethnicity in the American Cinema, 1935–1962," in *The Contemporary Hollywood Reader*, ed. Toby Miller (New York: Routledge, 2009), 325.
17. Leibman, 170; Christina Klein, *Cold War Orientalism: Asia in the Middlebrow Imagination, 1945–1961* (Berkley: University of California Press, 2003).
18. Gaylyn Studlar, "Discourses of Gender and Ethnicity: The Construction and De(con)struction of Rudolph Valentino as Other," *Film Criticism* 13, no. 2 (1989): 20; 23; for historical accounts of the importance of immigrant audiences in early movie houses, see, for example, Robert Sklar, *Movie-Made America: A Cultural History of American Movies* (New York: Vintage, 1994).
19. Studlar, 23.
20. In the case of Armenians, the Halladjian Decision of 1909 legally shifted the racial categorization of Armenian immigrants from "Asiatic" to "Caucasian" to work around the Asian Exclusion Act of 1882 and allow refugees of the Armenian genocides to enter the United States.
21. See Marling, "Autoeroticism: America's Love Affair with the Car in the Television Age," in *As Seen on TV*, 129–162, and Cotten Seiler, *Republic of Drivers: A Cultural History of Automobility in America* (University of Chicago Press, 2008).
22. Marling, 129; "West Coast Youth: Brawny and Buoyant, It Is a Bright Asset for the U.S. Future," *Life*, January 1951; "Back to Mexico Goes a Group of Serape-clad Wetbacks," *Life*, May 1, 1951.
23. Walter Shear, "Saroyan's Study of Ethnicity," *MELUS* 13, nos. 1–2 (1986): 45; Margaret Bedrosian, *The Magical Pine Ring: Culture and the Imagination in Armenian/American Literature* (Detroit: Wayne State University Press, 1991).
24. Stephanie Brown, "Anybody's Protest Novel: Chester Himes and the Prison of Authenticity," in *Invisible Suburbs: Recovering Protest Fiction in the 1950s United States*, ed. Joshua Lukin (Jackson: University Press Mississippi, 2008): 65.

25. George Freedley, review of *Rock Wagram*, by William Saroyan, *Library Journal* (February 1951): 17.
26. Saroyan, 2; for an in-depth portrait of Louis B. Mayer during this period, see Lillian Ross, *Picture* (New York: Rinehart, 1952).
27. Saroyan, 3; Rosten, 53.
28. Saroyan, 4; Ovalle, 10; Ken Nolley, "The Representation of Conquest: John Ford and the Hollywood Indian, 1939–1964," in *Hollywood's Indian: The Portrayal of the Native American in Film*, 2nd ed., ed. Peter C. Rollins and John E. O'Connor (Lexington: University of Kentucky Press, 2003); see also Robert F. Berkhofer, *The White Man's Indian: Images of the American Indian, from Columbus to the Present* (New York: Vintage, 1979), and *Seeing Red: Hollywood's Pixelated Skins*, ed. LeAnne Howe, Denise K. Cummings, and Harvey Markowitz (East Lansing: Michigan State University Press, 2013).
29. Saroyan, 201.
30. The novel's action does not include any detail about Rock's time in the service. After the visit to Fresno, the narrative again jumps forward eight years.
31. Lee and Gifford, 164.
32. Michael Gold, *Jews without Money* (New York: Carroll and Graf, 1996), 29.
33. Saroyan, 161.
34. Ibid., 78, 80–81.
35. Ibid., 69, 40; deCordova, 12.
36. Saroyan, 69, 71.
37. Ibid., 95,70.
38. Ibid., 155, 158; on Fordism and ethnicity see Sobchack and Martyn Lee, "The Political Economy of Fordism" and "Easing the Passage of Modernity," in *Consumer Culture Reborn*.
39. Saroyan, 120–121.
40. Saroyan 31; 117; R. L. Friedman, "Saroyan at a Hundred and One," *The Hopkins Review* 3, no. 1 (2010): 138.
41. Saroyan, 87–89, 107. For an in-depth exploration of the concept of "phoniness" in relation to "discourses of authenticity," see Abigail Cheever, *Real Phonies: Cultures of Authenticity in Post-World War II America* (Athens: University of Georgia Press, 2010).
42. Lee and Gifford, 164.
43. Saroyan, 301.

Chapter 5. Leaving the Dark Room in a Lighter Mood

1. Ralph Ellison, *Invisible Man* (New York: Vintage, 1990), 170; Alan Nadel, 8. This fantasy of nation building also accounts for the popularity of movies and television programming (1940s–1960s) that featured conquests in the West and frontier life, as in *Davy Crockett*.
2. William Lyne, "The Signifying Modernist: Ralph Ellison and the Limits of Double Consciousness," *PMLA* 107, no. 2 (1992): 320.
3. Lucy Fischer, "Three-Way Mirror: Imitation of Life," *Imitation of Life, Douglas Sirk Director* (New Brunswick, NJ: Rutgers University Press, 1991), 4.
4. "Sirk on Sirk," interview by Jonn Halliday, in *Imitation of Life, Douglas Sirk, Director*, ed. Lucy Fischer (New Brunswick, NJ: Rutgers University Press, 1991), 230.
5. Marina Heung, "'What's the Matter with Sarah Jane?' Mothers and Daughters in Douglas Sirk's *Imitation of Life*," in *Imitation of Life, Douglas Sirk, Director*, ed. Lucy Fischer, 307; "Imitation of Life: Production Notes," in *Imitation of Life, Douglas Sirk, Director*, 183.
6. "Imitation of Life: Production Notes," in *Imitation of Life, Douglas Sirk, Director*, 184; on African American response to the 1934 film, see Matthew H. Bernstein and Dana F. White, "Imitation of Life in a Segregated Atlanta: Its Promotion, Distribution and Reception," *Film History* 19 (2007): 152–178; see also Don Bogle on Fredi Washington as the "great black hope" of her day, in *Toms, Coons, Mulattoes, Mammies, and Bucks: An Interpretive History of Blacks in American Films*, 4th ed. (New York: Continuum, 2007), 60–62; Hiram Perez, "Two or Three Spectacular Mulatas and the Queer Pleasures of Overidentification," *Camera Obscura* (67) 23, no. 1 (2008): 113–143, 132.
7. Joseph R Urgo, *Novel Frames: Literature as Guide to Race, Sex, and History in American Culture* (Jackson: University Press of Mississippi, 1991), 5; Valerie Smith, "The Meaning of Narration in *Invisible Man*," in *New Essays on Invisible Man*, ed. Robert O'Meally (New York: Cambridge University Press, 1988), 41; Ellison, 498.
8. Bogle, 59.
9. I have transcribed all dialogue citations in this chapter from the continuity script reproduced in the anthology *Imitation of Life, Douglas Sirk, Director*, ed. Lucy Fischer.
10. Sandy Flitterman-Lewis, "*Imitation(s) of Life*: The Black Woman's Double Determination as Troubling 'Other,'" in *Imitation of Life, Douglas Sirk, Director*, ed. Lucy Fischer, 329.

11. Flitterman-Lewis, 334; Heung, 315. Marianne Conroy, "'No Sin in Lookin' Prosperous': Gender, Race, and the Class Formations of Middle-brow Taste in Douglas Sirk's *Imitation of Life*," in *The Hidden Foundation: Cinema and the Question of Class*, ed. David E. James and Rick Berg (Minneapolis: University of Minnesota Press, 1996): 114–137; Lauren Berlant, "National Brands/National Body: *Imitation of Life*," in *Comparative American Identities: Race, Sex, and Nationality in the Modern Text*, ed. Hortense Spillers (New York: Routledge, 1991), 110–140.
12. Borrowing Butler's and other feminist scholars' theories of gender performativity in application to performances of ethnicity has become fairly common—if not always directly acknowledging of its origins—in critical readings of ethic subjectivity.
13. Butler, 1–2; David Leiwei Li, *Imagining the Nation: Asian American Literature and Cultural Consent* (Stanford: Stanford University Press, 1998), 182.
14. Butler, 2.
15. Flitterman-Lewis, 333.
16. Medovoi, 285.
17. Flitterman-Lewis, 333.
18. Butler, 9–10; Butler spells the character's name without the "h," but I have used the spelling found in the original cast list.
19. Ryan DeRosa, "Black Passing and White Pluralism: *Imitation of Life* in the Civil Rights Struggle," in *American Cinema and the Southern Imaginary*, ed. Deborah Barker and Kathryn McKee (Athens: University of Georgia Press, 2011), 172.
20. Ellison explains this best in "The World and the Jug," his rebuttal to Irving Howe's comparisons of *Invisible Man* with Wright's work in *Collected Essays*, ed. John F. Callahan (New York: Modern Library, 1995).
21. Berlant, 130–132.
22. Heung, 314, 323; Rainer Werner Fassbinder, "Imitation of Life," in *Imitation of Life, Douglas Sirk, Director*, ed. Lucy Fischer, 245.
23. "Why Passing Is Passing Out," *Jet*, July 17 1952: 12–16; "Have Negroes Stopped Passing?" *Jet* Sept. 13, 1956: 10–12; Werner Sollors, *Neither Black nor White yet Both: Thematic Explorations of Interracial Literature* (New York: Oxford University Press, 1997), 230; most studies of passing place it within the approximate historical parameters of 1860–1940.
24. Bogle, 191–193; Susan Gilman, "The Mulatto, Tragic or Triumphant? The Nineteenth-Century American Race Melodrama," in *The Culture of Sentiment: Race, Gender, and Sentimentality in Nineteenth-Century America*, ed. Shirley Samuels (New York: Oxford University Press, 1992), 242; Fischer, 5.

25. Fischer, 4; Gilman, 223; DeRosa, 152.
26. Gilman, 242; Hazel Carby, *Reconstructing Womanhood: The Emergence of the Afro-American Woman Novelist* (New York: Oxford University Press, 1987), 89; Sollors, 230.
27. Conroy, 134; Flitterman-Lewis, 329.
28. Ralph Ellison, introduction to *Invisible Man* (New York: Vintage, 1990), xxii.
29. See, for example, Claudia Tate's feminist interpretation of the Invisible Man's attempts to emerge from underground as persistently aborted in "Notes on the Invisible Woman in Invisible Man," in *Speaking for You: The Vision of Ralph Ellison*, ed. Kimberly W. Benston (Washington, DC: Howard University Press, 1987),163–172; and Douglas Steward, "The Illusions of Phallic Agency: Invisible Man, Totem and Taboo, and the Santa Claus Surprise," *Callaloo* 26, no. 2 (2003): 522–535; Thomas R. Whitaker chooses, it seems, to accept the ambiguity inherent within the debate but maintains that some critics' "optimistic belief that his artistic 'self-definition' in this story will guarantee his emergence from hibernation is also unwarranted." "Spokesman for Invisibility," in *Speaking for You: The Vision of Ralph Ellison*, ed. Kimberly W. Benston, 394.
30. Ellison, 13; John Callahan, "Frequencies of Eloquence: The Performance and Composition of Invisible Man," in *New Essays on Invisible Man*, ed. Robert O'Meally (New York: Cambridge University Press, 1988), 87–88; Hortense Spillers, "Ellison's 'Usable Past': Toward Theory of Myth," in *Speaking for You: The Vision of Ralph Ellison*, ed. Kimberly W. Benston, 157; Valerie Smith, "The Meaning of Narration in *Invisible Man*," in *New Essays on Invisible Man*, ed. Robert O'Meally, 43.
31. Ralph Ellison, *Collected Essays*, ed. John F. Callahan, 299; Brown, 65.
32. Ellison, 18, 31; Robert B. Stepto, *From Behind the Veil: A Study of Afro-American Narrative*, 2nd ed. (Urbana: University of Illinois Press, 1991), 173.
33. Stepto, 175; Ellison, *Invisible Man*, 569.
34. Andrew Hoberek, "Race Man, Organization Man, *Invisible Man*," *Modern Language Quarterly* 59, no. 1 (1998): 103, 112.
35. Hoberek, 104; Ellison, *Invisible Man*, 33.
36. Ellison, *Invisible Man*, 19–20; Laura Mulvey, *Visual and Other Pleasures* (Bloomington: Indiana University Press: 1989).
37. Ellison, *Invisible Man*, 432–434, 19; Johnnie Wilcox, "Black Power: Minstrelsy and Electricity in Ralph Ellison's *Invisible Man*," *Callaloo* 30, no. 4 (Fall 2007): 994.

38. Lesley Larkin, "Postwar Liberalism, Close Reading, and 'You': Ralph Ellison's *Invisible Man*," *Literature, Interpretation, Theory* 19 (2008): 271; Wilcox, 98; Julia Sun-Joo Lee, "Knucklebones and Knocking-bones: The Accidental Trickster in Ellison's Invisible Man," *African American Review* 40, no. 3 (2006): 461–473.
39. Butler, 9; Ellison, *Invisible Man*, 431–433; Lee, 470; Smith, 39.
40. Daniel Y. Kim, "Invisible Desires: Homoerotic Racism and Its Homophobic Critique in Ralph Ellison's *Invisible Man*," *Novel* 30, no. 3 (1997): 315–316; Ellison, *Invisible Man*, 20. See also Ann Folwell Stanford, "He Speaks for Whom? Inscription and Reinscription of Women in *Invisible Man* and *The Salt Eaters*," *MELUS* 18, no. 2 (1993): 17–31.
41. Ellison, *Invisible Man*, 395, 153.
42. Ibid., 20; Wilcox, 995.
43. Ellison, *Invisible Man*, 164, 409.
44. Ibid., 10, 16, 170.
45. Medovoi, 66–67.
46. Ellison, *Invisible Man*, 388–390; Wilcox, 990.
47. Ellison, *Invisible Man*, 319; Hoberek, 107.
48. Ellison has written in his essays that he feels no connection to Africa because the Negro is culturally American, regardless of any desire to reconnect with a "homeland."
49. Bigsby, 176.
50. Ellison, *Collected Essays*, ed. John F. Callahan, 67; Greg Tate, "Preface to a One-Hundred-and-Eighty-Volume Patricide Note: Yet Another Few Thousand Words on the Death of Miles Davis and the Problem of Black Male Genius," in *Black Popular Culture*, ed. Michele Wallace and Gina Dent (New York: New Press, 1998), 244–245; DeRosa, 170–171.
51. Ellison, *Invisible Man*, 11–13.

Epilogue

1. Spillers, 146; Pierre Bourdieu, *The Field of Cultural Production: Essays on Art and Literature* (New York: Columbia University Press, 1993), 37–41; see also Evan Brier, *A Novel Marketplace*.
2. Bigsby, 173–174.
3. Urgo, 28; Wilcox, 998.
4. Urgo, 25.
5. See Michel Fabre, "From *Native Son* to *Invisible Man*: Some Notes on

Ralph Ellison's Evolution in the 1950s," in *Speaking for You: The Vision of Ralph Ellison*, ed. Kimberly W. Benston, 199–216 (Washington, DC: Howard University Press, 1987); and Ellison's *Collected Essays*, ed. John F. Callahan; *Invisible Man*, 4–5.

6. Christopher Breu, *Hard-Boiled Masculinities* (Minneapolis: University of Minnesota Press, 2005), 144.
7. Medovoi, 47.

Works Cited

Andersen, Kurt. "American Icons: *I Love Lucy*." Transcript. *Studio 360*. WNYC/Public Radio International. Aired October 8, 2010. Posted August 5, 2011. http://www.studio360.org/series/american-icons/.

Anderson, Douglas. "Nabokov's Genocidal and Nuclear Holocausts in Lolita." *Mosaic* 29, no. 2 (1996): 73–89.

Arac, Jonathan. "What Kind of History Does a Theory of the Novel Require?" *Novel: A Forum on Fiction* 42, no. 2 (2009): 190–195.

Archdeacon, Thomas J. *Becoming American: An Ethnic History*. New York: Free Press, 1983.

Arnold, Maxine. "The More the Merrier." *Photoplay*, January 1954.

The Atomic Café. The Archives Project, Inc. Thorn EMI Video, 1982.

"Back to Mexico goes a group of serape-clad wetbacks." *Life*, May 21 1951.

Baldwin, James. *Notes of a Native Son*. Boston: Beacon Press, 1955.

Balibar, Etienne, and Immanuel Wallerstein. *Race, Nation, Class: Ambiguous Identities*. Translated by Etienne Balibar and Chris Turner. New York: Verso, 1991.

Barnouw, Erik. *Tube of Plenty: The Evolution of American Television*. 2nd ed. New York: Oxford University Press, 1990.

Bedrosian, Margaret. *The Magical Pine Ring: Culture and the Imagination in Armenian/American Literature*. Detroit: Wayne State University Press, 1991.

Belletto, Steven, and Daniel Grausman, eds. *American Literature and Culture in an Age of Cold War: A Critical Reassessment*. Iowa City: University of Iowa Press, 2012.

Berlant, Lauren. "National Brands/National Body: *Imitation of Life*." In *Comparative American Identities: Race, Sex, and Nationality in the Modern Text*, edited by Hortense Spillers, 110–140. New York: Routledge, 1991.

Bigsby, C. W. E. "Improvising America: Ralph Ellison and the Paradox of Form." In *Speaking for You: The Vision of Ralph Ellison*, edited by Kimberly Bentson, 173–183. Washington, DC: Howard University Press, 1987.

Bogle, Don. *Toms, Coons, Mulattoes, Mammies, and Bucks: An Interpretive History of Blacks in American Films*. 4th ed. New York: Continuum, 2007.

Bourdieu, Pierre. *The Field of Cultural Production: Essays on Art and Literature*. New York: Columbia University Press, 1993.

Breu, Christopher. *Hard-Boiled Masculinities*. Minneapolis: University of Minnesota Press, 2005.

Brier, Evan. *A Novel Marketplace: Mass Culture, the Book Trade, and Postwar American Fiction*. Philadelphia: University of Pennsylvania Press, 2010.

Brooks, Gwendolyn. *Maud Martha*. New York: Harper, 1953.

Brown, Stephanie. "Anybody's Protest Novel: Chester Himes and the Prison of Authenticity." In *Invisible Suburbs: Recovering Protest Fiction in the 1950s United States*, edited by Joshua Lukin, 62–84. Jackson: University Press of Mississippi, 2008.

Butler, Judith. "Lana's 'Imitation': Melodramatic Repetition and the Gender Performative." *Genders* 9 (1990): 1–18.

Callahan, John. "Frequencies of Eloquence: The Performance and Composition of *Invisible Man*." In *New Essays on Invisible Man*, edited by Robert O'Meally, 55–94. New York: Cambridge University Press, 1988.

Carby, Hazel V. *Reconstructing Womanhood: The Emergence of the Afro-American Woman Novelist*. New York: Oxford University Press, 1987.

Chester, Alfred, and Vilma Howard. "The Art of Fiction: An Interview." In *Conversations with Ralph Ellison*, edited by Maryemma Graham and Amritjit Singh, 6–19. Jackson: University Press of Mississippi, 1995. Originally published in *The Paris Review* (Spring 1955).

Chow, Rey. *The Protestant Ethnic and the Spirit of Capitalism*. New York: Columbia University Press, 2002.

Christian, Karen. *Show and Tell: Identity as Performance in U.S. Latino/a Fiction*. Albuquerque: University of New Mexico Press, 1997.

Clarke, Susan. "Why They Are the Battling Sinatras." *Photoplay*, June 1952.

Cohen, Lizabeth. *A Consumer's Republic: The Politics of Mass Consumption in Postwar America*. New York: Knopf, 2003.

———. "From Town Center to Shopping Center: The Reconfiguration of Community Marketplaces in Postwar America." *American Historical Review* 101, no. 4 (October 1996): 1050–1081.

Conroy, Marianne. "'No Sin in Lookin' Prosperous': Gender, Race, and the Class Formations of Middlebrow Taste in Douglas Sirk's *Imitation of Life*." In *The Hidden Foundation: Cinema and the Question of Class*, edited by David E. James and Rick Berg, 114–137. Minneapolis: University of Minnesota Press, 1996.

Cross, Gary. *An All-Consuming Century: Why Commercialism Won in Modern America.* New York: Columbia University Press, 2000.

Dates, Jannette L., and William Barlow. *Split Image: African Americans in the Mass* Media. 2nd ed. Washington DC: Howard University Press, 1993.

Dávila, Arlene *Latino Spin: Public Image and the Whitewashing of Race*. New York: New York University Press, 2008.

deCordova, Richard. *Picture Personalities: The Emergence of the Star System in America*. Urbana: University of Illinois Press, 2001.

Denning, Michael. *The Cultural Front: The Laboring of American Culture in the Twentieth Century.* New York: Verso, 1996.

DeRosa, Ryan. "Black Passing and White Pluralism: *Imitation of Life* in the Civil Rights Struggle." In *American Cinema and the Southern Imaginary*, edited by Deborah Barker and Kathryn McKee, 151–173. Athens, University of Georgia Press, 2011.

Edney, Kathryn. "'Integration through the Wide Open Back Door': African Americans Respond to *Flower Drum Song* (1958)." *Studies in Musical Theatre* 4, no. 3 (2010): 261–272.

Ellison, Ralph. *Collected Essays*, edited by John F. Callahan. New York: Modern Library, 1995.

———. "Introduction." In *Invisible Man*, vii–xxiii. New York: Vintage, 1990.

———. *Invisible Man*. New York: Vintage, 1990.

Fassbinder, Rainer Werner. "*Imitation of Life*." In *Imitation of Life, Douglas Sirk, Director*, edited by Lucy Fischer, 244–246. New Brunswick, NJ: Rutgers University Press, 1991.

Fischer, Lucy, ed. *Imitation of Life, Douglas Sirk, Director*. New Brunswick, NJ: Rutgers University Press, 1991.

———. "Three-Way Mirror: *Imitation of Life*." In *Imitation of Life, Douglas Sirk, Director*, edited by Lucy Fischer, 3–28. New Brunswick, NJ: Rutgers University Press, 1991.

Fiske, John. *Television Culture*. New York: Methuen, 1987.

Flitterman-Lewis, Sandy. "*Imitation(s) of Life*: The Black Woman's Double

Determination as Troubling 'Other.'" In *Imitation of Life, Douglas Sirk, Director*, edited by Lucy Fischer, 325–335. New Brunswick, NJ: Rutgers University Press, 1991.

Foreman, Joel. Introduction to *The Other Fifties: Interrogating Midcentury American Icons*. Urbana: University of Illinois Press, 1997.

Frazier, Valerie. "Domestic Epic Warfare in *Maud Martha*." *African American Review* 39, nos. 1–2 (2005): 133–141.

Freedley, George. Review of *Rock Wagram*, by William Saroyan. *Library Journal* (February 1951): 17.

Friedman, R. L. "Saroyan at a Hundred and One." *The Hopkins Review* 3, no.1 (2010): 133–140.

Gilman, Susan. "The Mulatto, Tragic or Triumphant? The Nineteenth-Century American Race Melodrama." In *The Culture of Sentiment: Race, Gender, and Sentimentality in Nineteenth-Century America*, edited by Shirley Samuels, 221–43. New York: Oxford University Press, 1992.

Gold, Michael. *Jews without Money*. New York: Carroll and Graf, 1996.

Gray, Herman. *Watching Race: Television and the Struggle for "Blackness."* Minneapolis: University of Minnesota Press, 1995.

Haegert, John. "The Americanization of Humbert Humbert." In *Lolita*, edited by Harold Bloom, 120–133. Major Literary Characters Series. New York: Chelsea House, 1993.

Hall, Stuart. "What Is This 'Black' in Black Popular Culture?" In *Black Popular Culture*, edited by Michele Wallace and Gina Dent, 21–33. New York: The New Press, 1998.

Heung, Marina. "'What's the Matter with Sarah Jane?': Mothers and Daughters in Douglas Sirk's *Imitation of Life*." In *Imitation of Life, Douglas Sirk, Director*, edited by Lucy Fischer, 302–24. New Brunswick, NJ: Rutgers University Press, 1991.

Hoberek, Andrew. "Race Man, Organization Man, *Invisible Man*." *Modern Language Quarterly* 59, no. 1 (1998): 99–119.

hooks, bell. *Black Looks* Boston: South End Press, 1992.

Horkheimer, Max, and Theodor W. Adorno. *Dialectic of Enlightenment*. Translated by John Cumming. New York: Herder and Herder, 1972.

Imitation of Life. Directed by Douglas Sirk. 1959. Universal Studies Home Video, 2003. DVD.

"*Imitation of Life*: Production Notes." In *Imitation of Life, Douglas Sirk, Director*, edited by Lucy Fischer, 183–185. New Brunswick, NJ: Rutgers University Press, 1991.

Jameson, Fredric. *The Political Unconscious: Narrative as a Socially Symbolic Act.* Ithaca: Cornell University Press, 1981.

Joyrich, Lynne. "All That Television Allows: TV Melodrama, Postmodernism, and Consumer Culture." In *Private Screenings: Television and the Female Consumer*, edited by Lynn Spigel and Denise Mann, 227–251. Minneapolis: University of Minnesota Press, 1992.

Kim, Daniel Y. "Invisible Desires: Homoerotic Racism and Its Homophobic Critique in Ralph Ellison's *Invisible Man.*" *Novel* 30, no. 3 (1997): 309–328.

Klein, Christina. *Cold War Orientalism: Asia in the Middlebrow Imagination, 1945–1961*. Berkley: University of California Press, 2003.

Kozol, Wendy. *Life's America: Family and Nation in Postwar Photojournalism.* Philadelphia: Temple University Press, 1994.

Landay, Lori. *Madcaps, Screwballs, and Con Women: The Female Trickster in American Culture*. Philadelphia: University of Pennsylvania Press, 1998.

Larkin, Lesley. "Postwar Liberalism, Close Reading, and 'You': Ralph Ellison's *Invisible Man.*" *Literature, Interpretation, Theory* 19 (2008): 268–304.

Lee, C. Y. *The Flower Drum Song*. New York: Grosset and Dunlap, 1957.

Lee, Julia Sun-Joo. "Knucklebones and Knocking-bones: The Accidental Trickster in Ellison's *Invisible Man.*" *African American Review* 40, no. 3 (2006): 461–473.

Lee, Lawrence, and Barry Gifford. *Saroyan: A Biography*. New York: Harper and Row, 1984.

Lee, Martyn J. *Consumer Culture Reborn: The Cultural Politics of Consumption.* New York: Routledge, 1993.

Leibman, Nina C. *Living Room Lectures: The Fifties Family in Film and Television.* Austin: University of Texas Press, 1995.

Lewis, L. "The Wailing Syrian." *Colliers*, April 20, 1946.

Lhamon, W. T., Jr. *Deliberate Speed: The Origins of a Cultural Style in the American 1950s.* Washington, DC: Smithsonian, 1990.

Li, David Leiwei. *Imagining the Nation: Asian American Literature and Cultural Consent.* Stanford: Stanford University Press, 1998.

Ling, Amy. *Yellow Light: The Flowering of Asian American Arts*. Philadelphia: Temple University Press, 1999.

Ling, Jinqi. *Narrating Nationalisms: Ideology and Form in Asian American Literature.* New York: Oxford University Press, 1998.

Lipsitz, George. *Time Passages: Collective Memory and the American Popular Culture*. Minneapolis: University of Minnesota Press, 1990.

Lowe, Lisa. *Immigrant Acts: On Asian American Cultural Politics*. Durham, NC: Duke University Press, 1996.

Lui, Meihzhu, Bárbara Robles, Betsy Leondar-Wright, Rose Brewer, and Rebecca Adamson. *The Color of Wealth: The Story Behind the U.S. Racial Wealth Divide*. NY: The New Press, 2006.

Lukin, Joshua. "Introduction: Thirty-Three Years of the Fifties." In *Invisible Suburbs: Recovering Protest Fiction in the 1950s United States*, edited by Josh Lukin, ix–xxiv. University Press of Mississippi, 2008.

Lyne, William. "The Signifying Modernist: Ralph Ellison and the Limits of Double Consciousness." *PMLA* 107, no. 2 (1992): 319–330.

MacDonald, J. Fred. *Blacks and White TV: Afro-Americans in Television since 1948*. Chicago: Nelson-Hall, 1983.

Marable, Manning. "We Need New and Critical Study of Race and Ethnicity." *Chronicle of Higher Education* on-line. March 30, 2000 http://chronicle.com/weekly/v46/i25/25b00401.htm.

Marchetti, Gina. "Ethnicity, the Cinema, and Cultural Studies." In *Unspeakable Images: Ethnicity and the American Cinema*, edited by Lester D. Friedman, 277–307. Urbana: University of Illinois Press, 1991.

Marling, Karal Ann. *As Seen on Television: The Visual Culture of Everyday Life in the 1950s*. Cambridge: Harvard University Press, 1994.

Martiny, Erik. "The Unreachable 'Eden-Red Apple' of Nabokov's Film Technique in Versions of *Lolita* by Stanley Kubrick and Adrian Lyne." In *Lolita: From Nabokov to Kubrick and Lyne*, edited by Erik Martiny, 133–147. Paris: SEDES, 2009.

May, Elaine Tyler. *Homeward Bound: American Families in the Cold War Era.* New York: Basic Books, 1988.

McNally, Karen. *When Frankie Went to Hollywood: Frank Sinatra and American Male Identity*. Urbana: University of Illinois Press: 2008.

Medovoi, Leerom. *Rebels: Youth and the Cold War Origins of Identity*. Durham, NC: Duke University Press, 2005.

Meyerowitz, JoAnne. "Beyond the Feminine Mystique: A Reassessment of Postwar Mass Culture, 1946–1958." *Journal of American History* 79, no. 4 (March 1993): 1455–1482.

Miller, Toby. *The Well-Tempered Self: Citizenship, Culture, and the Postmodern Subject.* Baltimore: Johns Hopkins University Press, 1993.

Mulvey, Laura. *Visual and Other Pleasures*. Bloomington: Indiana University Press, 1989.

Nadel, Alan. *Containment Culture: American Narratives, Postmodernism, and the Atomic Age*. Durham, NC: Duke University Press, 1995.

Nabokov, Vladimir. *Lolita*. New York: Vintage International, 1989.

———. "On a Book Entitled *Lolita*." 1956. In *Lolita*, 311–317. New York: Vintage International, 1989.

Navasky, Victor. *Naming Names*. New York: Viking, 1980.

Nichols, M. "Danny, the Toothless Lion." *Coronet*, April 1960.

Nolley, Ken. "The Representation of Conquest: John Ford and the Hollywood Indian, 1939–1964." In *Hollywood's Indian: The Portrayal of the Native American in Film*, 2nd ed., edited by Peter C. Rollins and John E. O'Connor, 73–90. Lexington: University of Kentucky Press, 2003.

Noriega, Chon. "Citizen Chicano: The Trials and Titillations of Ethnicity in the American Cinema, 1935–1962." In *The Contemporary Hollywood Reader*, edited by Toby Miller, 320–333. New York: Routledge, 2009.

Ohmann, Richard. *Selling Culture: Magazines, Markets, and Class at the Turn of the Century*. New York: Verso, 1996.

Omi, Michael, and Howard Winant. *Racial Formation in the United States, from the 1960s to the 1980s*. New York: Routledge, 1986.

Oppenheimer, Jess, and Gregg Oppenheimer. *Laughs, Luck . . . and Lucy: How I Came to Create the Most Popular Sitcom of All Time*. Syracuse, NY: Syracuse University Press, 1996.

Ovalle, Priscilla Peña. *Dance and the Hollywood Latina: Race, Sex, and Stardom*. New Brunswick, NJ: Rutgers University Press, 2011.

Perez, Hiram. "Two or Three Spectacular Mulatas and the Queer Pleasures of Overidentification." *Camera Obscura* (67) 23, no. 1 (2008): 113–143.

Pérez-Firmat, Gustavo. *Life on the Hyphen: The Cuban-American Way*. Austin: University of Texas Press, 1994.

Polenberg, Richard. *One Nation Divisible: Class, Race, and Ethnicity in the United States since 1938*. New York: Viking, 1980.

Roberts, Shari. "The Lady in the Tutti-Frutti Hat: Carmen Miranda, a Spectacle of Ethnicity." In *The Contemporary Hollywood Reader*, edited by Toby Miller, 96–111. New York: Routledge, 2009.

Rodriguez, Clara E. *Changing Race: Latinos, the Census, and the History of Ethnicity in the United States*. New York: New York University Press, 2000.

Roediger, David. *Working toward Whiteness: How America's Immigrants Became White: The Strange Journey from Ellis Island to the Suburbs*. New York: Basic Books, 2005.

Rosten, Leo. "Extraordinary Jacobs." *Look* 17, 1953: 51–56.

Rubin, Joan Shelley. *The Making of Middlebrow Culture*. Chapel Hill: University of North Carolina Press, 1992.

Sacks, Karen Brodkin. "How Did Jews Become White Folks?" In *Race*, edited by Steven Gregory and Roger Sanjek, 78–102. New Brunswick, NJ: Rutgers University Press, 1994.

Said, Edward W. *Culture and Imperialism*. New York: Knopf, 1993.

Sanjek, Roger. "The Enduring Inequalities of Race." In *Race*, edited by Steven Gregory and Roger Sanjek, 1–17. New Brunswick, NJ: Rutgers University Press, 1994.

Saroyan, William. *Rock Wagram*. Garden City, NY: Doubleday, 1951.

Schiff, Stephen. "Nabokov's *Lolita*." In *A New Literary History of America*, edited by Greil Marcus and Werner Sollors, 866–871. Cambridge: Harvard University Press, 2009.

Shear, Walter. "Saroyan's Study of Ethnicity." *MELUS* 13, nos.1–2 (1986): 45–55.

Sirk, Douglas. "Sirk on Sirk." Interview by Jon Halliday. In *Imitation of Life, Douglas Sirk, Director*, edited by Lucy Fischer, 226–231. New Brunswick, NJ: Rutgers University Press, 1991.

Smith, Valerie. "The Meaning of Narration in *Invisible Man*." *New Essays on Invisible Man*, edited by Robert O'Meally, 25–53. New York: Cambridge University Press, 1988.

Sobchack, Vivian. "Postmodern Modes of Ethnicity." In *Unspeakable Images: Ethnicity and the American Cinema*, edited by Lester D. Friedman, 329–352. Urbana: University of Illinois Press, 1991.

Sollors, Werner. *Neither Black nor White yet Both: Thematic Explorations of Interracial Literature*. New York: Oxford University Press, 1997.

———. *The Invention of Ethnicity*. New York: Oxford University Press, 1989.

Spigel, Lynn. "Installing the Television Set: Popular Discourses on Television and Domestic Space, 1948–1955." In *Private Screenings: Television and the Female Consumer*, edited by Lynn Spigel and Denise Mann, 3–38. Minneapolis: University of Minnesota Press, 1992.

———. *Make Room for TV: Television and the Family Ideal in Postwar America*. Chicago: University of Chicago Press, 1992.

Spillers, Hortense. "Ellison's 'Usable Past': Toward a Theory of Myth." In *Speaking for You: The Vision of Ralph Ellison*, edited by Kimberly Bentson, 144–158. Washington, DC: Howard University Press, 1987.

Stephens, Michelle. "The First Negro Matinee Idol: Harry Belafonte and American Culture in the 1950s." In *Left of the Color Line: Race, Radicalism, and Twentieth-Century Literature of the United States*, edited by Bill V. Mullen and James Smethurst, 223–237. Chapel Hill: University of North Carolina Press, 2003.

Stepto, Robert B. *From Behind the Veil: A Study of Afro-American Narrative*. 2nd ed. Urbana: University of Illinois Press, 1991.

Studlar, Gaylyn. "Discourses of Gender and Ethnicity: The Construction and De(con)struction of Rudolph Valentino as Other." *Film Criticism* 13, no. 2 (1989): 18–35.

Takaki, Ronald, ed. *From Different Shores: Perspectives on Race and Ethnicity in America*. New York, NY: Oxford, 1987.

Tate, Greg. "Preface to a One-Hundred-and-Eighty-Volume Patricide Note: Yet Another Few Thousand Words on the Death of Miles Davis and the Problem of Black Male Genius." In *Black Popular Culture*, edited by Michele Wallace and Gina Dent, 243–248. New York: The New Press, 1998.

Urgo, Joseph R. *Novel Frames: Literature as Guide to Race, Sex, and History in American Culture.* Jackson: University Press of Mississippi, 1991.

Wald, Priscilla. *Constituting Americans: Cultural Anxiety and Narrative Form.* Durham, NC: Duke University Press, 1995.

Wallace, Michele. *Invisibility Blues*. New York: Verso, 1990.

Wallace, Michele, and Gina Dent, eds. *Black Popular Culture.* New York: The New Press, 1998.

Washington, Mary Helen. "'Taming All That Anger Down': Rage and Silence in Gwendolyn Brooks's *Maud Martha*." *Massachusetts Review* 24, no. 2 (1983): 453–466.

West, Cornel. Discussion. In *Black Popular Culture*, edited by Michele Wallace and Gina Dent, 85–91. New York: The New Press, 1998.

"West Coast Youth: Brawny and Buoyant, It Is a Bright Asset for the U.S. Future." *Life*, January 1, 1951.

Wheeler, Elizabeth A. *Uncontained: Urban Fiction in Postwar America*. New Brunswick, NJ: Rutgers University Press, 2001.

"Why Passing Is Passing Out." *Jet*, July 17 1952: 12–16.

Wilcox, Johnnie. "Black Power: Minstrelsy and Electricity in Ralph Ellison's *Invisible Man*." *Callaloo* 30, no. 4 (Fall 2007): 987–1009.

Whitfield, Stephen J. *The Culture of the Cold War*. Baltimore: Johns Hopkins University Press, 1996.

Wright, Richard. *Native Son*. New York: Harper, 1940.

Index